The People's Reformation

The People's Reformation

MAGISTRATES, CLERGY, AND

COMMONS IN STRASBOURG,

1500–1598

Lorna Jane Abray

Cornell University Press

Ithaca, New York

Cornell University Press gratefully acknowledges a grant from the Andrew W. Mellon Foundation that aided in bringing this book to publication.

First published 1985 by Cornell University Press.

Library of Congress Cataloging in Publcation Data

Abray, Lorna Jane.
   The People's Reformation.

   Bibliography: p.
   Includes index.
   1. Reformation—France—Strasbourg.   2. Strasbourg (France)—Church history. 3. Laity—France—Strasbourg—History—16th century.   I. Title.
BR372.S8A27   1985   274.4'3835   84–45805
ISBN 0–8014–1776–7 (alk. paper)

Printed in the United States of America

The paper in this book is acid-free and meets the guidelines for permanence and durability of the Committee on Production Guidelines for Book Longevity of the Council on Library Resources.

To Mary and Charles Abray

for a happy childhood and much else

Contents

Preface

Who shaped the reformation? What did the reformation mean to the men and women of the sixteenth century? This book explores the laity's contribution to the Lutheran reformation and investigates its effects on their ideas and their lives.

It is also a study of the Lutheran reformation in a particular place, the Free City of Strasbourg. Sixteenth-century Strasbourg, with a population of about twenty thousand, was one of the largest cities in the Holy Roman Empire and a nearly independent polity. Its religious struggles epitomized those of Europe as a whole. Catholics, Lutherans, Anabaptists, Schwenckfelders, Calvinists, people who were content to call themselves Christians, and others who were as indifferent to religion as the century allowed, all had their rendezvous in this frontier city. Strasbourg stood near the linguistic border dividing the French- and German-speaking lands, where the Rhine corridor connecting Italy and the Netherlands intersected the main overland route between France and the Empire. The Habsburg emperors, the Valois kings, and the Huguenot and Ligueur captains all kept covetous eyes on Strasbourg, while even that parsimonious sovereign Elizabeth Tudor parted with her pounds to maintain a resident agent there. The Strasburghers were not deluded in thinking that their city was of European importance.

In the course of the sixteenth century the Strasburghers reordered their church and changed their religious values and practices. Their story starts in the troubled years around the beginning of the century when the late medieval crisis began to produce a series of conflicting

[9]

programs to strengthen the church and the faith. In Strasbourg the evangelical reformers won out over their rivals and founded a new church. By the mid-1530s the Strasburghers had transferred control of their religious lives from the pope to their own secular rulers. In the process they set in motion a subtle dance of power in which the magistrates, the clergy, and the magistrates' lay subjects would constantly change partners for the rest of the century.

The local reformation settlement of the 1530s did not put an end to the arguments about the proper status of the clergy, about the definition of true doctrine, or about the creation of a Christian community pleasing to God. It did make the magistrates a party to those quarrels and also established them as the arbiters of religious debate. As a result, the laity had a strong voice in the evolution of the city's reformation. The clergy had a clearer sense than did the magistrates of what they wanted to accomplish by the reformation; most of the debates about religion resulted from the preachers' attempts to improve the original settlement by imposing their own vision of the reformation on the rulers and commons. Both preachers and secular rulers courted public support. Magistrates and clergymen could draft descriptions of how life should be in Strasbourg, but only the attitudes and actions of the mass of the people could determine what life would be at any given time. Their enthusiasm and their apathy both affected the course of the city's reformation.

The Strasburghers did not make their reformation in isolation, and during the course of the sixteenth century they had to learn harsh lessons about their city's decaying position in the wider world. From its inception to its completion, Strasbourg's reformation evolved in response to external pressures, with the demands of outsiders proving particularly important in the strangulation of organized dissent and in the elaboration of orthodox belief. In the end, the Strasburghers accepted a definition of their faith which had been made by strangers with little concern for the ebb and flow of life within the city's walls and embedded that definition, the Formula of Concord, in their second church ordinance. This ordinance of 1598 marked the official end of their reformation.

Yet the official reformation described in formal statements of things believed and of practices required or forbidden was never the whole reformation. The city's pastors accepted the authority of other Lutheran churches faster than did the city's magistrates, but even when both had bowed to forces outside their walls the people continued to think and act with considerable independence. They had their own sense of what it meant to be good Lutherans. Likewise, lay and clerical definitions of the good citizen never converged entirely. The Strasburghers' reformation began with a welter of competing visions of reform, and diversity long remained its essence. The reformation meant something different to each of the city's residents. For all of them—rulers and ruled, clergy and laity, rich and poor, men and women—it was much more than words on a page. It was a set of experiences against which and through which they defined the meaning of their lives.

The tens of thousands of men and women who lived and died in reformation Strasbourg can be split into three groups, each of which contributed something to the city's religious development. The two most obviously powerful were tiny fractions of the population. A total of fewer than 550 magistrates sat on Strasbourg's ruling council, the Senate and XXI, between the early 1520s and the end of the century.[1] Facing these magistrates, in opposition or in cooperation, were the men who created and sustained the Church Assembly, Strasbourg's Protestant clergy. From the early 1520s through the end of the century they counted no more than 150 pastors and preachers in their ranks.[2] The lives and ideas of members of these two elites are richly documented; we can know them as individuals. The commons of Strasbourg, the magistrates' subjects and the clergy's parishioners, rarely present themselves as individuals. We encounter them most often in groups: the congregation of St. So-and-so, the members of a particular guild, those who rioted over religion, those who would not bestir themselves to go to church. The laboring and artisanal families among them struggled to make ends meet, but the commons also included men and women who were comfortably off, or even rich. I have called the poor Strasburghers "the common people," and used "the burghers" as a convenient synonym for the commons as a whole, a usage that roughly reflects that term's legal and social meaning in Strasbourg.[3] At the top, the commons merged into the mag-

---

[1]Membership in the Senate and XXI can be traced with most accuracy after 1539, when the extant series of its minutes begins. Between 1539 and 1598 there were 449 magistrates. Appendix A provides information on the 115 men most active in setting religious policy. The city constitution is explained in Chapter 2, below.

[2]Again this is both an approximate and a maximum figure for clergymen who worked in the urban parishes as evangelicals or Protestants after 1520. Appendix B provides information about the 102 men who formed the core of the Church Assembly.

[3]See pp. 51–53.

isterial classes. Rulers and commons combined to form the laity, while the laity and clergy together constituted the people.

The Strasburghers' reformation was a long movement from late medieval Catholicism to Lutheran orthodoxy, a movement that occupied three generations. I have used this word "generation" with a certain disregard for the biological facts. In Strasbourg men and women were usually in their mid-twenties when they set about raising children, and a demographer's account of the sixteenth century would include five or six generations.[4] But the movement of ideas is more clearly seen as happening over three generations.[5] A first generation, already adult in the 1520s, created the city's original reformation settlement. Around the middle of the century these people's children took over and strove to protect and strengthen their legacy in the teeth of continental war and confessional wrangling. A third generation formulated Strasbourg's lasting answers to the questions about authority, doctrine, and discipline which had bedeviled the lives of their parents and grandparents. Within each of these generations there were younger and older members, with the magistrates older than the bulk of the population. Child-raising might begin when a couple were in their mid-twenties, but a magistrate was nearer forty when he began to exercise true power.[6] This fact has a bearing on the length of Strasbourg's reformation. Men of the third generation, men who came of age around the 1570s, did not take control of the council chambers until the 1590s.

Generational conflict thus had a role to play in the city's reformation, something that has long been acknowledged in a different form. The prevailing view of the city's evolution in the sixteenth century is built on a dichotomous periodization that runs like this: In the 1520s a small group of preachers proposed changes in the city's religious life which won the support of its commons and lay rulers. Popular enthusiasm was already waning in the 1530s, when magistrates and pastors built a new church. Through the thirties and forties Strasbourg re-

---

[4]Jean-Pierre Kintz, *La société strasbourgeoise du milieu du XVIe siècle à la fin de la guerre de Trente Ans, 1560–1650: Essai d'histoire démographique, économique, et sociale* (Paris, 1984), pp. 190, 197–200.

[5]Miriam Chrisman points out that an "intellectual generation" in Strasbourg lasted "from twelve to twenty years." *Lay Culture, Learned Culture: Books and Social Change in Strasbourg, 1480–1599* (New Haven, 1982), pp. xxi, 37–40. These shorter generations still produce a tripartite division of the sixteenth century in the overlapping groups she discusses in Parts 2–5.

[6]I have located birthdates for forty-one members of the Senate and XXI. The median lifespan was sixty-seven years; median age at entry to power was thirty-nine.

mained a major Protestant power, but the pioneering generation died out around the middle of the century. Thereafter, clergymen of limited vision and stifling orthodoxy dominated magistrates who lacked the will to assert themselves either at home or abroad. The golden age was gone. Strasbourg had ceased to be of any importance in cultural or political history. The second and third generations, in the persons of Church Assembly presidents Johann Marbach and Johann Pappus, had destroyed the vision of Martin Bucer's generation.[7]

The established interpretation grounds itself in painstaking and occasionally brilliant reconstructions of the early years of Strasbourg's reformation. Very few scholars have turned to the second and third generations, and as a result we are left with a misleading impression of the century as a whole. Strasburghers in the 1590s, looking back over a century of conflict and compromise, would have thought that the established interpretation raised more questions than it answered. If the ordinary laity dropped out of the reformation by the 1530s, who had threatened the magistrates with rebellion in defense of the faith in the 1540s and again in the late 1580s and early 1590s? If the doctrines and practices of the new church had been settled with the clergy's help in the 1530s, why had the clergy complained about a stalled and deformed reformation for the next sixty years? If the magistrates had lapsed into impotence around the middle of the century, how had they managed to keep the clergy in submission for the next four decades? Why had Strasbourg engaged in such a grandiose foreign policy in the latter half of the century if it had ceased to be a major Protestant power? What had Lutheran Strasbourg been doing when, much against the will of Marbach and Pappus, it supported the Huguenots and eventually allied itself with German and Swiss Calvinists? The Strasburghers of the late 1590s knew that the lay supremacy established in the 1530s had now been significantly altered so that control of the faith and of the church had passed back to the clergy. They also knew that the laity had not entirely abandoned the lay supremacy and that Strasbourg had not become the godly city of which their clergy had so long dreamed.

The key to understanding the evolution of Strasbourg's reformation is to be found in the interplay of magisterial, clerical, and popular power through three generations. Strasbourg did become a staunchly Lutheran city in more than name alone, but not quickly and not solely because of the clergy. All the Strasburghers had to grapple

[7]See Chapter 3, note 44, below.

with arguments about the preachers' authority, true religion, and Christian behavior; their struggles and their solutions to their problems tell us something about the larger history of the Lutheran denomination. That, in turn, tells us much about who made the reformation and what it meant to its creators.

This book falls into three parts. The first three chapters recount the origins of the initial reformation settlement of the 1530s and introduce the desires and powers of the magistrates, the clergy, and the commons. The next three chapters outline the events between the first and second church ordinances, concentrating on the influence of the outside world, the role of dissent within the city, and the establishment of Lutheran orthodoxy in the last decades of the century. The last three chapters analyze the Strasburghers' religious values, their understanding of the proper behavior for good Christians, and the impact of the reformation on their lives.

Names, Dates, and References

I have standardized the magistrates' and pastors' family names following Thomas A. Brady, Jr., *Ruling Class, Regime and Reformation at Strasbourg, 1520–1555* (Leiden, 1978), for the former and Marie-Joseph Bopp, *Die evangelischen Geistlichen und Theologen in Elsass und Lothringen von der Reformation bis zur Gegenwart* (Neustadt a.d. Aisch, 1959), for the latter. City names have been anglicized but village names have been left as they appear in the records.

All dates are old style.

Strasbourg editions of works published in the sixteenth century are cited by shortened titles throughout. Full bibliographical details can be found in Miriam Usher Chrisman, *Bibliography of Strasbourg Imprints, 1480–1599* (New Haven, 1982). The names of publishers and of series are omitted in the notes but included in the Bibliography. Most of the manuscripts cited are held by the Archives municipales de Strasbourg; see the list of abbreviations.

Acknowledgments

No documents, no history. My greatest debt is to the magistrates, clergy, and commons of Strasbourg for preserving their papers and making them accessible to scholars. François Joseph Fuchs, director of the Municipal Archives at the time I did the bulk of the research for this book, made me welcome in his domain and shared his expertise. Georges Foessel showed me every courtesy, while Edmond Ponsing helped me a great deal with paleographic problems.

Jean Rott, master of Strasbourg's reformation history, lent me transcripts, answered endless questions, and cracked jokes in his many languages. Jean-Pierre Kintz's wit brightened many a day, as did the kindness of his wife, Nicole; the reader will soon see how very much indebted I am to Professor Kintz's work on Strasbourg's demographic, economic, and social history. Stephen Nelson shared texts and insights, as did Werner Bellardi, Marc Lienhard, Rodolphe Peter, Francis Rapp, Bernard Roussel, and Bernard Vogler. At the Bibliothèque nationale et universitaire de Strasbourg, the Bibliothèque municipale, and the Archives départementales du Bas-Rhin I regularly encountered examples of the generosity of other Strasbourgeois.

Miriam Usher Chrisman has long been a steady purveyor of aid, comfort, texts, and—best of all—frank criticism; one could not ask for a better colleague. Thomas A. Brady, Jr., and Katherine Gingrich Brady have likewise encouraged me for more than a decade. Professor Brady's careful reading of the manuscript of this book prompted both large and small changes, making it far better than it would otherwise have been. A third member of the North American branch of the *Freundschaft,* James M. Kittelson, first set me on the road toward understanding the pivotal role of Johann Marbach and his generation.

As a graduate student at Yale University I had the great fortune to study under J. H. Hexter, Harry Miskimin, and R. R. Palmer. Steven Ozment, my thesis director, was always generous with his time, knowledge, and interest. I hope that I shall grow to be as useful to my own students.

Gerald Strauss and Cory Herrera both read this book in manuscript and offered me good advice. I am particularly grateful to John Ackerman and Brian Keeling of Cornell University Press for their expertise and good-will. John Grant, Ann Boddington, and Ursula Sherman, past and present colleagues in Scarborough College's Division of Humanities, each resolved problems of translation, while E. Patricia Vicari shared her command of the intellectual milieu of sixteenth- and seventeenth-century England, allowing me to see Strasbourg in a

[15]

broader perspective. Paul Gooch and Chantal Bertrand-Jennings both encouraged me by assuming that this project would not become the Endless Reformation. My fellow historians at Scarborough have given me the daily benefit of their reflections on our shared craft; at a difficult moment in my career they gave me hope and humor.

The librarians of the Sterling Memorial Library at Yale and the Bladen Library at Scarborough have been endlessly helpful, as have two secretaries in the Division of Humanities, Brigitte Wolter and Lois Pickup. I have benefited as well from the financial support of the old Canada Council doctoral fellowship program, Yale University, the Mrs. Giles M. Whiting Foundation, and the Office of Research Administration at the University of Toronto.

The boat trip crew, more inclined to think of themselves as experts at locks, docks, and emergency caulks, stand now revealed as involuntary editors, for individually and collectively they have heard every anecdote in this book, along with a quantity of other stories, judged tiresome, which the landlocked reader is to be spared. From them I learned the true force of the popular conviction that sermons should not go on so long that dinner is delayed.

My sister, brother-in-law, and niece have been patient with a project that has too often interfered with our chances of seeing each other. My parents have not only put up with the inconvenience of a scholarly daughter, they have encouraged me at every step of the way. It is my pleasure to dedicate this work to them.

LORNA JANE ABRAY

Scarborough College
University of Toronto

Abbreviations

ADBR	Archives départementales du Bas-Rhin
AMS	Archives municipales de Strasbourg
AMS AA	diplomatic correspondence
AMS N, AMS M	parish registers, births and marriages
AMS R	mandates
ARG	*Archiv für Reformationsgeschichte*
AST	Archives du Chapitre St. Thomas, AMS
BDS	Robert Stupperich et al., eds., *Martin Bucers deutsche Schriften* (Gütersloh, 1960–)
BNUS	Bibliothèque nationale et universitaire de Strasbourg
BSCMHA	*Bulletin de la société pour la conservation des monuments historiques d'Alsace*
BSHPF	*Bulletin de la société de l'histoire du protestantisme français*
KS	Kontraktstube, notarial archives, AMS
PC	Hans Virck et al., eds., *Die politische Correspondenz der Stadt Strassburg im Zeitalter der Reformation,* 5 vols. in 6 (Strasbourg, 1882–89, and Heidelberg, 1928–33)
RHPR	*Revue d'histoire et de philosophie religieuses*
RP	Ratsprotokolle, minutes of the Senate and XXI, AMS
SSARE	Société savante d'Alsace et des régions de l'est
TAE	Täuferakten, Elsass. *Quellen zur Geschichte der Täufer. Elsass. Stadt Strassburg, 1522–1535,* ed. Manfred Krebs and Hans Georg Rott, 2 vols. (Gütersloh, 1959–60)
XV	Minutes of the council of XV, AMS
ZGO	*Zeitschrift für die Geschichte des Oberrheins*

The People's Reformation

CHAPTER ONE

A City Converts

Strasbourg's original reformation settlement, in place by the mid-1530s, grew out of the strengths and weaknesses of European religious life in the generation before the reformation. Many of the men and women coming to maturity around the end of the fifteenth century cared passionately about God, their souls, and their church. They feared that their world had grown away from God or that God had allowed his church to go astray. Out of their anguish came a resolve to reshape Christendom which rocked empires and kingdoms in the early sixteenth century and swept even the resolutely secular into the upheaval. By the 1520s Strasburghers looking for answers to their questions about church organization, doctrine, and Christian morality could chose among five reforming currents: conservative, humanist, evangelical, radical, and spiritualist. Individuals took pieces from any or all of them to forge their own solutions to the religious crisis. Rapidly, in less than two decades, the majority had accepted an official consensus so that by 1536 the evangelicals had become the new establishment. They had two confessions of faith to define doctrine, a church ordinance to organize their institutions, and a disciplinary ordinance to regulate behavior. The Strasburghers had laid the foundation of their Protestant reformation.

Outwardly the late medieval church flourished in Strasbourg. Construction of the cathedral had come to a triumphant conclusion in 1439 when the stonemasons finished its spire, but a loving tinkering with details allowed the burghers to go on demonstrating their pious generosity. In the 1480s, for example, Hans Hammerer built an imposing stone pulpit, carved almost into laciness, for the use of the cathedral preacher. Bishop Wilhelm von Honstein ordered the construction of the St. Lawrence chapel on the cathedral's north side; work on the adjoining St. Martin's chapel went on until 1521. Local craftsmen cast a great new bell, blessed and hung to ring in honor of the Virgin Mary. It was the same story in most of the city's four collegiate churches, nine parish churches, nineteen religious houses, and nearly two hundred chapels. St. Thomas acquired an elaborate sculpture of the Mount of Olives for its cemetery, and around the turn of the century Old St. Peter gained new works of art, glass from Peter Hemmel's shop, and tapestries, as well as a new main altar executed by Veit Wagner. At New St. Peter one of the canons financed the construction of a chapel to the Holy Trinity, while rich and pious burghers contributed to the cost of a new convent, St. Mary Magdalene, for the Penitent nuns and saw to its decoration, notably with more of Hemmel's splendid glass.[1]

As patron of Strasbourg and its cathedral, the Virgin held a special place in the city's devotional life. The city's militia marched into battle under a large banner that showed her seated with the Christ child on her lap and her arms extended wide to embrace her people. Her image appeared on the city's seal and coins. A popular writer, the Franciscan Thomas Murner, wrote with great feeling about the annual procession in which thousands of peasants thronged into the city to unite with the clergy, commons, and magistrates honoring Mary. Strasburghers showered gifts on their patron. Hans Baldung and his wife Margrete Herlin were in good company when they donated an expensive camelhair altar cloth to the cathedral foundation of Unser Frauen Haus in 1510.[2]

In Strasbourg people had excellent opportunities to learn the elements of their religion, although we have no way of knowing to what degree they took advantage of this. The illiterate could hear sermons and "read" works of art, while the literate could draw on Strasbourg's lively printing industry. A Latin Bible came off the

---

[1]For information on particular churches see Roland Recht, Jean-Pierre Klein, and Georges Foessel, *Connaître Strasbourg* (Strasbourg, 1976). For the artists see Philippe Dollinger, ed., *Histoire de l'Alsace* (Toulouse, 1970), pp. 195–201.

[2]Paul Perdrizet, "La Vierge aux bras étendus," *Archives alsaciennes d'histoire de l'art,* 1 (1922), 7; Thomas Murner, *Ein andechtig geistliche Badenfart* (1514), in *Thomas Murners deutsche Schriften mit den Holzschnitten der Erstdrucke,* ed. Edouard Fuchs et al., 9 vols. (Berlin, 1918–31), 1^2:150; Marianne Bernhard, *Hans Baldung Grien: Handzeichnungen, Druckgraphik* (Munich, 1978), pp. 31–32.

presses here in 1466 and by the 1480s printers were selling German editions. The first Bible was expensive; at twelve florins its price equalled two months' wages for an artisan and it would have been beyond the reach of most young scholars and parish priests. By 1522 the price of a New Testament had fallen to no more than that of two rabbits for the pot.[3] Writing in 1520 to defend the Latin mass against Luther's attacks, Thomas Murner noted that German mass books were also readily available for those who did not understand the learned tongue.[4]

The Strasburghers of the last prereformation generations demonstrated their piety through a vogue for confraternities, mutual aid societies that looked after their members' temporal and spiritual welfare.[5] These bodies, which were open to both men and women, often linked people working in a particular trade with the members of one of the city's religious houses. For instance, the apprentice tanners' confraternity offered its members burial privileges in the Augustinians' cemetery. Other groups, like the locksmiths, chose to affiliate with a parish church. Whatever they chose, these lay bodies were firmly tied to existing religious institutions. Their members taxed themselves to create a relief fund on which they could draw in times of sickness or to meet their burial expenses. They promised to attend each other's funerals and to pray for the souls of the departed. Their common funds also paid for regular masses, altars, and candles to honor each confraternity's patron. The members' activities spilled out beyond their own circle, for example when they staged processions or miracle plays for the edification of the whole city.

The significance of these confraternities is ambiguous, even in their

[3]Rodolphe Peter, "Les groupes informels au temps de la réforme, types rhénans," in Les groupes informels dans l'eglise, ed. René Metz and Jean Schickle (Strasbourg, 1971), pp. 194–95.

[4]Ein christliche und briederliche ermanung von Doctor Martinus luters leren und predigen (1520), in Murner, Deutsche Schriften, 6:54. For an analysis of the religious material printed in Strasbourg before 1520 see Chrisman, Lay Culture, pp. 81–92.

[5]Francis Rapp, Réformes et réformation à Strasbourg: Eglise et société dans le diocèse de Strasbourg, 1450–1520 (Strasbourg, 1975), p. 469; Georg von Schanz, Zur Geschichte der deutschen Gesellenvereine im Mittelalter (Leipzig, 1876; reprint ed., Glashütten im Taunus, 1973), nos. 71, 74, 97; "Annales de Sébastien Brant," ed. Léon Dacheux, BSCMHA, n.s. 19 (1899), nos. 4395, 4397; Dollinger, Histoire de l'Alsace, pp. 181–82; Luzian Pfleger, "Zur Geschichte der Strassburger Passionsspiele," Archiv für elsässische Kirchengeschichte, 13 (1938), 70; Florenz Landmann, "Die St. Sebastians-Brüderschaft an St. Martin in Strassburg: Ihr Verhältnis zu Sebastian Brant," Archiv für elsässische Kirchengeschichte, 16 (1943), 107–28; Jean-Robert Zimmermann, Les compagnons de métiers à Strasbourg du début du XIVe siècle à la veille de la réforme (Strasbourg, 1971), pp. 28–29, 65–97.

religious dimension. On one hand they demonstrate the vitality of conventional piety. Their choice of patrons—God, the Virgin, and various plague saints like Roch were favorites—was thoroughly commonplace. So were their devotional practices: processions, altar-building, the lighting of candles, the purchase of masses. Indeed demands by these groups for the services of priests to say masses apparently exceeded the local supply, despite the city's multitudes of priests. Although these were lay groups, they had chaplains and placed themselves firmly within the structures of the church. On the other hand, the laity had created these organizations and added them to the old structures; they may reflect a sense of the insufficiency of those structures. A decade before the reformation Bishop Wilhelm von Honstein voiced reservations about the confraternities and ordered his clergy to keep a closer watch on them. They may have attracted particularly anxious or scrupulous souls. One of the most active was the "Fraternity of the Passion of Jesus Christ and of the Compassion of his Mother Mary, the Ever-Virgin"; some of its members, among them the magistrates Claus Kniebis, Martin Herlin, and Matthis Pfarrer, became early and zealous converts to evangelical teaching.

In Strasbourg, as elsewhere in the German-speaking lands, demonstrations of the vitality of the prereformation church coexisted with signs of institutional decline and spiritual uneasiness.[6] Vocations for the city's religious orders were falling off and the burghers made fewer and smaller gifts to them. Long before anyone in Strasbourg had heard of Martin Luther the local people had begun to turn away from the purchase of indulgences. In 1479–80 the Penitents took in 4,373 florins from the sale of indulgences for the building of their new convent; in 1481 the receipts plummeted to 382 florins. The next years saw some recovery, but never beyond a quarter of the first year's total. The problem was not peculiar to these nuns, this convent, and these indulgences. A papal indulgence for the ransoming of prisoners of war held by the Turks also began well and then faltered. In 1489 it brought in 1,800 florins and in 1502 2,300, but in 1509 the collectors could only raise 454 florins. Figures like these are just a small manifestation of the troubles in the prereformation church. The local upper clergy were rich and arrogant while the rank and file frequently lived in misery. Jealous of their privileges, the cathedral

---

[6]The following paragraph is based on Rapp, *Réformes et réformation*. The figures on donations and indulgences are from pp. 261, 398–401, 403–404; the quotation, p. 419.

A City Converts

and chapter canons blocked episcopal attempts to discipline the clergy and to improve religious life in the parishes. The numbers of religious in the city declined, but the financial power of their houses waxed, fattening on speculation in wine and grain and on investment in peasant and urban debt. The laity complained loud and long about clerical greed, clerical laziness, clerical immorality, clerical ignorance, clerical contempt for the laity, and the problems caused by absentee or incompetent pastors. Sometimes the laity took action: violently in the countryside, where a series of peasant revolts terrorized the rural clergy after 1493; pacifically in Strasbourg, where a group of prominent laymen endowed a preachership in the cathedral for Geiler von Kaysersberg to improve the quality of sermons by importing this master preacher. Geiler was one of the great figures of the late medieval church, and men and women went out of their way to hear him. Geiler, who owed his pulpit to the laity, found himself crying out to them, "You of the laity, you hate us clergymen!"

The rising tide of German anticlericalism is one of the most striking aspects of religious feeling in and around Strasbourg. As Francis Rapp has observed, it was in large measure created by clergymen and members of the laity anxious to reform the church.[7] Moralists like Geiler von Kaysersberg, Sebastian Brant, Jacob Wimpheling, and Thomas Murner did not spare the laity in their diatribes, but all reserved a very large place for the failings of the clergy precisely because they held the clergy to be the most important estate in Christendom. The views of conservative reformers like Geiler, Brant, Wimpheling, and other local intellectuals have received considerable attention from scholars.[8] The popular writings of Thomas Murner are not as well known although, like Geiler, he illustrates the anticlericalism some clerics pitched at the laity. In *Concerning the Four Heretics* (1509) this Franciscan gleefully related how four Dominicans in Bern had faked a series of visions at the expense of a credulous novice. Their goal, according to Murner, was to impress the laity and enhance the prestige of their order.[9] His *Guild of Delinquents* (1512)

[7]*Réformes et réformation,* book 5, takes up the problem at length.
[8]On the intellectual milieu see Miriam Usher Chrisman, *Strasbourg and the Reform* (New Haven, 1967), Chap. 4; Charles Schmidt, *Histoire littéraire de l'Alsace à la fin du XVe et au commencement du XVIe siècle,* 2 vols. (Paris, 1879). For Geiler, see Rapp, *Réformes et réformation,* passim, and Chrisman, *Strasbourg,* chap. 5. For Brant: Edwin Zeydel, *Sebastian Brant* (New York, 1967). For Wimpheling: Lewis W. Spitz, *The Religious Renaissance of the German Humanists* (Cambridge, Mass., 1963), Chap. 3.
[9]*Von den fier Ketzeren,* in Murner, *Deutsche Schriften,* vol. 1¹, esp. 32–34.

[25]

presented a broader canvas of clerical misdeeds. Preachers mocked serious things and neglected the Gospel. "When I want to hear God's word," Murner complained, "all I get is the reading out of documents excommunicating peasants for their debts." In his view, priests, monks, and nuns were all lazy and ignorant. As for the higher clergy, they cared for nothing but hunting.[10] In the same year that he catalogued the delinquents, Murner applied his talents to an *Exorcism of Fools*. Learned fools in the clergy urged the laity to fast while they stuffed their own bellies in secret. They flourished on money extorted from the laity by their ritual exhortation, "Give, everyone, give!" Surely if they had not been protected by their cloth they would have been hanged as thieves long before. Worse than ordinary robbers, the clerical thieves preyed on those poorer than themselves. Benefices, Murner claimed, went to children incapable of performing their duties, since the senior clergy used the church to support their kin. Nor did Murner spare the bishops. If they legislated against concubinage it was in order to collect fines, not to stop the practice. In Murner's view the bishops should be shepherds to their flocks, but since the Devil started giving mitres to nobles, that had all gone by the boards.[11]

Murner based his accusations on real events but his charges were exaggerated. Francis Rapp has examined the validity of the classic complaints against the clergy for the diocese of Strasbourg.[12] Charges of clerical greed can be substantiated, but there is little evidence that the burden of fees for religious services increased between 1450 and 1520. Nor does Rapp see signs of growing immorality when that is measured by sexual incontinence or brawling. As for the charges of ignorance and incompetence, there is solid evidence that the educational standards of the Strasbourg clergy improved in the decades before the reformation. According to Rapp, the increase in anticlericalism did not come from an increase in abuses. He points instead to structural changes in the economy manifested, for instance, in clerical investment in the increasing peasant debt and also to changes in the standards applied to the clergy.[13]

These changing standards grew out of a drive to reform the church

---

[10]*Die Schelmenzunft*, in Murner, *Deutsche Schriften*, 3:49, 73, 130.
[11]*Narrenbeschwörung*, in Murner, *Deutsche Schriften*, 2:134, 213–14, 220–21, 160, 238–39, 251.
[12]*Réformes et réformation*, pp. 421–34.
[13]Ibid., book 5, chap. 3.

which was a major part of Alsatian intellectual life in the decades
before the Protestant reformation. The keynote of this fundamentally
conservative campaign was a return to the strictest standards of the
medieval church. Successive bishops of Strasbourg tried to eliminate
the recognized failings of their subordinate clergy, while men like
Geiler, Brant, and Murner urged the laity to set their own lives in
order. Rapp has analyzed this long abortive campaign waged from
1450 to 1520; we may confine ourselves here to a representative
battle.

In 1509 Wilhelm von Honstein, elected bishop of Strasbourg in
1506, promulgated a major reforming text, which in many ways
anticipated the decisions made at Trent a generation later.[14] His aims
were to enhance his own control over the clergy and that of the clergy
over the laity, to improve the quality of services performed for the
laity, and to cut back on superstitious practices. Honstein ordered his
clergy to avoid the lay courts and the shelter of lay governments and
to submit themselves instead to his exclusive jurisdiction and protection. He demanded that they give up their concubines, and abandon
unseemly habits like swearing, brawling, and the wearing of secular
dress so that they could concentrate on their duties. The bishop told
his priests to restrict the processions demanded by villagers, to end
pilgrimages to unauthorized shrines, and to keep careful watch on the
confraternities. They were to be vigilant in enforcing canon laws
concerning the Easter duty, marriage, and excommunication. For
sermons Honstein recommended three themes: the contrast between
the eternal bliss the church offered to the saved and the unrelenting
agony reserved for the damned; Christian morality; and respect for
clerical privileges. He ordered special efforts to educate the laity.
Pastors were to have their congregations repeat the major prayers
aloud each Sunday, and they might consider displaying these prayers
on big posters in their churches. The clergy should see that parents
and godparents provided religious instruction for their charges. Heterodox ideas were to be rooted out.

Honstein's text contained little that was original, and his attempt at
reform met an entirely typical fate: the canons of New and Old St.
Peter complained to Rome and Rome quashed the bishop's effort.
Outside his immediate circle Honstein had no supporters. His clergy
were hostile or unenthusiastic and the laity did not rally to him;

[14]Ibid., pp. 378–81.

[27]

indeed it is unlikely that more than a handful of them knew anything about the project. The Strasbourg council did, and it sided with the canons. For the next decade the stalemate continued, and the conservative reform proposals produced no results.

Early in the sixteenth century men like Honstein, Brant, Geiler, and Murner addressed three problems that were to dominate the sixteenth-century religious crisis: the proper relations of clergy and laity, the enforcement of Christian discipline, and the imposition of orthodox belief. While the conservative solutions to these problems offered the laity the promise of an improved clergy more capable of carrying out its functions, they also demanded a great deal from the laity in return. Conservative reformers called on men and women outside holy orders to meet stringent standards of piety and morality. The people who heard Murner's sermons or read his books found recitals of their own shortcomings mixed in with those of the clergy. According to Murner, ignorance, immorality, laziness, superstition, violence, lack of charity, and sharp business practices were commonplace among the laity. The Franciscan also knew very well that some of the church's problems were caused by the laity and that the laity got the kind of church it deserved. For example, the laity urged priests to say masses for secular ends like changing the weather, thus wasting a precious tool for salvation in a presumptuous attempt to tell God how to run his universe. Laymen and laywomen encouraged the multiplication of penances and the whole notion of works-righteousness through their unwillingness to trust in God's forgiveness. They balked at learning the elements of their faith. In church they ignored the services to gossip about the Italian wars. The greed of the nobility had destroyed the episcopal office and turned the women's convents in particular into hostels for the nobles' younger children. Lay lords contributed to the financial cost of religious life by siphoning off indulgence money, taxing pilgrims, and impropriating tithes.[15] To reform the church would entail sacrifices by the laity as well as changes in the clergy.

To a man, the conservative reformers defended clerical privileges against lay encroachments. Honstein objected to lay governments' attempts to extend their jurisdiction over the clergy. In Strasbourg around 1500, Geiler preached that the magistrates had been inspired by the Devil in their efforts to restrict clerical privileges and clerical

---

[15]*Von den fier Ketzeren*, p. 109; *Narrenbeschwörung*, pp. 384, 158, 251, 262–65, 248–50.

incomes. Summoned to justify this assault, he submitted a list of twenty-one unchristian policies pursued by the city council.[16] The cathedral preacher attacked city legislation restricting the flow of money into convents in the form of novices' dowries, restrictions on the right of religious to inherit from their families, interference in priests' right to dispose of their property, and the taxes imposed on the clergy. Murner declared that the real motive behind lay interest in church reform was greed: "You want to reform us so you can collect our revenues for yourselves."[17] Whatever their motives, many of the laity had grievances against the clerical privileges that the conservative reformers defended. The laity also showed little sympathy for the drive to extend monastic ideals of fasting, prayer, and confession to ordinary Christians. Geiler himself observed that the canon law had grown into an oppressive tangle in which human elaborations had all but buried the simpler requirements of the Ten Commandments.[18] No one in conservative reform circles, however, had concrete proposals for change in church law or doctrine.

The reform proposals emanating from Erasmus of Rotterdam and his younger disciples in many ways came closer to the hopes of the laity. Erasmus had no sympathy for the monastic ideals and the scholastic theology praised by the conservative reformers. To the Christian humanists who followed him, as to the conservatives, reform meant a return to old standards, but where the conservatives were comfortable with medieval standards, these humanists wanted to push back to the age of Christ, the apostles, and the church fathers. The backward journey could be accomplished by a serial progression. The revival of good letters would engender good theology to tell the people how to live lives pleasing to Christ. Purged of scholastic obscurantism, the simple Gospel message would convert the people. Thus the long-desired reformation of Christendom could be accomplished.

Reform was to be achieved by scholarly work and education, tasks in which the laity were included. While Geiler condemned the circulation of German Bibles and objected on principle to the notion that the lay people could understand Scripture by reading it themselves, Erasmus based his hopes for reform on the spread of Scrip-

---

[16]*Die aeltesten Schriften Geilers von Kaysersberg,* ed. Léon Dacheux (Freiburg im Breisgau, 1882; reprint ed., Amsterdam, 1965), pp. 1–76.

[17]*Narrenbeschwörung,* p. 379; see also pp. 389–91.

[18]Schmidt, *Histoire littéraire,* 1:491.

ture. In the introduction to his 1516 edition of the New Testament he argued that Scripture accommodated itself to the capacity of its readers, nourishing both the simple and the wise. "Only a very few can be learned, but all can be Christian, and all can be devout, and—I shall boldly add—all can be theologians."[19] Against the idea of a special clerical estate, Erasmus nurtured the vision of a Christian society all of whose members had enlisted in a common holy order at their baptism.[20] Where the conservatives would keep the laity in a state of tutelage, perpetual children to be taught by the clergy, Erasmus would raise at least some of them to the level of teachers and partners in the enterprise of reform.

A Christian humanist reform of religious life would not necessarily have touched church doctrine. Nor would it necessarily have demanded alterations in the organization and structure of the church, since its goal was primarily pedagogic and moral. Once better instructed, Christians in all walks of life would live better and suffuse the church with new vitality. Superstitions, legalism, and mechanical devotional practices would dry up like puddles under the summer sun. In their own view, the Erasmians proposed a more thorough reform than did the conservatives because they attacked the causes of religious problems, not just their symptoms. While the ideals of Erasmus's *Handbook of a Christian Knight* probably remained too demanding for most laymen—certainly the soldier to whom it was dedicated showed little inclination to practice the philosophy of Christ—the Christian humanists had taken a long step away from the older counsels of perfection and toward the values of prosperous burghers. Erasmus's descriptions of pleasant feasts in comfortable villas bore little resemblance to Geiler's warnings that those who savored the taste of their food committed sin.[21]

In the last decades before evangelical preaching began in Strasbourg there was little sign of any local Erasmian movement. Certainly the city had its humanists who corresponded with Erasmus and

[19]Ibid., 1:422; "Paraclesis" in *Christian Humanism and the Reformation: Selected Writings of Erasmus with the Life of Erasmus by Beatus Rhenanus,* ed. and trans. John C. Olin, rev. ed. (New York, 1975), pp. 92–106, esp. 96–97 and 100.

[20]Desiderius Erasmus, *Collected Works of Erasmus,* vol. 2, *Correspondence, 1501–1514* (Toronto, 1974–), no. 296 (1517); "On the Well-to-do- Beggars" (1524) in *The Colloquies of Erasmus,* ed. and trans. Craig R. Thompson (Chicago, 1965), p. 216.

[21]*Enchiridion Militis Christiani* (1503) in *The Essential Erasmus,* ed. and trans. John P. Dolan (New York, 1964), pp. 24–93; Geiler, *Die siben hauptsund* (Augsburg, 1510), sig. BBi recto-verso; Erasmus, "The Godly Feast" (1522) in *Colloquies,* pp. 42–78.

entertained him when he visited in 1514.[22] Nevertheless, as a group they were closer to the conservative reform movement than to the philosopher of Christ.[23] Indeed the conservative reform movement depended to a large extent on the energies of humanists like Brant and Wimpheling. The local humanists shared the Erasmians' enthusiasm for educational reform, and they made several attempts to found a Latin school, all without much result. Like the conservative reformers, they were unable to enlist the support of the people or to move the magistrates to action.[24] Humanism did not become an effective force in Strasbourg until the evangelical reformation began and the younger partisans of Erasmus replaced the older humanists at the head of the city's intelligentsia.

In Strasbourg in the 1520s the voices of the conservative reformers and their humanist allies were drowned out by the evangelicals. By now Geiler and Brant were dead and Wimpheling, hostile to the new ideas, soon left the city, leaving Murner alone to keep up the conservative fight. In his writings against Luther and his supporters Murner continued to denounce bad practices in the church, like the use of excommunication for temporal purposes and the persistence of pluralism, while rejecting Luther's remedies.[25] His campaign proved short, for violence and the threat of violence speedily silenced defenders both of the old church and of conservative reform. Humanism, meanwhile, took on a new face and new power. Many of the new evangelicals, in and out of the clergy, were old Erasmians, among them Martin Bucer, Wolfgang Capito, Caspar Hedio, and Jacob Sturm.[26] Even after Erasmus disassociated himself from the evangelical cause, he continued to be respected by many of the city's intellectuals. Through the work of Jean Sturm his pedagogical princi-

---

[22]Erasmus, *Collected Works*, vol. 2, nos. 302, 305; Chrisman, *Lay Culture*, pp. 45–46, 92–102.

[23]Francis Rapp, "Die elsässischen Humanisten und die geistliche Gesellschaft," in *Die Humanisten in ihrer politischen und sozialen Umwelt*, ed. Otto Herding and Robert Stupperich (Bonn, 1976), pp. 87–108.

[24]Chrisman, *Strasbourg*, pp. 62–66, and *Lay Culture*, pp. 98–99.

[25]*An den grossmechtigsten und durchlüchtigsten Adel tütschen nation*, in Murner, *Deutsche Schriften*, 7:81, 104–5, 112.

[26]Bernd Moeller, "Die deutschen Humanisten und die Anfänge der Reformation," *Zeitschrift für Kirchengeschichte*, 70 (1959), 46–61; Martin Bucer, *La correspondance de Martin Bucer*, ed. Jean Rott (Leiden, 1979), nos. 2, 8; Nicole Peremans, *Erasme et Bucer d'après leur correspondance* (Paris, 1970); James M. Kittelson, *Wolfgang Capito: From Humanist to Reformer* (Leiden, 1975); Thomas A. Brady, Jr., "Jacob Sturm of Strasbourg (1489–1553) and the Political Security of German Protestantism, 1526–1532" (Ph.D. diss., University of Chicago, 1968), pp. 12–32, 38.

ples, at least, won an enduring success in the new Latin school, founded at last in 1538.[27] Christian humanism was to remain a live force in reformation Strasbourg. At mid-century Georg Wickram offered Strasburghers the fictional portrait of a prosperous and godly peasant who had learned his religion from Erasmus.[28] As we shall see, the religious values of some real Strasburghers were closer to those of Erasmus than to those of the clergy in the new established church.

The reform proposals that carried the day in Strasbourg were more novel and dramatic than those of the conservatives or the humanists. The evangelical faction that coalesced behind Martin Luther and his scattered sympathizers in the clergy branded the doctrines of the old church an obstacle to salvation and attacked its structures as inimical to Christian life. Luther's followers joined him in expanding, refining, altering, and spreading this message. These evangelicals took their case directly to the common people instead of working only among the educated and the powerful. All over the Empire men and women welcomed the new theology, which promised them surety of salvation and relief from the maddening psychological and financial demands of the old religious establishment.[29] In town after town the argument that the detested aspects of the old order had no scriptural foundation convinced Germans that they could and should be abolished.

After a stuttering start, the new reform program made rapid progress in Strasbourg.[30] When Matthis Zell, the most popular preacher in the city, took up the cause, neither the canons nor the bishop could stop the spread of revolt.[31] Zell drew large crowds, and preacher

[27]Anton Schindling, *Humanistische Hochschule und freie Reichstadt: Gymnasium und Akademie in Strassburg, 1538–1621* (Wiesbaden, 1977); Chrisman, *Lay Culture,* pp. 99, 192–201.

[28]*Der Irr Reitend Bilger* (1556), in *Georg Wickrams sämtliche Werke,* ed. Hans-Gert Roloff, 12 vols. (Berlin, 1967–75), vol. 1, chaps. 8–12.

[29]Steven Ozment, *The Reformation in the Cities* (New Haven, 1975).

[30]Marc Lienhard and Jean Rott, "Die Anfänge der evangelischen Predigten in Strassburg und ihr erstes Manifest: Der Aufruf der Karmeliter Tilmann von Lyn (Anfang 1522)," in *Bucer und seine Zeit: Forschungsbericht und Bibliographie,* ed. Marijn de Kroon and Wilhelm Krüger (Wiesbaden, 1976), pp. 54–73.

[31]Chrisman, *Strasbourg;* Thomas A. Brady, Jr., *Ruling Class, Regime and Reformation at Strasbourg, 1520–1555* (Leiden, 1978); William Stafford, *Domesticating the Clergy: The Inception of the Reformation in Strasbourg, 1522–1524* (Missoula, Mont., 1976); Georges Livet, Francis Rapp, and Jean Rott, eds., *Strasbourg au coeur religieux du XVIe siècle: Hommage à Lucien Febvre* (Strasbourg, 1977). Taken together, these studies make any detailed account here of events in the 1520s and 1530s superfluous.

after preacher went over to his side. Martin Bucer arrived from Wissembourg, already a convert and already married. Wolfgang Capito, the provost of the St. Thomas chapter, added his voice, and his protégé Caspar Hedio joined in as well. By 1524 the core of the future Church Assembly had united and won a substantial popular following.

The program the new preachers expounded was as straightforward as it was revolutionary. According to it, the Christian church had nearly disappeared under the grime of centuries of human additions to Scripture. The clergy who defended these accretions were parasites, determined to keep the people in blindness for their own profit. The Bible explained that salvation came from faith, and faith alone. Anything else the priests demanded was mere human invention. The Bible taught that the church was the fellowship of believers, not the pompous hordes of lazy, rich, and selfish prelates who claimed to speak for Christ. As Bucer explained it: "All the law and the prophets are based on two commandments: Thou shalt love the Lord thy God with all thy heart and thou shalt love thy neighbor as thyself. . . . But how does the love of God come to mean that people should have to build churches, provide for Masses, endow brotherhoods, purchase good works, burn candles, and all sorts of absurdities, and all at great expense?"[32]

The reformation as Bucer and his colleagues preached it was as concerned with morality and ethics as was any series of sermons Geiler ever delivered or any exhortation Erasmus ever uttered. Their reading of the Bible taught them that the doctrines and institutions of the church were corrupt and led them to foment direct and violent attacks that Geiler would not have countenanced and that Erasmus rejected. With the authority of God's word behind them, they taught their listeners that the old ways were ungodly and must be destroyed. Monks and nuns wasted their time in senseless works—liberate them from their prisons. Images befuddled the ignorant who worshiped them instead of Christ—destroy them. The priests were lazy—make them work. The old formula of salvation by works, which the new preachers said the old priests taught, was claptrap—sweep it away and let the Gospel in its simplicity reach out to the people and bring them to God. The mass rested on a misreading of Scripture and dazzled the simple with its pomp and mumblings in a foreign

---

[32]*Summary seiner Predig* (1523), quoted by Chrisman, *Strasbourg*, pp. 122–23.

tongue—let Christ's words ring out in German. Tithes had been misused—return them to their proper purposes. The church refused to allow priests to marry, although neither Christ nor the Apostles forbade this—let those who could not be chaste take wives, and so put an end to the sorry tales of concubinage and seduction. The priests had surrounded themselves with spurious privileges—let the clergy become citizens and subjects like other Christians. The people wanted this, the preachers said, and it was the city council's duty to oversee the return of the true church.

The magistrates were not so sure.[33] They decided to protect Matthis Zell from his ecclesiastical superiors on the grounds that he was simply preaching the Gospel. But as the Gospel became more radical it became a new thing, and innovations were never to the magistrates' taste. These preachers clamored "Martin," but Luther was a heretic, excommunicated by the pope and condemned by the emperor. Certainly the new preachers flattered the lay rulers, praised their office and pronounced them competent to rule on church matters. The magistrates could see some advantages to take from the new movement. Sweeping away the church courts and making the clergy become citizens seemed like a sound idea to them, for they had been working in that direction for years. Letting priests marry might end the offensive spectacle of men of God living in sin. Some magistrates showed an enthusiasm for the new gospel early in the twenties, but as a group they were loath to accept the consequences of an open break with the emperor's church. The lay rulers hesitated to accept the authority in church matters which the evangelicals pushed upon them. And when Caspar Hedio married Augustin Drenss's own sister, that senator knew things had gone too far, even if his senior colleague Claus Kniebis had blessed her marriage to a priest.[34]

Zealous evangelicals like Kniebis and supporters of the old religious order like Drenss battled in the council chambers, while cooler heads like Bernhard Wurmser and Jacob Sturm begged for a little calm.[35] Confusion reigned: what did Christ require? When calm

[33]The two following paragraphs draw heavily on Brady, *Ruling Class*, chap. 6.

[34]The fullest account of this incident is Stafford's *Domesticating the Clergy*, pp. 210–18, but he is wrong in describing Drenss as a common citizen. See Brady, *Ruling Class*, pp. 231–32 and Appendix A, no. 18.

[35]Thomas A. Brady, Jr., "'Sind also zu beiden theilen Christen, des Gott erbarm': La mémoire de Jacques Sturm sur le culte public à Strasbourg (août 1525)," in *Horizons européens de la réforme en Alsace./Das Elsass und die Reformation im Europa des XVI Jahrhunderts: Mélanges offerts à Jean Rott pour son 65e anniversaire*, ed. Marijn de Kroon and Marc Lienhard (Strasbourg, 1980), pp. 69–79.

won out, it was because the magistrates all agreed that change must not endanger their control of Strasbourg and that the refusal of all change provoked violence. The rioters and the iconoclasts might turn against the secular authoritites next, and the Peasants' War of 1525 made this threat very real. Throughout the 1520s the magistrates also worried that Charles V might invoke his imperial authority and step in to pacify the city at the ruling families' expense.

The evangelical preachers certainly taxed the magistrates' willingness to make concessions. These preachers wanted radical changes in religious life, and that meant change in the social fabric as well. Although they blamed the street fights, the tavern brawls, and the attacks on the churches on the resistance of the loyalists, it was obvious that they were the *agents provocateurs.* Conservatives like Thomas Murner tried to save the old church by charging that the evangelicals fomented revolution. Murner again and again laid responsibility for the violence on the shoulders of the converted clergy, revived memories of the Hussite wars in Bohemia, and exploited the terrifying memories of recent alliances of peasant rebels claiming religious inspiration well before the Peasants' War began in Alsace. Murner warned that the evangelical preachers would expand the priesthood of all believers into the lordship of all subjects. This heresy, he argued, would engender mob rule and destroy property rights.[36] Murner was right to link the evangelical sermons and the violence. He was wrong to assume that the new preachers would support a thorough social and political revolution. While the evangelical clergy were willing to become pastors by popular election and preached a doctrine of property rights which emphasized the obligations of the rich to the church and to the poor, they also preached respect for constituted secular authority, cooperated in the city council's takeover of nomination rights in urban and rural parishes (a process that put election in the hands of the better-off laity), and did not attempt to force the rich to share their property with the poor. Without making any statement remotely comparable to Luther's *Against the Murdering, Robbing Hordes of Peasants,* they acted to discourage the local bands. The new preachers chose to live with the old political and social powers in secular life.

The conservative reformers had had very little desire to alter the distribution of power and wealth within their society beyond their interest in beating back lay infringements on clerical authority. Like-

---

[36]*Ein christliche und briederliche ermanung,* pp. 40–41, 113–15. *Von den babstenthum* (1520), in Murner, *Deutsche Schriften,* 7:48; *An den . . . Adel,* pp. 63, 66–68, 72, 78.

wise, the humanist reformers were only tangentially interested in the power structure of early modern Europe. The evangelicals planned more sweeping changes, but whether deliberately or not their program was driving toward an increase in the prerogatives of the lay rulers. Alongside these three groups was a fourth approach to reform, fragmented, disorganized, and much more revolutionary. The radical current certainly wished to see the sway of the old priests broken, but their reformation of Christendom also involved the erosion or destruction of the power of their temporal lords. Thomas Murner's criticism of the old church had tied its failings to the ruling classes' control of religion, and Strasbourg's urban mobs and peasant bands struck at their lay lords as well as at their priests in the 1520s.

The iconoclasts whose axes ripped across religious paintings or smashed statues were not only destroying holy symbols, they were purging their church of a symbol of the prestige of the wealthy families who had decorated the churches with these objects. The blows that annihilated the faces of saints also obliterated the faces of ruling class donors, frequently the ancestors of men now sitting on the city council.[37] When several hundred craftsmen and laborers seized Carthusian wine in transit to the city, stormed the Charterhouse and the convent of St. Arbogast, then ate and drank themselves into a stupor on the spoils, they irrefutably demonstrated that their sense of reformation involved a redistribution of ecclesiastical wealth.[38] Strasbourg's gardeners' guild, the city's largest and poorest guild, distinguished itself by its violent support for change in the 1520s; many members sympathized with the peasants in 1524–25. Clemens Ziegler, a Strasbourg gardener who later became a spiritualist, at this time was touring the countryside, preaching reform and attacking the tithe to such effect that the peasants of Truttenhausen marched into battle under a banner reading "Evangelium, Christus, Clemens Ziegler."[39] A captured peasant, Martin Küffer-

---

[37]Brady, *Ruling Class,* pp. 217–21, 233–34. Carl C. Christensen, "Patterns of Iconoclasm in the Early Reformation: Strasbourg and Basel," in *The Image and the Word: Confrontations in Judaism, Christianity and Islam,* ed. Joseph Gutmann (Missoula, Mont., 1977), pp. 107–48, does not address the issue directly but provides considerable evidence linking Strasbourg iconoclasts to the peasants and showing the initial magisterial opposition.

[38]Rodolphe Reuss, ed., "Les éphémerides de Jacques de Gottesheim, docteur en droit, prébendier du grand-choeur de la cathédrale (1524–1543)," *BSCMHA,* n.s. 19 (1899), p. 269; Léon Dacheux, ed., "Les chroniques strasbourgeoises de Jacques Trausch et de Jean Wencker," *BSCMHA,* n.s. 15 (1892), no. 2672.

[39]Rodolphe Peter, "Le maraîcher Clément Ziegler, l'homme et son oeuvre," *RHPR,* 34 (1954), 255–82. Ziegler withdrew his support when the peasants turned to violence.

knecht of Rappoltsweyer, affirmed his belief that only the imperial levies on the peasants were legal and that seigneurial and clerical taxes need not be paid; indeed he claimed that only the emperor had legitimate temporal authority. Put into practice, Küfferknecht's ideas would have destroyed the corporate rights of the Strasbourg council over its dependent villages as well as the rights of individual urban seigneurs (a group that overlapped the Strasbourg ruling class). Küfferknecht's was not an isolated voice in Alsace.[40]

The peasants challenged lay as well as clerical lordship and they had supporters in Strasbourg.[41] So did the Anabaptist movement that began to take shape here in the 1520s.[42] Here again we find groups of "little people," craftsmen and laborers, who were drawn by the idea of a reformation that would overhaul social as well as ecclesiastical structures on a grand scale. Against the idea of a broad church, taking in all citizens, which was supported by both the old priests and the new preachers, the Anabaptists came to demand gathered churches of committed believers, real Christians who shaped their lives by obedience to Biblical commandments and lived them outside the jurisdiction of the temporal government. Their literalist reading of Scripture led them to refuse to take oaths, the cement of early modern communal life, and to reject the use of coercion among Christians, two positions which would have destroyed the city's whole political and judicial apparatus. Their emphasis on stewardship and sharing was equally incompatible with the realities of the urban economy.

Like the conservative reformers, Strasbourg's peasants and poor were speedily silenced. The former had helped to create the anticlericalism on which the victorious evangelical reformation fed. The latter, by their desire to turn religious change into a thorough restructuring of society, pushed the city council into the hands of the evangelical preachers, who appeared moderate by contrast. After 1525 there was almost no evidence of violent social radicalism in Strasbourg. The Anabaptists, however, had a long career ahead of them. For decades their groups would continue to offer the

---

[40]Gunther Franz, ed., *Quellen zur Geschichte des Bauernkrieges* (Munich, 1963), no. 70, on Küfferknecht, who attributed his ideas to Zell, and no. 71, the articles of the peasants of Hagenau, Bitsch, Hanau-Lichtenberg, and the right bank of the Rhine. Zell and Hedio had both preached against the misuse of tithes, but not against their legality.

[41]Jean Rott, "Artisanat et mouvements sociaux à Strasbourg autour de 1525," in *Artisans et ouvriers d'Alsace* (Strasbourg, 1965), pp. 137–70, and Rapp, *Réformes et réformation*, pp. 473–79. For an index of radical sentiment in the city see Brant, "Annales," no. 4616.

[42]Source material has been published through 1535 in *TAE*. Brant, "Annales," nos. 4677 (1525), 4707 (1526).

Strasburghers a vision of a different reformation and to remind the clergymen of the established church of the limitations of their achievements.

The fifth current that emerged in Strasbourg in these early years was the spiritualist.[43] For the spiritualists, even more than for the humanists, the reformation was an individual matter. What counted was a personal relationship with God, not the creation of public institutions like churches and schools, although they did not necessarily object to institutions. To spiritualists the Bible itself could become a tyrant when it was used to deny the direct revelation God sent to the believer. The conservative struggle to enforce church law, the humanist drive for a faith formed by education, the preachers' campaign to purify the church and its doctrines, the radical emphasis on biblical literalism and social egalitarianism, all became more or less irrelevant to men like Clemens Ziegler, Caspar Schwenckfeld, and Eckard zum Treubel. This indifference to the causes of others permitted the spiritualists to take up an attitude of being above controversy and allowed them to carry on with whatever institutional structures emerged from the quarrels. As Eckard zum Treubel, a Strasbourg patrician, advised one of his children in 1528:[44]

> Hold yourself true to the corporate body of the Christian church and to your chief parish church. Wherever it is, attend it. For the great St. Peter's cathedral in Rome, with all its court and court followers, is not the Christian church, nor the great church chapter in Strasbourg. . . . But where pious believing Christians come together, whether it be in wild woods or in the fields, that is the true Christian church. . . . It consists in faith and in the love of God and one's neighbour. But your rightful parish, dear son, is in the cathedral of Strasbourg and you should do what it does and what it teaches.

This sort of advice had an obvious charm in the confusion of the early reformation. Some Strasburghers did accept the outward forms of the established church while at the same time keeping an inner distance from it.

These five reforming streams, conservative, humanist, evangelical, radical, and spiritualist, overlapped at many points. The evangelical

[43]*TAE* includes material on the spiritualists.
[44]Quoted by Miriam Usher Chrisman, "Lay Response to the Protestant Reformation in Germany, 1520–1528," in *Reformation Principle and Practice: Festschrift for Geoffrey Dickens,* ed. Peter Newman Brooks (London, 1980), pp. 48–49.

solution to the religious crisis bore enough resemblance to the old church for its proponents to be branded "new papists." It incorporated the humanist pedagogic program and shared something of the radicals' concern to help the downtrodden. The humanists for their part often opted for the old faith, as did Erasmus himself. In Caspar Schwenckfeld they had a spiritualist brother, and indeed their own piety had an individualist flavor. The radicals could have claimed Thomas Murner as an Alsatian Müntzer had the Franciscan converted and continued his attacks on the lay lords. Spiritualists, as zum Treubel shows, could coexist with any church order. At the same time, differing theories about the relations of the clergy and the laity, the standards and enforcement of morality, and the definition and policing of orthodoxy separated the five streams.

Strasbourg's rulers chose to support the evangelicals, although that did not mean that every magistrate, then or later, personally accepted the clergy's religion (see Appendix A). The magistrates' official commitment to Capito, Bucer, Zell, and Hedio had roots both idealistic and practical. The magistrates of the 1520s had grown up in a society permeated with Christian values; when the preachers quoted Scripture they listened, and slowly a majority converted. Their conversion was made easier by the preachers' manifest willingness to defer to secular authority. Demanding as they were, the preachers were less radical than many of their followers and rivals, and this fact also swayed the magistrates. The city's lay rulers managed to use the preachers to channel Strasbourg's reformation in directions where it did the least harm to the status quo and where more of the damage was borne by the clerical than by the lay lords. They made concessions to the preachers, counting on their influence to calm the rebellious crowds in their streets, and at the same time made sure that the preachers recognized that the price of religious reform was social peace. The magistrates would make the preachers pastors and give them parishes, provided that the newly created pastors reined in their parishioners.

After 1523, when the magistrates decided to protect Matthis Zell, change came rapidly. Evangelicals acquired pulpits. The clergy were compelled to take out citizenship, a move the evangelicals heartily supported. Citizens were aided in their efforts to talk relatives out of the religious houses, monks and nuns were offered pensions, and the city took over the administration of their property. In 1525, at the height of the Peasants' War, the magistrates restricted the celebration of the mass to the chapels of the four chapter churches. They allowed the churches to be stripped of their works of art and whitewashed, while ensuring that as much as possible of the banished property returned to its donors or their heirs. They passed legislation to muzzle debate and did their best to ensure that if change there must be to suit their subjects, then change would go forward in an orderly fashion. With each concession they lowered the risk of violence a little more.

One by one, individual magistrates went over to the new faith. In 1526 the city council could still muster a bare majority to prevent the total abolition of the mass.[45] In all likelihood the magistrates, conscious of the emperor's devotion to the old ways, lagged behind their subjects at this time. On the other hand, it is hard to believe that the absolute prohibition of the mass could have been postponed until 1529 if a large majority of Strasburghers had accepted the gospel of the evangelical reformers wholeheartedly by the mid-twenties. The zealots who broke chairs over priests' heads catch the historian's eye; they are allowed to speak loudly for the mute majority. Yet Strasbourg's biggest reformation riot involved only three to six hundred people, at most only 3 percent of the population.[46] Of course, one could support the new ideas without taking to the streets. Certainly by the end of the decade the majority of Strasburghers had accepted the new faith.

After the decade of destruction, the work of rebuilding took over as the Strasburghers began to pull together a new church from the conflicting ideas of the advocates of reform. Catholic theology, and with it conservative reform, had been rejected by the majority. The defeat of the radical movements meant that the egalitarian notion of the priesthood of all believers would be confined to the religious sphere and have limited consequences there. The humanist drive for pedagogical reform was to survive in evangelical translation, but the wishes of the spiritualists were denied by the consolidation of a state church with its obligatory orthodoxy. The new church was to be Protestant in its doctrines, structures, and definition of Christian morality.

The exact doctrines of this Protestant church would remain a matter of controversy until the end of the century. The central question at first was where Strasbourg stood in the eucharistic quarrel between

[45]Brant, "Annales," no. 4701.
[46]See note 38, above.

the Swiss and the Saxons.[47] By the end of the 1520s Martin Bucer, now a leading Strasbourg theologian, had decided that his own and Luther's views agreed in the essentials. Luther was not convinced. Strasbourg's exclusion from the circle of Wittenberg orthodoxy continued, and the city had to submit its own confession of faith to the Diet of Augsburg in 1530. In this Tetrapolitan Confession Bucer and Wolfgang Capito struggled to come close to the Wittenberg explanation of the eucharist while leaving the wording ambiguous enough for the Swiss to accept.[48] The Swiss never rallied, but the Saxons did thaw and in 1532 they finally allowed Strasbourg to sign their Augsburg Confession. Four years later Bucer made his personal submission to Luther in the Wittenberg Concord.[49]

A certain ambiguity continued to hang over the city's doctrinal position. In 1536 Bucer had proclaimed the essential unity of the Tetrapolitan and Augsburg Confessions, and no one had seen any reason to disavow the former. In 1548 the local clergy could refer to "our two Augsburg Confessions" (since both had been submitted to the emperor in 1530), and the city council did not publicly reject the Tetrapolitan Confession until 1598.[50] The *Tetrapolitana* lent itself to conflicting interpretations, and between 1536 and 1598 there were Strasburghers who chose to construe it in a distinctly Swiss manner. The result was more than a generation of discord among the city's intellectuals, in and out of the clergy, over what exactly constituted orthodox belief in Strasbourg.

The reorganization of church structures was relatively easier. The number of places of worship was pared back. Thirteen out of nineteen religious houses disappeared, as did most private chapels, three parish churches, and the weakest of the collegial churches, All Saints. The new established church held the chapter of St. Thomas and the seven remaining parish churches. The magistrates took over patronage rights in these churches and created lay parish wardens to oversee parish activities. They promulgated a church ordinance embodying these changes in 1534.[51]

[47]Ernst Bizer, *Studien zur Geschichte des Abendmahlstreits im 16ten Jahrhundert* (Gütersloh, 1940) remains a useful introduction.
[48]*BDS*, vol. 3.
[49]Text in Bizer, *Abendmahlstreits*, pp. 117–19. On its introduction in Strasbourg see J.-V. Pollet, *Martin Bucer: Etudes sur la correspondance avec de nombreux textes inédits*, 2 vols. (Paris, 1959–62), vol. 1, nos. 19–23.
[50]AST 49/1c, f. 64 r (1548). For 1598, see Chapter 6, at note 49.
[51]Text, *BDS*, 5:15–41. See François Wendel, *L'église de Strasbourg, sa constitution et son organisation, 1532–1535* (Paris, 1942), and Chapter 3, below.

Along with the new established church, which from 1529 to 1549 had a monopoly on public religious services, Lutheran Strasbourg contained other churches of varying legality. A truncated version of the old structures survived in the chapters of the cathedral and New and Old St. Peter, in the remaining religious houses (the Teutonic Knights, the Knights of St. John, and the Carthusians, as well as the Dominican nuns of St. Margaret and St. Nicolas, and the Penitents of St. Mary Magdalene), and in at least one of the beguinages. These Catholic corporations were still recognized in law. Catholic services, from which the public was banned after 1529, continued in private in these corporations and in the homes of adherents of the old faith. After 1549 the mass again enjoyed legal status in the city. A third church order, entirely illegal, also existed. A noticeable minority of Strasburghers, unimpressed by the condemnation of religious radicalism, rejected the parish churches and joined the clandestine sectarian communities. Late in the 1530s a French refugee parish, nominally part of the established church but increasingly at odds with Lutheran doctrine and eventually deprived of any legal existence, completed the array. While Strasbourg's two confessions of faith fueled doctrinal quarrels among the intellectuals, the common people could vote with their feet for Lutheran, Catholic, sectarian, or Calvinist services.

The new established church also redefined the standards of Christian morality. Communion and confession ceased to be obligatory, as did the observance of the Lenten fast and most saints' days. Under the new order Strasburghers found it easier to marry and possible to remarry after divorce.[52] However, the city continued to enforce legislation against blasphemy, adultery, and fornication, and to demand respect for the Sabbath; it still claimed to regulate business life as well in a spirit indistinguishable from that of the prereformation period. In 1535 the magistrates issued a disciplinary ordinance that brought together a series of statutes enacted in the twenties and thirties, most of which renewed existing late medieval legislation.[53] Throughout the century the model burghers remained like their ancestors peaceful, god-fearing, moderate in their pleasures, and honest in their

[52]François Wendel, *Le mariage à Strasbourg à l'époque de la réforme, 1520–1692* (Strasbourg, 1928), and Walther Köhler, *Züricher Ehegericht und genfer Konsistorium,* 2 vols. (Leipzig, 1932), vol. 2, passim.

[53]Text in Timotheus Wilhelm Roehrich, *Mittheilungen aus der Geschichte der evangelischen Kirche des Elsasses,* 3 vols. (Paris, 1855), 1:244–84.

dealings with their fellows. What constituted proper piety certainly varied from one territory to another in the sixteenth century, but moral standards were generally something upon which Europeans found themselves in substantial agreement. Still, there was room in Strasbourg for serious disagreement about who was to police morality and how strictly to enforce ideals. Zealots criticized the established church because it numbered sinners in its ranks, the Lutheran clergy hectored the magistrates to use the law to create a city of saints, and the magistrates joined the majority of their subjects to steer a middle course between the saints and the sinners.

The Strasburghers' new church did not give full victory to the advocates of any of the conflicting reform programs of the early sixteenth century. Those who championed conservative reform had lost badly in the city and had yet to make gains in the surrounding diocesan lands. Strasburghers who remained faithful to the Catholic church had to resign themselves to life in a nest of heretics. The humanists had been swallowed up by the evangelical movement, and until the magistrates acted to improve the educational system in the late thirties their hopes were thwarted. Disappointed radicals surveyed a city where the ancient divisions between rich and poor survived and where the preaching of the Gospel had not produced the great desideratum of all the reformers, a population wholly committed to Christ. Spiritualists denounced the elements of coercion and dogmatism already evident in the new order. As for the evangelical preachers, they found in the thirties that they had paid a high price for the defeat of their rivals in reform. They had developed arguments more potent to achieve change than those of their conservative and humanist predecessors. They had helped the magistrates to beat back the radicals and spiritualists. They had mobilized a zealous minority of supporters whose visible, often violent demand for change had pushed the magistrates to make concessions. Nevertheless the magistrates, not the evangelical preachers, had emerged as the real victors in the early phase of the reformation. In the space of fifteen years the secular rulers of Strasbourg had established a control over the church and religious life that would have been unthinkable a generation earlier.[54] As they struggled to complete their reformation, Strasbourg's Protestant pastors would have to master the rules of their city's new balance of power.

[54]Compare the late medieval situation as described by Rapp, *Réformes et réformation*, pp. 108–14 and 410–20, with the changes in the early twenties, pp. 473–77.

CHAPTER TWO

Religion and Power

B y the 1530s, when Strasbourg's religious life began to settle into its new patterns, it was clear that most of the Strasburghers had turned away from their preachers' demands for a continuing reformation. Many people had delivered themselves from the pope's yoke without taking up the Gospel, complained Caspar Hedio in 1534.[1] Indeed, Martin Bucer echoed, they understood Christian freedom only as the license of the flesh; as soon as someone mentioned "church discipline" or "church order" they began to scream against the restoration of human laws and obligations. Bucer blamed the magistrates for this state of affairs. The German ruling classes, he said in a bitter judgment near the end of his life, had learned only two things from the Gospel: to throw off the tyranny of pope and bishop, and to abandon all discipline and penance. In their carnal wisdom they preferred reason of state to Scripture.[2]

With the benefit of hindsight Bucer had located the fatal error lurking in the evangelical preachers' campaigns of the 1520s. They had rallied popular support for their reformation and forced the city council's hand, obliging the magistrates to accept changes faster than they thought politic. The Strasbourg magistrates did not like to be coerced by anyone. They were determined to neutralize the power of clergy and commons, and used the evangelicals' own ideas to do so. While

---

[1] *Radts Predig* (Strasbourg, 1534), sig. C iv recto. For the circumstances prompting this sermon see Wendel, *L'Eglise*, pp. 108–9.

[2] *Von der waren Seelsorge* (1538), BDS, 7:94, 95; *De Regno Christi* (1550) in *Melanchthon and Bucer*, ed. and trans. Wilhelm Pauck (Philadelphia, 1969), pp. 212–13, 259–60.

struggling to eliminate the mass, the reformers flattered the magistrates and exalted their prerogatives over the church. They had argued that the magistrates could regulate the external aspects of religious life, and that lay magistrates could judge whether or not given doctrines were correct Christian theology. The "shrewd tacticians" of the early reformation thus dealt away many cards they soon regretted losing.[3] By 1536 the lay magistrates had taken control of doctrine, discipline, and church organization.

The evangelicals had appealed to the laity to judge the truth of the doctrines on which they and their rivals based their reform proposals. They were particularly anxious to win the magistrates' approval and thus obtain official sanction for their theology. The magistrates, of course, were not theologians. Jacob Sturm, who was one of the few magistrates with any expertise in doctrine, knew that his colleagues were incapable of absorbing the nuances of a confession of faith when one was presented to them.[4] Nevertheless, when papal authority collapsed, they were the only group able to make doctrinal formulae binding on the city. Thus the city's original Protestant confession, the *Tetrapolitana,* was presented to the emperor at Augsburg in 1530 not as the opinions of its authors, Martin Bucer and Wolfgang Capito, but as those of the city's ruling council.[5] The Sixteen Articles became doctrinal norms in Strasbourg not when the clergy drafted them in 1533, but when the magistrates approved them in 1534.[6] The right to pronounce upon doctrine was not just an aberration of the early reformation. For twenty years at the close of sixteenth century the lay rulers refused to accept the Formula of Concord proposed by Jacob Andreae in 1577, although their own pastors repeatedly begged them to grant it legal standing.

Just as the lay rulers reserved to themselves the last word on doctrine, they also took sole control of the policing of morality under the terms of the original settlement. The old church courts vanished and the magistrates permitted no consistory to replace them. Sins were punished now, when they were punished, as crimes, and punishment was dispensed by the lay courts. For several decades excommunica-

---

[3]Ozment, *Reformation in the Cities,* pp. 125, 131–38.
[4]*TAE,* vol. 2, no. 503 (1534).
[5]Text and supporting documents: *BDS,* vol. 3. Thomas A. Brady, Jr., "Jacob Sturm of Strasbourg and the Lutherans at the Diet of Augsburg (1530)," *Church History,* 42 (1973), 1–20.
[6]Text: *TAE,* vol. 2, no. 371. See also Wendel, *L'Eglise,* and *BDS,* vol. 5.

tion was reduced to a half measure, purged of its power to inflict social ostracism. The clergy strove to recover their lost power to discipline the laity, but their progress would be slow.

Through their 1534 Church Ordinance the magistrates established the new church's structure and spelled out their control of its personnel.[7] Legislation on these matters bristled with devices to keep the clergy firmly under lay control, and to ensure that lay control meant magisterial control. The city council turned the preachers into civic employees and made use of their new status as citizens to police them. It created a new lay office, that of church warden, to monitor the preachers' opinions and behavior. Not content with that, the magistrates designated one pastor to lead the clergy, with the intention of using him to control his fellows. Mindful of the preachers' success in mobilizing support among their lay subjects in the twenties, the magistrates took steps to limit the clergy's freedom to communicate with parishioners.

The city council began to take charge of the appointment of pastors to the urban parishes as early as 1524. Modifying the early evangelical idea of popular election by the congregation, the secular authorities developed a procedure that emphasized their own power and eliminated most parishioners from the selection process. First the council summoned two or three candidates to preach trial sermons before the whole congregation. Then, under the supervision of two or more magistrates delegated to collect the vote, the most prominent and respectable parishioners elected their new pastor or assistant pastor. The city council ratified the election, made the formal appointment, and arranged for the payment of a salary. Shortly thereafter the lay church wardens, acting in the name of the council, presented the man to his congregation.[8] If he later proved unsatisfactory it was up to the magistrates, not his fellow clergymen or his parishioners, to dismiss him.[9]

The magistrates tended to treat the clergy they appointed like senior members of the civic bureaucracy, on a par with the city lawyers

[7]Text: *BDS*, 5:15–41.
[8]AST 87/14 and 47-1/8. For a typical election see RP 1548, ff. 11r–12r, 216v–217r, 219r-v, 222r-v. See also Jean-Pierre Kintz, "Eglise et société strasbourgeoise du milieu du XVIe siècle au milieu du XVIIe siècle," *Annuaire de la société des amis du vieux-Strasbourg*, 11 (1983), 40–44.
[9]In practice, the magistrates dismissed clergymen only at the request of their fellows; the only exceptions occurred in 1549, when fear of Charles V brought about the exile of Bucer and Paul Fagius.

or secretaries. Like the members of those two groups, the clergy were professional men, employed by the magistrates, consulted in their areas of expertise, and even on occasion sent off to foreign territories to represent the city.[10] The clergy, like the lawyers and secretaries, were supposed to remain subordinate; they could suggest a course of action but could not dictate policy. When policy conflicted with their own desires they were expected to defer to their employers' will.

The Protestant preachers' status as citizens of Strasbourg reinforced their subjection to the lay rulers. Early in 1525 the magistrates had ordered all clergymen resident in the city to become burghers, an order that had the warm support of the leaders of the evangelical party.[11] By taking out citizenship the preachers accepted the jurisdiction of the lay courts. They agreed to pay taxes and to join guilds. Most important, they bound themselves by solemn oath to obey the magistrates without reservation. Nothing in the burgher's oath gave them legal grounds to refuse an order for reasons of conscience. Like any other citizen, they could be punished if they disobeyed.

The magistrates planned to use their church wardens to keep track of the clergy's activities. After 1531 each parish had three lay *Kirchenpfleger* whose task was to supervise the doctrine, morals, and work of the parish clergy and to discipline the laity.[12] The senior warden in each parish was a member of the city's standing executive councils, and the second was a guild official eligible for election to the city's Senate; only the junior man was not part of the regime. The city council chose church wardens for life terms, without consulting the clergy. The wardens' primary responsibility was to police the clergy, but they were also expected to work with their pastor and his assistant to ensure the smooth running of the parish, for instance by organizing the elections of new clergymen. In addition, the wardens were to take turns attending the clergy's regular meetings; at least four times a year all twenty-one wardens were to attend one of these meetings en masse. The clergy had orders to defer to the opinions of the lay wardens and not to make important decisions, even if the wardens approved their projects, without getting permission from the city council itself. The wardens were to act as the magistrates'

---

[10]Lorna Jane Abray, "The Long Reformation: Magistrates, Clergy, and People in Strasbourg, 1520–1598" (Ph.D. diss., Yale University, 1978), Appendix A.

[11]Bernd Moeller, "Kleriker als Bürger," in *Festschrift für Hermann Heimpel*, 3 vols. (Göttingen, 1972), 2:205–6, 211–14; Ozment, *Reformation in the Cities*, pp. 86–87.

[12]*Kirchenpflegerordnung*, in Roehrich, *Mittheilungen*, 1:257–60.

regular liaison with the clergy, reporting problems in their parishes and carrying instructions from the council back to the preachers.

A decade after creating the office of church warden the magistrates decided to add another structure of control. They could not imagine a group without a leader, and took it upon themselves to supply the clergy with one. Following the examples of Saxony and Hesse they appointed one preacher to be "superintendent over all the pastors."[13] In Saxony and Hesse the superintendents had coercive powers over their colleagues, but in Strasbourg the magistrates arranged matters differently. Within a year of creating the position they decided that "superintendent" meant "person in charge" and transferred the title back to themselves.[14] The head clergyman found himself reduced to "president," and the magistrates insisted that the president's power was very limited. "The president only chairs the clergy's meetings; other than that he has no authority unless we later decide to grant other powers to him."[15] Appointed by the magistrates, the president was intended to be their tool.

In the 1520s the magistrates had received an unsettling demonstration of the new preachers' ability to arouse the Strasburghers' emotions and to mobilize public opinion to coerce the ruling classes. They had responded quickly with measures designed to ensure that the preachers' eloquence would be harnessed and used to pacify, not inflame, their subjects. In 1523 the magistrates declared that nothing could be preached in the city except the Gospel. This apparently innocuous statute, enacted to cool the bitter evangelical-conservative quarrels, bound preachers not to lead the faithful into controversy, but to encourage them in the love of God and their fellows.[16] For the

---

[13]RP 1541, f. 522r–v; Heinrich Nobbe, "Das Superintendentenamt, seine Stellung und Aufgabe nach den evangel. Kirchenordnungen des 16. Jahrhunderts," *Zeitschrift für Kirchengeschichte,* 14 (1894), 404–29, 526–77; 15 (1895), 44–93; Irmgard Höss, "The Lutheran Church of the Reformation: Problems of Its Formation and Organization in the Middle and North German Territories," in *The Social History of the Reformation,* ed. Lawrence P. Buck and Jonathan W. Zophy (Columbus, 1972), pp. 317–39. On Hesse and Saxony, see Wilhelm Pauck, "The Ministry in the Time of the Continental Reformation," in *The Ministry in Historical Perspective,* ed. H. Richard Niebuhr and Daniel D. Williams (New York, 1956), pp. 122–24.

[14]RP 1542, f. 239v, "Zeigen herr Sturm, h. Pfarer und Andres Mieg als super attendenten in kirchen sachen. . . . "

[15]RP 1576, f. 669r. See also RP 1573, ff. 878v–881v; AST 79/53 and 54; and RP 1581, ff. 544v–546r.

[16]Bernd Moeller has published the text and demonstrated that it was a pacification edict, not an endorsement of evangelical theology. "L'édit strasbourgeois sur la prédication du 1er decembre 1523 dans son contexte historique," in Livet et al., eds., *Strasbourg au coeur religieux,* pp. 51–61.

remainder of the century the magistrates interpreted this statute quite broadly. In practice it set a number of limits on the clergy's freedom to preach. They could not, for example, take up "private matters" from the pulpit; naming delinquent individuals was forbidden. Nor could they criticize their local doctrinal opponents by name. They could not take up matters of politics and diplomacy without the magistrates' permission, and they could not criticize the magistrates. They were not to preach on the limits they saw to the magistrates' power over the church. Naturally the preachers committed all these offenses, but each time the magistrates reprimanded them and compelled them to stop. When necessary, the council could suspend a recalcitrant preacher.[17]

The city council also monitored the written word. Again the original legislation went back to the battles of the twenties, when Strasbourg's printers turned out floods of exuberant manifestos, pointed dialogues, and inflammatory broadsheets. The magistrates declared in 1524 that nothing could be printed without the approval of their censors. A printer who violated this ordinance would suffer the confiscation of his press run and other unspecified but "appropriate" penalties.[18] This law, too, was used later to muzzle the clergy. The magistrates forced Johann Marbach to tone down his *Three Sermons* against the Calvinists; they forbade Matthis Negelin to be "sharp" in his exposé of a local visionary prophet; sometimes they struck out whole sections of a text, like the Preface to Marbach's *Bishop's Sermon* of 1569.[19] Just as they inserted themselves between preachers and parishioners, the magistrates made themselves a filter between clerical authors and their readers. Their objectives were obvious: to impede alliances between clergy and commons and to keep all their subjects in a properly subordinate position. Neither objective was new.

Strasbourg's magistrates had developed a system to keep people in their places well before the reformation allowed them to take control of the church. The measures they devised to regulate the clergy fitted

[17]*Privat-sachen,* RP 1543, f. 399v; doctrinal quarrels, AST 84/73, 75, both from 1561, and RP 1562, ff. 212v–213r; politics and diplomacy, RP 1547, f. 153f and RP 1549, f. 266r; criticism of magistrates, RP 1556, ff. 98v, 99v; limits to the magistrates' powers, RP 1572, ff. 623r, 624r–625r; suspension of Matthis Negelin, AST 72/5, 6, and RP 1572, ff. 623, 675–676r, 743r, 801v.

[18]Text of the ordinance in Aloys Meister and Aloys Ruppel, eds., "Die strassburger Chronik des Johann Georg Saladins," *BSCMHA,* n.s. 23 (1911), 307–9.

[19]RP 1565, ff. 432v–433v, on the *Drey christlichen Predigen;* RP 1566, f. 263v, on an attack on the Steinbachian sect of which I have found no further trace; RP 1569, f. 468v on *Von dem bischofflichen Ampt* and its deleted Preface, AST 178/4.

into a larger pattern of secular rule which restricted power to the small group of families who dominated the city's economic and political life. Strasbourg's oligarchs were determined to protect their power, and the nature of oligarchical rule helped shape the city's religious evolution throughout the century.[20]

Each year on a Tuesday morning early in January, the magistrates and citizens of Strasbourg met to mark the most solemn moment in the calendar of their secular public life. Through the ritual of mutual oaths, citizens and rulers reaffirmed their commitment to each other and to the fundamental laws of their community. In the *Schwörtag's* ceremonies the burghers acted out an idealized version of the balance of power within their walls. The Schwörtag portrayed a Strasbourg united by a balanced and benevolent regime, and blessed by God. Behind these myths was another Strasbourg, internally divided, controlled by a few families whose conception of the common good was shaped by individuals' sensitivity to their own interests, and a city where God's blessings occasionally included religious discord, riot, and even war. Orchestrated by the oligarchs, the Schwörtag conveniently masked the real nature of their power and told little about how they exercised it.

The Schwörtag began at nine o'clock with the ringing of the council hall's bell.[21] Out of the city hall came the Ammeister and the four Stettmeisters, Strasbourg's highest-ranking magistrates. Behind them marched the members of the council of XXI, the city's standing executive committee. With due pomp the oligarchs paraded to the cathedral square, where they mounted a platform decked with the city's colors, red and white. Then the members of the twenty guilds entered the square, group by group, saluted by trumpets and kettledrums. At the head of each contingent came a standard-bearer, followed by the guild's officials and the masters with their journeymen and apprentices. As the officials, who included the guild's representatives on the city Senate, joined the city's executive on the platform, the guildsmen found their places below. Finally the members of the two noble corporations, accompanied by liveried municipal valets, made their way to a place of honor in the square.

---

[20]Otto Winckelmann, "Strassburgs Verfassung und Verwaltung im 16ten Jahrhundert," *ZGO*, n.F. 18 (1903), 493–537, 600–642, and Ulrich Crämer, *Die Verfassung und Verwaltung Strassburgs von der Reformationszeit bis zum Fall der Reichstadt 1521–1681* (Frankfurt, 1931) describe the constitution. For the way it worked in practice, Brady's *Ruling Class* is essential.

[21]Hans Meyer, *Die strassburger Goldschmiedezunft von ihrem Entstehen bis 1681: Urkunden und Darstellung* (Leipzig, 1881), no. 28 (1538).

When all these several thousand men had been brought to order, the city secretary read out the *Schwörbrief,* a concise statement of the city's constitution.[22] The citizens listened to the old provisions designed to prevent their rulers from favoring their private interests instead of the common good. They heard of their duty to defend the city, to uphold its laws, and to obey the magistrates. When he had completed these readings the secretary stepped back, and the newly elected Ammeister moved forward to take his oath of office. That done, he turned to the crowds below to extend his New Year's greetings to his fellow citizens. At his command, every man in the square raised two fingers and swore to God to abide by the laws that had been read out to him. The secretary then sealed this collective oath with a prayer: "May God grant you and all of us luck, health, prosperity, and long life." The trumpets and drums sounded again, the officials took their leave, and the crowd dispersed.

The Schwörtag served the oligarchs' purposes well. It provided a focus for civic patriotism and left many burghers thinking of themselves as part of the city's ruling class. To the several thousand men looking up at their representatives on the official platform, Strasbourg could look like a polity in which power was broadly based and widely shared. In fact only a minority of the city's people were welcome in the cathedral square for the oath-taking ceremony, and few among them exercised any formal power. A closer look at the full range of urban judicial categories and social classes is necessary to unravel the workings of the city's political life.

Sixteenth-century Strasbourg, with its population of twenty to twenty-five thousand people, was too large to be homogeneous.[23] The magistrates' subjects within the walls fell into three judicial groups: full burghers or citizens, *Schultheissenbürger,* and inhabitants.[24] Full burghers could be nobles or commoners, men or women. They were either the children of burghers or immigrants who had acquired their status by purchase or marriage. Non-citizens who arrived with, or acquired, property worth more than the low value of £10 were expected to purchase citizenship. Probably a majority of city families had at least one representative in the cathedral square for

[22]Text in Carl von Hegel, ed., *Die Chroniken der oberrheinischen Städte: Strassburg,* 2 vols. (Leipzig, 1870–71), 2:946–50.

[23]Philippe Dollinger, "La population de Strasbourg et sa répartition aux XVe et XVIe siècles," in *Die Stadt in der europäischen Geschichte: Festschrift Edith Ennen,* ed. Werner Busch, Klaus Fehn, et al. (Bonn, 1972), pp. 521–38. For the latter part of the century see Kintz, *La société,* pp. 233–36.

[24]François Joseph Fuchs, "Droit de bourgeoisie à Strasbourg," *RA,* 101 (1962), 19–50.

the Schwörtag.[25] Possession of *Bürgerrecht* thus told little about a Strasburgher's economic position; there were quite poor burghers as well as very rich ones. Adult male burghers enjoyed complete political enfranchisement: they could vote within their guilds or corporations and hold office. Women burghers, on the other hand, were excluded from public life. Schultheissenbürger also did not belong to the political class. They were poor men and women who were allowed to settle permanently in the city. In return for the right to live and work there, they promised to be obedient and self-supporting. Admission to the status of Schultheissenbürger remained under the control of an episcopal official throughout the century.[26] The third and smallest fraction of the resident population is divisible into two subgroups. The city extended temporary residence permits to individuals who ran the gamut from wealthy foreign nobles and merchants to penniless refugees. Strasbourg also guaranteed legal protection to the monks, nuns, and canons associated with the religious houses and chapters that survived the reformation.

The judicial hierarchy of full burghers, Schultheissenbürger, and inhabitants bears little relationship to the city's complicated class structure. Much of the relevant evidence is no longer extant, but one helpful document is a 1628 sumptuary law that divided the city's people into six ranks.[27] At the top came the members of the Senate and XXI, all the nobles, and the regime's legal counselors, along with their wives and children. One step down came the families of "distinguished citizens," that is, the pool of families which had contributed members to the Senate and XXI over the past century but which temporarily had no active magistrate. Ranked with them were those with university degrees, rentier families who lived without working, wholesalers, and important civil servants. The third group included families belonging to the richer guilds whose members were merchants or exercised skilled trades in their own shops, innkeepers, stewards, notaries, and the middle rank of civil servants. Below them were the families of the "common guilds," like the gardeners and fishermen, along with the lesser civic employees. Day laborers

[25]Erdmann Weyrauch, *Konfessionelle Krise und soziale Stabilität: Das Interim in Strassbourg, 1548–1562* (Stuttgart, 1978), pp. 93–95.

[26]AMS II/271/8 gives an incomplete 1546 census of *Schultheissenbürger* and the 1530 version of their oath of allegiance.

[27]*Der Statt Strassburg Policeij Ordnung* (Strasbourg, 1628), Titullus VIII, pp. 41–56. See also AMS R29/126, an extract from a 1568 sumptuary law.

formed a class by themselves. In the lowest rank came women, single or widowed, who worked to support themselves. The text did not take note of the real bottom of the urban population, the unemployed and the unemployable.

Jean-Pierre Kintz's analysis of the Strasburghers' wills and testaments allows us to regroup the six ranks into three: the poor, the comfortable, and the rich.[28] A high proportion of families—41.7 percent—lived in poverty or even in debt. An almost equal group ranged themselves above the poverty line (property worth £150) but below the rich. Another 18.5 percent of Strasbourg's families owned property worth more than £1,500. The very rich among this group, worth more the £12,000, amounted to fewer than 2 percent of the city's families. The top 5 families in Kintz's sample were worth as much as the bottom 227 together. Overall, only 10 percent of the Strasburghers controlled 70 percent of the city's wealth. The magistrates belonged to that 10 percent. The poverty line probably ran through the sumptuary law's fourth level, that of common guildsmen. The gap between a great merchant and a poor gardener was enormous, although both might take the same oath on the Schwörtag. Poor gardeners rarely rose from the cathedral square to the oligarchs' platform.

At the base of the city government was a council of three hundred *Schöffen,* made up of fifteen representatives from each guild. This body continued to meet throughout the sixteenth century, and settled such important issues as the timing of the abolition of the mass. Nevertheless it had no voice in day to day decisions, and in times of crisis came to rubber stamp the views of the senior magistrates. The oligarchs summoned the Schöffen to give their policies a veneer of popular approval, and they were not above concealing information to ensure that approval for their plans would be forthcoming.[29]

A *cursus honorum* ran upward from the Schöffen to the regime's highest rank. The Schöffen of each guild took turns serving two-year terms on the city Senate, where they joined ten representatives of the noble corporations. Three times weekly these thirty senators sat in joint session with the members of the standing executive councils, who were collectively known as the XXI. By the sixteenth century

---

[28]Kintz, *La société,* pp. 460–77, 521–22, on a sample of Strasburghers who died between 1598 and 1621.

[29]Brady, *Ruling Class,* pp. 166–68; Crämer, *Verfassung,* pp. 27–28; RP 1591, ff. 360v–364r, on manipulation of briefings to the Schöffen.

the XXI was little more than a convenient, if peculiar, name for all the members of the councils of XV and XIII together. XVers and XIIIers each met on their own, the XVers to administer internal affairs and the XIIIers to manage external affairs. When the senators, XVers, and XIIIers all assembled in one body, they called themselves the Senate and XXI. This was the workhorse of the regime, exercising a general right of review over finance, defense, law, education, poor relief, and the rural territories. In the 1520s it gained jurisdiction over religious affairs as well. The senators were the junior partners in this body; the dominant voices belonged to the XVers and XIIIers. At the summit of the regime was the Ammeister, a commoner elected by the guildsmen in the Senate to serve a one-year term as head of the government. Assisting him were noblemen acting as Stettmeisters, the ceremonial heads of state.

At every step up the ladder written and unwritten rules guaranteed that important offices would fall to the sons of established ruling families. For example, a provision that commoners could hold memberships in two guilds at once permitted upper-class families to move into the poorer guilds and take over their political offices. Carl Mieg, a prosperous cloth merchant, sat first for the merchants' guild *zum Spiegel,* then switched to the clothmakers' guild. One of his sons rose to be Ammeister, representing the clothmakers although he was a rentier, not a weaver. Another son, likewise a rentier, sat on the Senate and XXI as a barrelmaker. A real barrelmaker might hope to join the Schöffen, with its carefully restricted authority; he might even manage to serve a few terms on the Senate. That was the limit of any realistic ambition for the majority of guildsmen.[30]

As a result of mechanisms like these formal power in Strasbourg was the preserve of the prosperous; even the simple senators who never progressed to the inner circle of the XXI were more substantial citizens than most of the city's inhabitants.[31] Government remained the work of men with a commitment to the status quo. What was true of the senators was even more striking in the members of the standing councils who held the real power in Strasbourg. Thomas A.

---

[30]Brady, *Ruling Class,* pp. 118–21, 173–78; Philippe Mieg, *Histoire généalogique de la famille Mieg, 1395–1934* (Mulhouse, 1934). For Carl Mieg, Sr. and Jr., see Brady, *Ruling Class,* Appendix A, nos. LXI, LXII; for Sebastian, *Histoire généalogique,* pp. xix, xxx–xxxiii, 20–22.

[31]Thomas A. Brady, Jr., has worked out the details for one senator in "The Social Place of a German Renaissance Artist: Hans Baldung Grien (1484/85–1545) at Strasbourg," *Central European History,* 8 (1975), 299–315.

Brady, Jr., has analyzed the social position of the men of the XXI in the first half of the sixteenth century.[32] Brady describes the core of the ruling elite as "a rentier-merchant aristrocracy."[33] At this rarefied level distinctions between nobles and commoners had nearly evaporated. Family ties bound the two, for the great merchant families married into those both of nobles and of lesser merchants, and it was not unheard of for prominent commoners to enter the nobility. The magistrates of Strasbourg were practical men, worldly, pragmatic, and convinced of the legitimacy of their rule. All this played into their original response to the reformation and would guide them as they exercised their new powers over religious life, for the patterns Brady found among the magistrates in the early decades of the reformation persisted through the century.[34]

The reformation put these men at the center of three generations of religious strife and a seemingly endless struggle to balance the demands of their God and of their world. They had to fit religious problems into an already overloaded agenda. A local writer, Johann Fischart, elaborated on Saint Paul to describe the duties of rulers: "to legislate wholesome laws and customs, to appoint good men to the councils, the church, and the schools; to reconcile citizens who quarrel with each other; to administer justice; to protect the dutiful and the pious; to punish miscreants; to watch over the poor, widows, and orphans . . . ; in short, to foster the common tranquility, security, calm, and peace."[35] Meeting daily in one capacity or another, the magistrates labored to fulfill the perennial promise of good rulers to provide their subjects with peace, order, and good government. The religious dimensions of their duties cropped up again and again, but the oligarchs could never give a religious problem their undivided attention or consider a religious issue in isolation from its secular consequences.

Keeping the peace meant protecting Strasbourg from external threats. The council of XIII took charge of the city's fortifications and

[32]Brady, *Ruling Class,* Part 1.

[33]Ibid., p. 195.

[34]I discuss the careers of Sebastian Mieg and Johann Schenckbecher, two examples from the latter half of the century, in "The Long Reformation," pp. 21–25. Two important changes in the ruling classes should be noted: the oligarchy found it increasingly difficult to recruit patricians for active careers in the second half of the century, and as a whole, the upper classes were less wealthy in the later decades, although they retained their local preeminence. See Brady, *Ruling Class,* pp. 76, 288–89, and Kintz, *La société,* passim, on the contraction of the city's economy.

[35]*Ordenliche Beschreibung* (Strasbourg, 1588), sig. Aii recto–Aiii verso.

[55]

war matériel, its militia and occasional mercenaries, and diplomacy.[36] Strasbourg's rulers practiced a delicate balancing act throughout the sixteenth century, playing off the rulers of France and the Holy Roman Empire, the Protestant and Catholic powers within the Empire, and the Saxons and the Swiss. The magistrates' support for the Protestant cause provoked many crises, of which the Schmalkaldic War of the 1540s, which pitted the Protestants against their Catholic emperor, was only the most spectacular. In precarious times, assuring the survival of their city became almost the sole order of the magistrates' business. Military force was not the only means to protect the city and its people. The magistrates were alert to any encroachment on the Strasburghers' traditional privileges and used all their diplomatic resources to defend the legal and economic advantages of their citizens.[37]

The magistrates also guaranteed their subjects order at home. The oldest city constitution began with the promise that everyone, native or foreign, would always enjoy peace within the city.[38] The Senate and XXI maintained a rudimentary police force,[39] and dealt harshly with those who tried to divide its subjects or to incite them to violence. The magistrates exhorted their people to preserve "civic calm and unity" at the annual Schwörtag and thereafter in the preambles to ordinances and in the judgments pronounced by the courts.[40] The Senate sat alone as a court, the Senate and XXI offered guidance on tricky and important cases, and the XIII was a sovereign imperial court.[41] It was Strasbourg's boast that "no one shall be judged without a hearing."[42] Much of the magistrates' routine activity in religious affairs rose from this promise, for even heretics had a right to defend themselves. Dissidents—from lowly Anabaptists through the pastors of the Calvinist refugee church to important men like the

---

[36]The minutes of the XIII are extant only from 1599.

[37]For example, RP 1539, ff. 249v–250r and following, concerning Hans Esslinger and other rural subjects whom the cathedral canons accused of Anabaptism. The case dragged on into the 1550s. For commercial privileges see, as examples, *PC,* vol. 1, nos. 55, 122, 153.

[38]Wilhelm Weigand, ed., *Urkunden und Stadtrechte bis zum Jahre 1266. Urkundenbuch der Stadt Strassburg* (Strasbourg, 1879), p. 467.

[39]Crämer, *Verfassung,* pp. 55–56.

[40]AST 80/94, a 1581 mandate against religious quarrels, invokes the Schwörtag oaths. Arbitration of private quarrels: KS 46[ii], f. 97r-v; KS 48[i], loose piece inserted after f. 101; KS 70[iii], ff. 56v–57r.

[41]Crämer, *Verfassung,* pp. 55–80. Only fragments of the court records are extant.

[42]ADBR, G370A, f. 10v (1471), repeated in G371, f. 17r (1563–64).

Latin school's rector, Jean Sturm, and Senator Adolff Braun—regularly demanded and received the judgment of the magistrates. The Senate and XXI acted as the final arbiter of all the city's quarrels, secular and spiritual.

Strasbourg's rulers appeared to be all-powerful and secure, but despite their wide powers and their many mechanisms to keep control in the hands of a few families, the oligarchs remained vulnerable. While there was no legal means to turn out a Senate and XXI that consistently flouted public opinion, there was the possibility of a popular revolution. Strasbourg's rudimentary police force could cope with individual criminals, but not with large-scale violence, and the Senate and XXI did not maintain a standing mercenary garrison. The city militia was just that, the burghers in arms. If the people and their magistrates clashed, there was no way to guarantee that the militia would side with the oligarchs. In short, if the Strasburghers chose to stage a coup, the magistrates could do little to save themselves. They knew this very well and sensibly assumed that their best defense lay in prophylactic measures designed to convince their subjects that the oligarchs provided good government.

What the magistrates particularly wanted to communicate to their subjects was the conviction that the oligarchy ruled fairly, in the interests of all. Again and again in their mandates and other public pronouncements the oligarchs underlined their fatherly concern for their people and reiterated their claim to resolve all issues, secular or spiritual, in the interest of the common good and in accordance with God's will. They all swore, on taking office, that they would put the public interest before their private advantage, and they donated their time, wisdom, and experience to the city for the most minimal remuneration. Or so it seemed. In fact the common good invariably coincided with what was good for the ruling families as a class, and they can scarcely be said to have neglected their collective interests. For example, the tax system they used to finance their operations was gentle to the wealthy at the expense of those of more modest means, for they relied heavily on indirect taxes.[43] Nor were they above profiting individually from their offices, despite their own rules against this. Claus Kniebis slid some of the convent property taken over in the 1520s into his own hands. Michael Lichtensteiger, who served in the regime between 1562 and 1589, abused his privileges

---

[43]Crämer, *Verfassung*, pp. 128–33.

shamelessly. He fell into debt and milked what he could from his offices, even trying to secure his household wine at public expense. In the 1590s Nicolas Fuchs was accused of using the knowledge he had acquired as administrator of the rural territory of Barr to engage in what amounted to insider trading on the land market.[44] Security of property and the magistrates' own prosperity could take precedence over respect for the clergy's version of religious truth, as the exodus of so many members of the ruling families demonstrated during the Schmalkaldic War crisis.[45]

Despite incidents like these, the magistrates' claim to rule in accordance with the common good and the divine will was not a cynical boast. If it had been, they could not have survived. They firmly believed that what was good for the privileged also benefited the humble. They were equally sure that their policies protected the true church, contributed to the salvation of the souls in their care, and discharged their obligation to God to rule benevolently. Their system of poor relief provided a demonstration of the care they took to protect the standard of living of their poorer and poorest charges. In the twenties the magistrates reorganized the city's welfare arrangements, and thereafter poor people, native and foreign, could get help from the hospitals, the orphanage, and the General Alms which the Senate and XXI administered.[46] The magistrates also took pains to keep down the cost of living. Strasbourg maintained municipal storehouses that supplied grain at subsidized prices during the inevitable famines. Even in normal times the magistrates regulated the price and quality of goods in the market places and made some attempt to restrict speculation.[47] Brotherly love, Christian duty, and self-interest merged in these policies. Protecting the struggling from human and natural disasters dampened their resentment of the rich. By helping the weak the magistrates kept the city safe for the powerful.

The oligarchs dealt harshly and speedily with anyone who challenged their claims to exercise legitimate power and evenhanded justice. Their critics could expect immediate punishment, ranging from tongue-lashings or a spell in the prison towers on bread and water to

---

[44]For Kniebis, Brady, *Ruling Class,* p. 146; for Lichtensteiger, XV 1586, f. 61r and passim through 1578, f. 178v; for Fuchs, Kintz, *La société,* p. 451.

[45]Brady, *Ruling Class,* pp. 285–90.

[46]Otto Winckelmann, *Das Fürsorgewesen der Stadt Strassburg vor und nach der Reformation bis zum Ausgang des sechzehnten Jahrhunderts,* 2 vols. in 1 (Leipzig, 1922).

[47]Kintz, *La société,* pp. 296–300, 509–21.

exile or even execution.[48] Publishers who hoped to make a living learned to obey the censors and probably exercised considerable self-censorship as well. The magistrates did what they could to police less formal methods of communication with or among their subjects. Anyone who could write could scribble a graffito on a wall or tack up a poster, and the Senate and XXI was prepared to investigate mysterious threats like "Caspar, smarten up!" when Caspar was one of their minor functionaries.[49] The magistrates had ears as well as eyes; they kept themselves informed of what was said in the city's marketplaces and taverns, as well as in the public baths. Rumor-mongers and gossips never knew when their idle chatter might strike the magistrates as being disruptive of good order and result in their being hauled in and upbraided.[50]

The care the magistrates took to monitor and maneuver public opinion indicated the extent of their fear of popular revolution. This fear had been sharpened by the turmoil of the 1520s when the commons had had their say in politics and the Peasants' War had erupted around Strasbourg. Throughout the century news of the tribulations of other urban rulers—those of Münster, Geneva, Lyons, and the Dutch cities were well known in Strasbourg—reinforced these worries, and events within the walls could turn nervousness into something approaching panic. In the 1520s the magistrates managed to ride out the popular passions of the early reformation and to preserve, indeed expand, their own authority. In the late 1540s, while the Protestant Schmalkaldic League to which Strasbourg belonged went down to defeat at the hands of the Catholics, and the magistrates struggled to make peace with the emperor, men and women gathered in the streets and public places to denounce the oligarchs. Anti-Catholicism and fears for the survival of the local church carried burgher after burgher into sedition; threats against the oligarchs circulated freely. In the 1580s and 1590s the foreign policy pursued by the Senate and XXI again outraged public opinion, and this time disgruntled subjects accused their rulers of selling out the city to the Calvinists. Once again they threatened to revolt. These disturbances all rapidly took on an economic dimension, with the poorer

---

[48]RP 1547, ff. 481v, 18v, 22r; RP 1551, f. 99r. Johann Adam, *Evangelische Kirchengeschichte der Stadt Strassburg bis zur französische Revolution* (Strasbourg, 1922), pp. 145–46, on the execution of Georg Frey.

[49]RP 1578, f. 429v.

[50]RP 1569, ff. 764v, 800r-v, 831r.

Strasburghers menacing the rich. This conflict was obvious at the time of the Peasants' War, and it reappeared dramatically at mid-century in the charges that the oligarchs intended to abandon the faith to protect their fortunes. Toward the end of the century the popular anti-Calvinism that contributed to the final triumph of Lutheran orthodoxy blended with complaints that the rich magistrates showed neither concern for nor charity toward the suffering of those at the bottom of the economic scale.

Three times in three generations the Strasburghers came close to overthrowing the oligarchs' regime. In each case the threat to the ruling families' control followed on the heels of Bible-thumping sermons in the city churches. Throughout the century religion remained the spark that could ignite the common people's resentments. The magistrates naturally sought to prevent this from happening. On one hand, as we have seen, they tried to tame the clergy by various devices, while on the other hand they worked with the preachers to develop the Christian religion's potential to support the status quo.

The clergy had their own place in the Senate and XXI's efforts to make sure that the commons accepted the regime. Thus the oligarchs repeatedly forbade their preachers from criticizing secular authority at any level, from preaching about political issues like the legitimacy of oath-taking, from taking up prophetic texts that encouraged apocalyptic or millenarian excitement, and, above all, from challenging specific magisterial policies.[51] The Senate and XXI expected the pastors to concentrate instead on reminding their parishioners of the lessons of Romans 13: God had created temporal authority and Christ insisted that his followers respect it. In 1531 the city rulers provided the clergy with a particularly spectacular forum for this teaching when they decided to inaugurate an annual magistrates' sermon to replace the mass formerly held on the day after the Schwörtag.[52] Magistrates and commons would gather in the cathedral to hear a preacher expound the obedience required of Christians, and then magistrates, clergy, and commons all joined in solemn prayer for the regime. The pastors were usually willing to inculcate the gospel of obedience in their flocks; certainly it had a place of honor in their catechizing.[53] As Wolfgang Capito put it in 1527, "The Christian

---

[51]AST 84/9 (1526); AST 75/52 (1539); RP 1548, f. 634r-v; AST 67/Heft 6, ff. 40v–45v (1571).

[52]Brant, "Annales," *BSCMHA*, n.s. 19 (1892–1901), nos. 4900, 4958.

[53]August Ernst and Johann Adam, *Katechetische Geschichte des Elsasses bis zur Revolution* (Strasbourg, 1887) summarizes the contents of the catechisms.

accepts civil orders from his temporal authority to which he is obedient and loyal . . . , and knows that he who resists authority resists the very order of God."[54]

From the 1520s on, powerful forces encouraged the magistrates and preachers to draw together in an alliance of authorities. In the twenties the preachers and the Senate and XXI had engaged in an uneasy cooperative effort to purify the church by removing the old clerical power and its abuses. They acted in concert to beat back the radical and spiritualist challenges. In the process the secular rulers committed themselves to Protestantism. Thereafter, for military and diplomatic reasons, the oligarchs needed the clergy to vouch for their orthodoxy, and that meant that the magistrates required their clergy's help just as the clergy needed the magistrates' protection. The magistrates took their new responsibilities in religion very seriously. They were as anxious as their preachers to ensure that Strasbourg's church was Christian and that it flourished to God's honor. Finally, in the sixteenth century religion was the foundation of morality, and morality was the underpinning of public order. When the preachers urged their parishioners to be sober, hard-working, and honest, they made a powerful contribution to keeping the peace within the walls. Clergy and magistrates saw a common enemy in the irreligious and disrespectful elements among the commons.

Even so, the magistrates' commitment to the clergy was never wholehearted. They recognized that the preachers were the one group in the city with the potential to emerge as rivals to the civil authorities. Furthermore, for most of the century the magistrates balked at the clergy's drive to turn Strasbourg into a fortress of orthodox belief where the populace would conform to all the clerical notions of good behavior. There was room in Strasbourg for a loose lay alliance against clerical pretensions, and that alliance was based on a general consensus about the day to day regulation of religion.

Anticlericalism had been a hallmark of the early reformation in Strasbourg, and it persisted well past the middle of the century. The old anticlericalism that fueled the revolt against the pope's church had been founded on a hatred of clerical power and on resentment of the clergy's alleged ignorance, immorality, and greed. The new preachers created remarkably few scandals after their tumultuous appearance as rebels in Strasbourg had given way to their new dignity as pastors in the city parishes. Some of the city's Catholic minority

---

[54]Quoted by Kittelson, *Wolfgang Capito*, p. 141.

may have continued to regard a married clergyman as inherently immoral, but the great majority of Strasburghers abandoned their attacks on the clergy's behavior, accepted them as learned, and found them cheaper to support than the old priests, canons, and religious. Yet memories of the priests' abuses of their power remained fresh, and the Strasburghers did not trust the sincerity of the new pastors' renunciation of the old clerical powers. Pastor Caspar Hedio, preaching the annual magistrates' sermon to the assembled rulers and burghers in 1534, lamented that the clergy were constantly accused of wanting to erect a "new papacy." Six years later, along with Bucer and Capito, he would repeat to the Senate and XXI his complaint that fear of reestablishing something like the pope's yoke was preventing rulers and the commons from accepting Christ's will.[55] For the magistrates the chief terror of the "new papacy" lay in the possibility that the clergy might "seize the sword," that is, challenge the magistrates' secular authority.[56] To most of the laity the "new papacy" had more to do with the clergy's attempts to discipline their parishioners, to stamp out old customs like the parties held to celebrate baptisms and marriages, and to renew old obligations like private confession. The magistrates' fear of the clergy's potential political power led them to restrict the pastors' efforts to discipline the laity, to the relief of many ordinary Strasburghers.

The rulers and commons also shared a tacit agreement that religious services should be strictly limited to a few hours each week, concentrated on Sunday morning. When the clergy complained that few people came to the weekday services the magistrates replied that this was the preachers' own fault, because the services were too long.[57] The laity, preoccupied with their temporal affairs, rationed the hours they would spend in church. Few of them could afford to take much time away from their work, and most of them resented the suggestion that their limited holidays should be spent standing in their churches, absorbing the preachers' lessons. Church attendance never measured up to the clergy's demands, although as the decades passed the pastors slowly reduced those demands.[58] The magistrates, who often skipped services themselves, were not prepared to use the

---

[55]*Radts Predig,* sig. Bi verso–Ci recto; RP 1540 f. 303v.
[56]RP 1559, ff. 326v–327r; RP 1562, ff. 105v, 116v–117r; RP 1564, ff. 440v–441v.
[57]RP 1555, ff. 453r, 454r.
[58]René Bornert, *La réforme protestante du culte à Strasbourg au XVIe siècle (1523–1598): Approche sociologique et interprétation théologique* (Leiden, 1981), pp. 148–50, 173, 178–79.

law to bully their lay subjects into better performance.[59] When the clergy urged the members of the Senate to set a good example by coming regularly to their Tuesday prayer services, the Senate and XXI simply announced that the Senators were too busy with their judicial work.[60] The clergy never managed to convince the lay Strasburghers that religious exercises ought always to take priority over secular business.

When they did turn their minds to pious thoughts, the Strasburghers showed a marked indifference to the clergy's efforts to create and expound a coherent theology. Faced with the task of censoring a stack of theology books, the magistrates Carl Mieg and Johann Carl Lorcher decided to read only the titles. To read the texts, they protested, would take years.[61] If retention of the material taught is any guide, many of the laity long showed equally little enthusiasm for the simplified version of Protestant doctrines patiently expounded by preachers and by pastors catechizing their flocks. For decades after the evangelical triumph, the clergy grumbled over the commons' ignorance of their new faith.[62] When the Strasburghers found the preachers' sermons dull, they were apt to wander about in the churches and gossip—or even buy sauerkraut—until something caught their attention.[63] But evidence of the laity's interest in religion abounded, for example in the popularity of plays based on Bible stories.[64] Questions of doctrine could arouse interest, but when this happened the laity were all too likely to rearrange the clergy's theories, preferring to modify or even reject the canons of orthodoxy. For all that, the majority remained deeply attached to their reformation, as their anxiety about its survival at mid-century and in the eighties and nineties eloquently testified.

The Strasburghers' loyalty to their reformation combined with the realities of oligarchical rule to allow a third alliance that cut across the normal groupings of magistrates/preachers and magistrates/commons. The preachers never became the docile instruments of lay authority dreamed of by the Senate and XXI. The alliance of magistrates

---

[59]RP 1540, ff. 302v–304v; RP 1544, f. 523r.

[60]RP 1545, f. 359r, 359v.

[61]RP 1563, f. 393r.

[62]*TAE*, vol. 2, no. 523 (1534); AMS N26, pp. 309, 393 (1563), and 469 (1565).

[63]RP 1540, f. 201r; RP 1541, f. 395r, 395v; RP 1544, f. 350r; RP 1546, f. 556r.

[64]Miriam Usher Chrisman, *Bibliography of Strasbourg Imprints*, pp. 196–201 lists more than thirty such plays printed between 1533 and 1599 against only twenty on all other themes for the whole century.

and commons slowing their reformation outraged them, and they strove to counter it by reviving the unusual coalition of the 1520s which had allowed preachers and commons to unite and force change on the oligarchs. From time to time the clergy did manage to recruit at least a militant minority of the population to back their projects.

One of the clergy's tactics in their attempt to reshape the balance of power was to abandon their usual support for the oligarchs as purveyors of good government. The city's rulers felt an understandable terror before the popular preacher who could tie his gospel to the possibility of leveling the distinctions between rich and poor. Strasbourg's clergy, motivated both by concern for the poor and by their antipathy to commercial capitalism, used their pulpits to snipe at the city's economic order. When the clergy denounced abuses in the marketplaces, the magistrates, who regulated trade, were an obvious target. In the 1540s Matthis Zell attacked the oligarchs for permitting and practicing speculation on the commodities market which drove up the cost of living for the poor. His successor at the cathedral, Ludwig Rabus, preached that the magistrates worshiped only Mammon. In the next generation young Tobias Speccer accused the oligarchs of selling stockpiled grain to foreigners at a profit when they should have distributed it to the city's needy families.[65] The preachers found an attentive audience for these charges in the great mass of the city's poor and struggling commons. Sermons like these simultaneously weakened the bonds between upper- and lower-class laity and encouraged the people to accept the preachers as the real champions of the common good.

The major focus of the clerical campaign for popular support naturally centered around religion rather than the economy. The oligarchs claimed to protect God's church, while the pastors sought to demonstrate that their performance was unsatisfactory in God's eyes. The preachers stressed that the magistrates were negligent in defense of the truth, for they allowed dissenters to live and agitate within the walls. They also argued that the lay rulers permitted the wicked to misbehave freely, scandalizing both God and the good burghers. Throughout the century the clergy sought to mobilize confessional bigotry and the fear of God in support of their own reformation.

The magistrates, who had profited greatly from the original reformation crisis, were alert to the clergy's attempt to combine secular and spiritual grievances to alter the balance of power in the city. They

[65]RP 1545, f. 348r; RP 1552, f. 310r; AST 84/108, 84/109b (1594).

remained convinced that religion was a volatile problem, rife with possibilities for sedition unless religious zeal, economic distress, and the clergy themselves could all be kept under control. At the same time, like their lay and clerical subjects, the magistrates recognized the need to accomplish God's will. In the end the highest authority the Strasburghers knew was always their God.

No sixteenth-century Strasburgher ever managed to divorce religion from power. The settlement of the 1530s gave the magistrates control of the church, but popular pressure had contributed to that settlement and popular pressure would shape its continuing evolution. Throughout the next decades the clergy would struggle to recover some of the authority seized by the magistrates in the tumultuous years between the first mention of Luther in the city and the announcement of the Wittenberg Concord. The pastors labored to create a new alliance of pious Strasburghers in and out of the council chambers, an alliance that would allow them to lead the city toward a more Christian life. They dug away at the lay obduracy blocking their reformation. They underlined the areas where clerical and magisterial goals coincided, striving to teach the magistrates to use their authority properly. They exploited sources of friction between the magistrates and the common people, using popular support to wrest concessions from the oligarchs in the 1550s and again in the 1590s. Throughout this long campaign they always relied on their own considerable power. No matter how the Senate and XXI struggled to tame the clergy, the preachers remained God's spokesmen on earth.

CHAPTER THREE

The Clergy's Reformation

The evangelical preachers who began Strasbourg's reformation in the early 1520s had labored to create a triple regeneration. They intended to rebuild the clerical estate, to clarify pure doctrine, and to oversee the renewal of the burghers' spiritual and secular lives. By the mid-1530s they had achieved a partial and, in their view, unsatisfactory reformation settlement. After the reorganization of the church in Strasbourg the clergy had no area of exclusive jurisdiction left to them. Instead of belonging to a mighty international institution that overshadowed the city state, they now made up a vulnerable parochial body, dependent on the magistrates for protection against their enemies outside the city and their opponents within it. Even as the pieces of the original settlement began to come together in the 1530s, the clergy noted its defects and resolved to improve it. For the next six decades they would struggle to rebuild their own power and to impose good doctrine and good discipline on the laity. The cornerstone of these attempts was the drive to escape from the tutelage to the laity embodied in the original settlement.

The early evangelical preachers had had no intention of robbing the clergy of their power to direct the laity. Matthis Zell, for example, sought to enhance the independence of pastors and took care to separate religious and secular jurisdictions.[1] In his first reforming tract, *No One Should Live for Himself, but for Others,* published in 1523, Martin Bucer had argued: "The best and most nearly perfect estate on

[1]Stafford, *Domesticating the Clergy,* pp. 38–40.

earth, the most holy calling . . . is the spiritual. Just as spiritual matters are more important than secular affairs and service to the community greater than service to individuals, so the clergy's office is the most perfect, for we serve the community and its eternal salvation."[2] Wolfgang Capito, always fearful of the dangers of letting the ignorant masses judge religious policy, insisted that in doctrinal matters even the secular rulers must defer to the expertise of theologians.[3] Caspar Hedio agreed with his colleagues: divine law must take precedence over human law and the clergy over the laity.[4] In their theoretical statements about the proper relationship of church and state the reformers emphasized separation, while hoping for cooperation between the spiritual and secular authorities.[5] Political realities in Strasbourg forced these men to suffer dependence and to face magisterial opposition as often as they experienced cooperation. As Bucer observed late in his life, until the secular rulers submitted wholeheartedly to the laws of Christ, a confused and truncated church order was to be expected.[6] The preachers recognized their obligation to teach their lay masters how Christ wanted his church to operate. They told the Senate and XXI again and again, "We must obey God before we obey men."

Capito summed up their enduring conviction in 1528 when he told the magistrates, "I speak as a preacher and one with authority from God."[7] In the beginning the evangelical preachers had stressed their desire to serve the laity, but undoubtedly they intended to serve the community as leaders. As the years passed, they became more and more careful to underline the independence and prestige of their calling, and to stress their obligation to discipline all the laity, of whatever rank. Late in the 1530s Bucer prepared an entire treatise, *On True Pastoral Care*, to clarify the clergy's rights. In it he reminded his readers that God had set pastors over the church with a divine commission to refute error and to bring in Christ's kingdom.[8] The preachers developed their claim to independence from lay inter-

---

[2]*BDS*, 1:51–54.

[3]Kittelson, *Wolfgang Capito*, pp. 85–86, 138.

[4]Stafford, *Domesticating the Clergy*, pp. 213–14.

[5]Bucer, for example, continued to hope for a collaboration that would transcend jurisdictional boundaries. T. F. Torrance, "Kingdom and Church in the Thought of Martin Bucer," *Journal of Ecclesiastical History*, 6 (1955), 48–59.

[6]*De Regno Christi*, in *Melanchthon and Bucer*, ed. Wilhelm Pauck, pp. 211–12.

[7]Kittelson, *Wolfgang Capito*, p. 138.

[8]*Von der waren Seelsorge* (1538), *BDS*, 7:69, 112, 141–239; Jacques Courvoisier, *La notion d'église chez Bucer dans son développement historique* (Paris, 1933), pp. 57, 74–75, 81.

ference in petitions to the Senate and XXI in the 1540s.[9] Their successors continued to insist that as the servants of Christ they were required to instruct the entire city about Christ's demands and to chastise all those who failed to conform to Christ's desires.[10]

The clergy felt themselves to have been personally called by God to preach his word and convert his people. From this conviction they drew the strength to carry on the long battle against lay worldliness. In it, too, Bucer, his colleagues, and their successors found their best justification to hammer at the doors of the council chambers, seeking official assistance in their drive to reform Strasbourg. The city's laws gave the clergy little support for their exalted conception of their office. The preachers generally found themselves on firmer ground when they cited Scripture rather than statute as the basis for their authority, but for decades even Scripture could not always make the magistrates defer to their clergy. The proper limits of clerical authority remained very much part of the reformation debates as late as the 1580s and 1590s.

The early evangelical preachers had begun the work of rebuilding the prestige of the clerical estate by denouncing the weaknesses and abuses of the hierarchical church of the late middle ages. Skillful appeals to lay anticlericalism allowed them to destroy the old church organization.[11] At the same time, anticlericalism led the magistrates to elaborate a series of measures by which the laity could control the clergy. If they were to recover their independence, the clergy would have to demonstrate that these controls were unnecessary by showing that they could police themselves and guarantee the laity an honest, trustworthy, and hard-working set of pastors and preachers. They found the means to accomplish this in the *Kirchenconvent* or Church Assembly.

The Church Assembly began with informal meetings of the evangelical preachers in Matthis Zell's home in the 1520s.[12] The magistrates granted it legal recognition as a corporation in 1531, when they ordered the lay church wardens to attend its meetings.[13] The wardens

[9]AST 87/49 (1544), pp. 43, 49, 61; "Von der kirchen Mengel und Fähl" (1546), *BDS*, 17:159–64, 180; AST 84/53 (1547).
[10]AST 100/unnumbered, first of a series of pieces about Tilemann Hesshus (1565), ff. 14r–15v; AST 84/85, ff. 496r–497r and AST 84/88, ff. 4r, 7r-v, 32r, 34r, both from 1572.
[11]See, for example, Stafford's analysis (*Domesticating the Clergy*, pp. 7–46) of Zell's 1523 *Christliche Verantwortung*.
[12]AST 79/3, ff. 16–51, "Beschreibung des strasburgischen Kirchen Convents" (1576). "Ordnung und Kirchenbreuch" (1534), *BDS*, 5:30–31.
[13]*Kirchenpflegerordnung* in Roehrich, *Mittheilungen*, 1:257–60.

never made their presence felt, and the Church Assembly remained the clergy's council. Once a week the president, the seven pastors and their assistants, and the preachers without pastoral charges met to discuss the assignment of duties, the disciplining of the laity, the education of the young, and the means to spur the magistrates to further reform of the church.[14]

The Church Assembly slowly worked out ways to discipline its members' behavior and to ensure that all were orthodox in their beliefs. By 1533 the clergy had already begun to practice a fraternal correction of each other's weaknesses. Eventually five members of the clergy came to act as "censors" of the rest, meeting monthly to investigate everyone's teaching and life. Twice a year the whole Assembly devoted sessions to reciprocal criticism.[15] New recruits had to undergo an examination of their beliefs before the full Assembly and to subscribe to the Augsburg Confession before being admitted.[16] By testing new members and by rigorous policing of old members, the Church Assembly maintained its cohesion. Dissidents were driven out. Among the first to go were the so-called "epicureans," such as Wolfgang Schultheiss and Anton Engelbrecht, who fought against the intrusion of the magistrates into religious life. The majority of the city's pastors in the early 1530s wanted the magistrates to use the law to compel people to respect the new church and to destroy the sectarians' opposition to it. Schultheiss and Engelbrecht denounced this and left the church.[17] Other men who balked at accepting the administrative authority of the Assembly, like Beatus Gerung, also lost their jobs.[18] In the 1580s the Assembly discharged Michael Philipp Beuther when he refused to join its campaign to obtain Strasbourg's ratification of the Formula of Concord.[19]

The Church Assembly (which is analyzed in more detail in Appendix B) became a close-knit body that rarely split into factions. Its members tended to serve long terms. Twenty-nine men had clerical

[14]Fragments of the minutes survive in AST 67 and BNUS ms. 998.

[15]*TAE,* vol. 2, no. 373, pp. 49–54, and no. 392 (1533); *Kirchenordnung* (Strasbourg, 1598), pp. 330–36.

[16]AST 52/2, f. 24r-v (1561); AST 72/4, f. 8r (1562); AST 69/190, f. 487v (1588). This examination of new recruits began in 1545.

[17]Werner Bellardi, *Wolfgang Schultheiss: Wege und Wandlungen eines strassburger Spiritualisten und Zeitgenossen Martin Bucers* (Frankfurt am Main, 1976) and "Anton Engelbrecht (1485–1558): Helfer, Mitarbeiter und Gegner Bucers," *ARG,* 64 (1973), 183–206; Wendel, *L'Eglise.*

[18]RP 1555, f. 95r; RP 1557, ff. 77v–78r and passim through ff. 216v–217r.

[19]Otto Jung, *Michael Philipp Beuther: Generalsuperintendent des Hertzogtums Zweibrücken (1564–1619)* (Landau, 1954), pp. 11–19.

careers of more than twenty years; the Methuselah was Conrad Hubert, a member of the Assembly from 1531 to 1577. Men who had worked with Bucer still participated in meetings into the 1570s, and the senior man in 1598 had been at work since 1561.[20] Stability of personnel engendered continuity of ideas, and shared education reinforced this. After the opening of Strasbourg's Latin school in 1538 the city increasingly educated the lion's share of its own clergy; those who went abroad for the doctorate tended to pursue their studies at only two universities, Wittenberg and Tübingen.

Practical training provided the clergy with another set of shared experiences. Once the new church had been organized the Church Assembly promoted its members through the sort of *cursus honorum* followed by Johann Lipp.[21] Lipp was born in Strasbourg in 1554, and was the son of a master shoemaker. He studied in the Latin school for five years, was ordained in 1573, and took his Master's degree in 1576. The Church Assembly then sent him out to work in one of the rural parishes. In 1579 he married Susanna Clemens, whose father was a clergyman in Kirweiler. Lipp was called back to the city in 1583 and elected assistant pastor at New St. Peter, an office he held for fifteen years until his election as the parish's pastor. He retired in 1618 and died four years later. Many of his colleagues in the Church Assembly were not native Strasburghers, and others had more formal education. Some had spent part of their training as chaplains in the city hospital and some had been obliged to work in the villages, but Lipp's experiences were becoming typical of the careers of Strasbourg's clergy. Naturally, not all could hope to become pastors; Johann Frey remained an assistant pastor for almost forty years.[22] Lipp's retirement was also unusual, for most of the clergy died in office.

Lipp was not alone in marrying a preacher's daughter, but several of his colleagues went him one better. At least ten of them married the daughters of colleagues in the Assembly, and at least four more married widows of colleagues. The Church Assembly could not boast nets of family ties as intricate as those that bound the magisterial clans, but even by 1598, when its members had been at the

---

[20]Marie-Joseph Bopp, *Die evangelischen Geistlichen und Theologen in Elsass und Lothringen von der Reformation bis zur Gegenwart* (Neustadt a.d. Aisch, 1959) provides biographical sketches.

[21]Bopp, *Geistlichen*, no. 3211.

[22]Ibid., no. 1465.

games of marital politics a scant three generations, they had shown themselves adept at bringing their sons into the fold; nine men followed their fathers into the Assembly. Nor were a young man's relatives his only source of support there, for President Johann Marbach made himself the patron to a generation. Of the thirty-four men who entered the Assembly during the first twenty years of Marbach's presidency (1552–72), fifteen had boarded at his house as young men.[23]

Fired by the conviction that their work was God's work, united by internal discipline, shared education and experiences, and the ties of marriage and friendship, Strasbourg's clergy could mount lengthy and eventually effective campaigns to make the city's reformation correspond to their vision. They were particularly successful at subverting the institutions of lay control created by the Senate and XXI. As the century wore on, the office of church warden decayed, while that of church president grew more powerful. Slowly the Church Assembly gained control of clerical appointments. From the beginning of the reformation its members had found ways to evade the censorship of their writing and preaching so that they could speak directly to the laity.

The church wardens had been created to police the clergy's lives and teaching and had authority from the magistrates to discipline parishioners. They were to monitor what went on in the Church Assembly's meetings and to act as the link between the Assembly and the Senate and XXI. For several reasons the system never worked properly. The wardens tended to skip the Assembly meetings.[24] It is likely that these laymen felt themselves ill-equipped intellectually to deal with theology and ecclesiastical matters, particularly in a forum where the clergy usually outnumbered them. Throughout the century the Senate and XXI and the Church Assembly preferred to keep up direct relations, sending only routine messages to one another through the wardens. The magistrates, who often left vacancies in the wardens' ranks unfilled for months, hardly encouraged their agents to consider their work vital.[25] The Senate and XXI twice tried to

---

[23]AST 63/1, pp. 73–82.

[24]RP 1547, ff. 162r, 681r–682r; AST 67/2, f. 6r (1566); AST 67/5, ff. 26v, 27r, 33v, 35v (1569); AST 67/8, f. 11r (1572).

[25]It took almost two years to appoint wardens to the parish opened in the Prediger Kirche as a substitute for the cathedral during the Catholic restoration of 1549–59. RP 1552, ff. 421r, 427r.

bolster the wardens' authority, but with little result.[26] Meanwhile the Church Assembly undermined the wardens' disciplinary powers over the clergy by developing its own procedures to regulate its members' behavior and orthodoxy; the Assembly's internal discipline rendered the wardens' surveillance of these matters quite superfluous. The wardens did retain the power to investigate and reprimand parishioners, but in this they came to act more and more as the pastors' agents.[27]

While the church wardens lost ground, the president of the Church Assembly emerged as the real leader of the clergy, although the Senate and XXI refused to recognize this in law before 1598. The magistrates always kept the right to decide who was to be president, but in four tries in the sixteenth century they only once managed to select a truly cooperative man. Perhaps, as the clergy claimed, the Senate and XXI merely ratified the Church Assembly's own choice of a leader.[28]

The magistrates installed Martin Bucer as the Assembly's first president in 1541, citing his service to the Protestant churches and his great learning.[29] Bucer was the obvious choice, although by now he had grown disillusioned with the progress of the reformation in Strasbourg and in particular with the performance of the Senate and XXI. He was soon deeply involved in efforts to mobilize the support of zealous laymen organized in "Christian fellowships" within the established church. Through these groups Bucer hoped to revive the religious enthusiasm of the twenties, but the magistrates rightly regarded this as a challenge to their power and set out to thwart the plan.[30] Relations between Bucer and his masters took a further turn for the worse toward the end of the Schmalkaldic War, when Bucer led the preachers in public opposition to the magistrates' attempts to appease Charles V and capitalized on popular opposition to concessions to try to block the Augsburg Interim.[31] When Bucer tendered his resignation in 1549, the Senate and XXI must have been relieved to see him leave the city.

[26]AMS R3, ff. 262r–264r (1539); Weyrauch, *Konfessionelle Krise*, pp. 112–13.
[27]See Chapter 8, below, at note 63.
[28]AST 79/3, ff. 18r–20v, 1576. There is no evidence from the magistrates to support this claim, but the clergy did produce short lists for other church positions, and if the claim is valid it would explain the magistrates' otherwise puzzling choices of Marbach and Pappus.
[29]RP 1541, f. 522r–v.
[30]Werner Bellardi, *Die Geschichte der "christlichen Gemeinschaft" in Strassburg (1546/1550): Der Versuch einer "zweiten Reformation"* (Leipzig, 1934).
[31]*BDS*, 17:346–620. Werner Bellardi, "Bucer und das Interim," in *Horizons européens*, ed. Marijn de Kroon and Marc Lienhard, pp. 267–311.

In Bucer's place the magistrates appointed Caspar Hedio, a veteran of the early reformation who had preferred historical writing to pastoral activism in the 1540s.[32] During the crisis over the fellowships Hedio had shown himself ready to compromise, and in the difficult early days of the Catholic restoration he again avoided picking quarrels with the Senate and XXI. The revived menace of Catholic power, the briefness of his tenure, his age, and his mild disposition combined to make Hedio the least troublesome of the sixteenth-century presidents.

At Hedio's death in 1552 the magistrates offered the post first temporarily, then permanently to Johann Marbach.[33] Marbach had worked with Bucer to organize the parish movements in the mid-forties and the two had united in opposition to the Interim; he may have been Bucer's preferred successor.[34] Marbach brought a young man's energy and an admirable administrative flair to his work. He had a strong sense of what needed to be done to strengthen the church in Strasbourg and was soon engaged in running battles with the magistrates over the elimination of Catholicism, sectarianism, and Calvinism and over the need to make lay behavior match pastoral standards. Some of the worst clashes between the clergy and the magistrates arose during his presidency.

When Marbach died in 1581 the Senate and XXI rather unaccountably chose Johann Pappus to replace him, apparently for lack of a better candidate at home and from inability to attract a man from outside. As the magistrates noted, he was one of the least experienced members of the Church Assembly.[35] They must have known that youth did not make him respectful of authority, for Pappus had spent the previous two years carrying the clergy's standard in a raging public battle against the aged school rector, Jean Sturm.[36] Pappus and Sturm had conducted much of their struggle in flat defiance of the magistrates' orders to keep silent in public. Once in office, with Sturm defeated, Pappus proved to be less flamboyant. He continued

---

[32]Hedio has been almost entirely ignored by historians. Emil Himmelheber, *Caspar Hedio: Ein Lebensbild aus der Reformationsgeschichte* (Karlsruhe, 1881) says little about his years as president.

[33]RP 1552, f. 448r–v. In 1555 the magistrates were still discussing who should replace Hedio, and Marbach was not on their short list (RP ff. 285v–286r). Wilhelm Horning, *Dr. Johann Marbach* (Strasbourg, 1887) is dated and marred by confessional bias.

[34]So Marbach claimed. AST 55/2, f. 24r–v (1561).

[35]RP 1581, ff. 544v–546r. Wilhelm Horning, *Dr. Johann Pappus von Lindau* (Strasbourg, 1891); again, this should be consulted with caution.

[36]See Chapter 6.

Marbach's efforts with greater discretion and greater success. Pappus was the better strategist and also the beneficiary of circumstances; by concentrating his forces he was able to reap where Marbach had sown, winning a new Church Ordinance in 1598. His tenure in office lasted until his death in 1610, by which time the Church Assembly had turned the original reformation settlement inside out.

The Senate and XXI always managed to deny the title of "superintendent" to Bucer, Hedio, Marbach, and Pappus. As late as 1581 the magistrates still insisted that the president of the Church Assembly was no more than the pastor appointed to chair its meetings.[37] With the consent of their colleagues and through the accumulation of duties, the presidents came to exercise far more power than this. By the last quarter of the century the president had become chief censor of his colleagues. He drafted documents in the Assembly's name and presented petitions to the magistrates on its behalf; once a year he joined two magistrates to inspect the rural parishes. He attended meetings with the clergy of other territories and usually preached the annual magistrates' sermon. All of the presidents took an active role in the school system, as lecturers or inspectors. From time to time the magistrates grumbled about the extent of the president's influence, but as long as he operated with his colleagues' consent there was little that could be done to change this. In Saxony and Hesse the superintendents policed their subordinates to the benefit of the territoral rulers, but in the smaller theater of a free city the president, a close and trusted friend of the other preachers, did not play the role of an enforcer for the magistrates.[38] Instead he became the spokesman for clerical opposition to official policies.

The president and Church Assembly came to exert considerable influence over appointments to the city's parishes. According to the law, appointments were made by the Senate and XXI in ratification of choices made by prominent lay parishioners.[39] By the 1570s at the latest, responsibility for drawing up the short list of candidates to present to the parishioners had drifted into the hands of the Church Assembly, which kept a careful watch on potential preachers. The presidents secured the right to be present at the elections, and the Assembly began to examine new recruits on their doctrinal ideas before admitting them to the clerical corps. At the ceremony to

[37]RP 1542, f. 239v; RP 1573, ff. 878v–881v; RP 1576, f. 669r; RP 1581, ff. 544–546r.
[38]See Chapter 2, note 13, above.
[39]See Chapter 2, note 8, above.

introduce the winning candidate to his flock the president replaced the church wardens as his sponsor.[40]

Bit by bit in the decades after the original reformation settlement crystallized in legislation, the clergy rearranged the organization of the church to enhance their own independence. While these maneuvers went on behind the scenes, the preachers openly evaded the magistrates' efforts to censor their sermons and books. Again and again they took to their pulpits to denounce specific magisterial policies, like the compromises made with the emperor in the 1540s and the alliances made with the Calvinists in the 1580s. They criticized the behavior, in particular the business practices, of individual magistrates. They denounced the lay magistrates' invasion of what they defined as the spiritual sphere of jurisdiction.[41] The magistrates could reprimand preachers after the fact, but they had no way of gagging them while they were in their pulpits. As for the censorship of the written word, the clergy found it easy enough to arrange to have controversial works printed outside the city, as Pappus did with his open letter to the burghers in defense of the Formula of Concord.[42]

The Church Assembly's efforts to escape lay tutelage and to rebuild the authority of the clerical estate were a means to an end. The end was to reform the city's religious life by leading its people to orthodox belief and pious practice. Dissent had to be smashed, true doctrine proclaimed, and discipline strengthened. The clergy's drive to reform the city was unrelenting, as can be seen from the analysis in Appendix C of a sample of their many petitions to the Senate and XXI. One such petition broke down the main themes of authority, doctrine, and discipline into specific problems, illustrating the range of the clergy's campaigns in the sixteenth century.[43] The Assembly accused the magistrates of neglecting their responsibility to protect the church and pointed to no less than ten areas where the laity's performance was unsatisfactory. The Senate and XXI allowed the nuns in the remaining convents and the Knights of St. John to practice their superstitious abominations as freely as if they lived in the papal territories. The Anabaptists carried on with equal boldness, while the Schwenckfelders did no less damage to the true church. A

[40]AST 79/3, ff. 34r–51v (1576); *Kirchenordnung*, pp. 282–90.
[41]RP 1547, ff. 41r, 63v, 153r; AST 84/103 (1587); AST 72/5 (1572), Matthis Negelin's sermon on St. Peter's keys.
[42]*Bericht und Warnung . . . an eine christliche Burgerschafft* (Tübingen, 1581).
[43]AST 84/88, ff. 35v and following.

great number of Zwinglians and Calvinists flourished in the city, although these people were fundamentally opposed to its Augsburg Confession. Blasphemy and swearing continued unabated among the common people. Murderers and other criminals, who under both divine and imperial law deserved execution, instead got off nearly scot-free. The magistrates' record for punishing the sexually immoral, such as prostitutes and adulterers, was no better. Drunkenness and gluttony caused great scandals. Usury, speculation, and other economic abuses persisted unchecked, injuring both the poor and the city's reputation. Moreover, the magistrates blocked the clergy's efforts to defend the church; for more than a year now the city censors had been sitting on their reply to attacks on them by a Catholic controversialist.

This 1572 petition was an epitome of the Church Assembly's program since the beginning of the reformation. It highlighted the three themes of the clerical reformation: the authority of those who preached God's word and could call even magistrates to task, the need to stamp out heterodox opinion and disseminate true doctrine, and the drive for moral regeneration. Except for the reference to the Zwinglians and Calvinists, the petition could have been drafted in the 1520s as easily as in the 1570s.

The clergy's program showed great constancy from the 1520s through the 1590s, yet many scholars who have taken up the reformation in Strasbourg have argued that the history of the local church breaks at mid-century. They insist that a first period of constructive work, tolerance, and ecumenism under Bucer's direction gave way to a period of rigidity, intolerance, and confessional persecution dominated by Marbach and Pappus.[44] As we shall see, this claim has its roots in the sixteenth century, in the contention of Jean Sturm, rector

---

[44]For example, Ernst and Adam, *Katechetische Geschichte des Elsasses,* pp. 13, 127; Charles Engel, *Les commencements de l'instruction primaire à Strasbourg au moyen âge et dans la première moitié du 16e siècle* (Strasbourg, 1889), p. 41, and *L'école latine et l'ancienne académie de Strasbourg, 1538–1621* (Strasbourg, 1900), p. 63; Wilhelm Horning, *Handbuch der Geschichte der evang.-luth. Kirche in Strassburg unter Marbach und Pappus* (Strasbourg, 1903), pp. 1–2; Winckelmann, *Das Fürsorgewesen der Stadt Strassburg,* 1:168; Lucien Febvre, "La France et Strasbourg au XVIe siècle," *La vie en Alsace,* 5 (1926), 36–37; Wendel, *L'Eglise,* pp. 237–38; Crämer, *Verfassung,* pp. 193–94; Henri Strohl, *Le protestantisme en Alsace* (Strasbourg, 1950), pp. 77–80; Pierre Mesnard, "La pietas litterata de Jean Sturm et le développement à Strasbourg d'une pédagogie oecuménique (1538–1581)," BSHPF 111, (1965), 289. Horning is the only one to prefer Marbach and Pappus. The Catholic historian Nikolaus Paulus condemns all the Strasbourg Protestants in *Die Strassburger Reformatoren und die Gewissensfreiheit* (Strasbourg, 1895).

of the Strasbourg school, that Marbach abandoned Bucer's ideals and sought to impose foreign values and his own tyranny on the local church.[45] Out of the Sturm-Marbach debates grew the legends of Marbach's innovations and of pronounced changes in the policies of the Church Assembly after Bucer's departure in 1549.

The problem centers on Strasbourg's confessional history and the relation of the local church to an evolving Lutheran orthodoxy. Certainly the city's confessional history is not as straightforward as that of Nuremberg or Zurich, for instance. It was complicated by Strasbourg's position in the sacramentarian quarrels of the 1520s, when Strasbourg leaned to Zwingli rather than to Luther. This break with the Lutheran mainstream had been repaired by 1536, when the Wittenberg Concord was signed. What followed was the working out of the implications of this agreement, a process begun by Bucer, not Marbach. Johann Adam, the scholar most familiar with the long-term course of church history in Strasbourg, rightly concluded: "The Lutheranization of Strasbourg was not first begun, as it is often claimed, by Marbach. Its beginnings are to be sought much more in Bucer's work at the time of the Wittenberg Concord. In the last decade of his service in Strasbourg Bucer turned more and more to Luther."[46] Contemporary testimony supports Adam's judgment. Richard Hills, an English cloth merchant who had been living in the city since 1540, wrote to Heinrich Bullinger in 1546, "You mention . . . that Marbach is altogether a Lutheran: but this is no new thing among us because almost all the preachers here are chiefly imbibing and inculcating Lutheranism."[47] The Church Assembly's attacks on the Zwinglians and Calvinists in Marbach's day were not particularly different from Bucer's colleagues' attacks on the Anabaptists; moreover, they derived naturally from Bucer's movement into the Lutheran camp. In the second half of the century the Church Assembly broadened the range of groups whose errors it wished to root out, but the idea that orthodox belief had to be protected was pure Bucer.

The idea of orthodoxy—that is, that religious truth can be defined, and once defined, must be defended—was not a concern peculiar to the second generation of Protestants. Sixteenth-century book titles,

[45]Chapter 5, below, at note 74.

[46]Adam, *Kirchengeschichte,* p. 315.

[47]Hastings Robinson, ed., *Original Letters Relating to the English Reformation,* 2 vols. (Cambridge, 1846–47), vol. 1, no. 115.

those parades of "True Accounts," "True Histories," and "True Descriptions," reflect an obsession with accuracy and betray a fear of deception as well as an anxiety over standards. Nothing could have been more natural in this climate than attempts to fix authorities and to separate what was right from what was wrong. The reformation, after all, sprang from such a search for truth and standards in religion.

In Strasbourg as elsewhere, the evolution of the new orthodoxy was a slow process, the fruit of a consistent effort to define by negating and to purify by ostracizing. In the 1520s Catholicism had been stamped false; by the 1530s Anabaptism had been rejected. Then, after 1536, the symbolic interpretation of the eucharist upheld by the Swiss was identified as erroneous. Orthodoxy in Strasbourg was fluid in content for decades. Only in the Formula of Concord did the clergy achieve a consistent, fixed, full, and enduring doctrinal formulation, but the desire for orthodoxy did not come into Strasbourg in Johann Marbach's saddle bags. Bucer was just as anxious to see the suppression of Catholicism, sectarianism, and Judaism as Marbach and Pappus were to add Calvinism to the list of proscribed doctrines.[48] From the beginning of the reformation the evangelicals had intended to clarify, disseminate, and defend true doctrine.

The preachers' concern to teach true piety and morality was likewise a part of the clergy's reformation from its inception. The early evangelicals had expected the preaching of God's word to produce moral regeneration, and from the first they had attacked evil practices among the laity as well as among the clergy. They assumed that their sermons would cause the Strasburghers to remodel their lives so that all their thoughts and actions would be directed to the accomplishment of God's will. Zell and Bucer, for example, strove to create a lasting religious commitment among their listeners. They were convinced that those who heard the Word of God would love God, pray and feel real repentance, participate in the life of the church, and practice the works of Christian charity toward their neighbors.[49] The laity disappointed them. Just as they flirted with heterodoxy, individuals also resisted the call to moral reform. The city's collective voice, the magistrates, generally refused to order compulsory performance of religious exercises and, in the preachers' view, did not

---

[48]On Bucer's intolerance see Paulus, *Gewissensfreiheit*, pp. 1, 2, 67; Charles B. Mitchell, "Martin Bucer and Sectarian Dissent" (Ph.D. diss., Yale University, 1960); see also Hastings Eells, "Bucer's Plan for the Jews," *Church History*, 6 (1937), 127–36.
[49]Stafford, *Domesticating the Clergy*, pp. 41, 100.

punish moral lapses with sufficient rigor. Furthermore, they declined to let the clergy take over the latter task. Changing the burghers' moral standards and practices proved to be the most difficult part of the clergy's struggle to reform Strasbourg.

Throughout their long campaign to reform the city the clergy benefited from their special position as the spokesmen for God's will. As preachers they enjoyed a unique advantage. The church services gave them a regular opportunity to address a cross-section of the city's population, and they did so some fifty times each week.[50] No other group in the city, including the magistrates, had any mechanism to assemble the population in such numbers for regular instruction. Since the clergy coordinated the themes of their Sunday sermons in the weekly Church Assembly meetings, they could send an idea into almost every household in the city on any given Sunday. Very few of their thousands and thousands of sermons have survived, but a tiny number were published, and traces of others survive in the magistrates' records. In simple terms the preachers explained again and again what the laity should think and how they should behave, varying routine exhortation with stinging rebukes to backsliders and vehement denunciations of the wickedness of those who opposed the clergy. (The themes of these sermons are outlined in Appendix D.)

As pastors the clergy participated in the most intimate family events of their parishioners. They married people and baptized their children. When sickness came the pastor followed to console the sufferer and other family members; when death arrived it was the pastors who took charge of funeral services and sought to strengthen the survivors. Their own family backgrounds made it possible for the clergy to understand the troubles and joys of their parishioners' lives. Unlike the leading magistrates, who were set off from their ordinary subjects by wealth and secular majesty, the pastors often came from artisanal families, and their skimpy salaries helped them appreciate the realities of life for Strasbourg's majority.[51]

As educators the clergy also had important means to influence the evolution of public opinion in Strasbourg. Books allowed them to develop the points raised in their sermons more thoroughly and in a lasting form. Although the rate at which religious books were writ-

---

[50]Bornert, *La réforme protestante du culte à Strasbourg*, p. 149.

[51]Kintz, "Eglise et société strasbourgeoise," pp. 37, 47–49. AST 173/48 (1558) and AST 177, ff. 20v–22r (1554), Marbach describes the plight of clerical families and affirms that the meanest tradesmen often earned more than a member of the Church Assembly.

ten and published in Strasbourg slowed dramatically after the flood of the 1520s, the members of the Church Assembly continued to turn out vernacular works for the laity.[52] This production was aimed at the literate and most of it was for adults, but the clergy also worked to educate children and youths. They had been involved since the beginning in the organization of a school system for reformed Strasbourg and remained active at every level, from the surveillance of ABC books to the administration of the Latin school.[53] The most vital part of this work was the least glamorous: the steady effort to drill ideas into the heads of class after class of catechumens. The clergy knew very well that if adults failed them in the present, properly educated children might serve them in the future.[54]

While the clergy's work as teachers brought them into contact with the laity, their learning set them apart from most of their fellow citizens. In the early reformation Wolfgang Capito cringed at the notion of untrained laymen evaluating theology, although most of his colleagues enthusiastically submitted their ideas for lay appraisal. Bit by bit, as the doctrinal debates grew more and more technical, Capito's position won out among the clergy. Few of the laity could follow the arguments of doctors of theology sparring over sacramental theology, predestination, or the salvific force of human works, and few showed much interest in trying to participate. When they did try, the clergy slapped them down.[55] The religious debates of the early reformation were open to all comers, but by mid-century only the learned could keep up, and by the end of the century the clergy argued that only theologians counted as learned in this arena.

Doctrinal expertise gave the clergy a particularly good lever to move the magistrates. By law the secular rulers had to choose what

---

[52]Chrisman, *Lay Culture,* pp. 289, 298. She notes (p. xx) that after 1530 the preachers returned to Latin. Still, they did not entirely abandon the vernacular. Among the later works are Bucer, *Seelsorge;* Melchior Speccer, *Von der herrlichen Zukunfft Jesu Christi* (Strasbourg, 1555); Isaac Kessler, *Kurtz Examen und underricht vom Sacrament des heyligen Abentmals . . . Für die christliche Jugendt* (Strasbourg, 1556); Marbach, *Christlicher und warhaffter Underricht* (Strasbourg, 1566) and *Von Mirackeln und Wunderzeichen* (Strasbourg, 1571); Pappus, *Christlicher und notwendiger Bericht von der zweybrueckischen zu Heidelberg newlich gedruckten Erklaerung des Catechesmi* (Tübingen, 1588).

[53]AST 67/6, ff. 36v–37v (1571) and AST 67/7, f. 11v (1572); Schindling, *Humanistische Hochschule.*

[54]For an overview of the Lutheran clergy's efforts see Gerald Strauss, *Luther's House of Learning: Indoctrination of the Young in the German Reformation* (Baltimore, 1978). His pessimistic conclusions do not apply to Strasbourg; see Chapter 9, below. For Strasbourg catechisms see Ernst and Adam, *Katechetische Geschichte des Elsasses.*

[55]See Chapter 6, below, at note 16.

was and was not orthodox in Strasbourg, but as the debates escaped their comprehension they were forced into a growing dependence on the clergy. In the 1550s and 1560s they could appeal to outside experts—Philipp Melanchthon or the Basel theologians—as a counterweight to their own clergymen.[56] By the 1570s it was becoming impossible to find Lutheran theologians who disagreed with the advice of the Strasbourg Church Assembly. The magistrates held firm for another twenty years, rejecting the clergy's calls to ratify the Formula of Concord, but this was the rearguard campaign of an aging generation of magistrates unwilling to abandon the lay supremacy.

The clergy used a variety of lobbying techniques to win over the magistrates. Sometimes an individual pastor would present a magistrate, often one of the wardens in his parish, with a particular problem to bring to the Senate and XXI. Social occasions gave the clergy an opportunity to approach magistrates informally; Johann Marbach made a point of having senior members of the councils to dinner to discuss church affairs.[57] The clergy's preferred technique was to draw up a formal petition and then send a delegation to present it to the Senate and XXI. (See Appendix C for an analysis of one hundred such petitions.) When private intercession and official petitions did not move the magistrates, the clergy returned to their basic weapon, the sermon. The magistrates' sermon allowed them a special occasion to call their rulers to heel. Hedio used it in 1534 to chastise the Senate and XXI for its failure to implement the recommendations of the first Strasbourg synod, held the year before. Marbach used it in 1558 to upbraid the magistrates for allowing the Catholic services restored in 1549 to continue so long.[58] Naturally the clergy did not limit their criticism of official policy to one sermon in the year. Throughout the century the magistrates received regular criticism, both direct and indirect, of their policies, and faced the danger that sermons would rouse the populace against the ruling class.

The clergy had one last device through which to compel lay collaboration, and that was the threat of God's wrath. An individual sinner

[56]In the 1550s they flung Melanchthon's acceptance of the Interim in the faces of the Church Assembly members who opposed accommodations to the emperor; in the 1560s they imported theologians from Basel to settle a clash over predestination between Marbach and Girolamo Zanchi. See Chapter 5, below.

[57]AST 198, "Diarium Marbachii," ff. 53r, 99r, 164r. This sort of information is rare; Marbach's notes cover only October 1552 to March 1556, with gaps.

[58]Hedio, *Radts Predig;* RP 1558, ff. 27v–28v; AST 173/48.

or opponent faced the menace of damnation, and the Strasburghers believed their preachers when the latter argued from the pulpits that God held communities collectively responsible for their attitudes and actions. Bad weather, disease, and invasion struck sixteenth-century people as proof of God's anger, and all of them knew the awful lesson of Sodom and Gomorrah.[59] Whenever natural or human catastrophe threatened the city the pastors and preachers attributed it to the obstinacy and backsliding of the Strasburghers.[60] The clergy's final lesson was simple and terrifying: if the laity ignored God's will, disaster would follow. Famine, plague, and war were the fruits of disobedience.

God's will was the ultimate foundation of the clergy's program to reform Strasbourg, and God's wrath their ultimate threat to their opponents. From the beginning, Strasbourg's clergy had a consistent program for their city, but their drive to create a true church in a fortress of piety met with resistance from the laity at every step. The magistrates were reluctant to acknowledge the authority of any human rivals, and lay families from the humblest to the most powerful showed every sign of doubting that God really demanded from the faithful exactly what the clergy claimed. The Strasbourg reformation had begun in a conflict of ideas about the nature of a proper reformation, and the settlement of the 1530s had not ended the arguments. The Strasburghers continued their debates about what God wanted, always influenced by the contributions of their neighbors.

[59]RP 1539, f. 212r; RP 1541, f. 180r; RP 1589, f. 115v.
[60]AST 80/41, the clergy request a day of special prayers, blaming all wars and calamities, particularly the recent Turkish victories, on the lack of piety among Christians; the magistrates agreed, RP 1546, ff. 385r–386v and AST 80/42. See also RP 1546, f. 618v; RP 1547, f. 52v; RP 1547, ff. 178v–183v.

CHAPTER FOUR

The World outside the Walls

The Strasburghers prided themselves on their independence. Civic rituals like the Schwörtag encouraged them in this delusion, for when the burghers gathered in the cathedral square to renew their loyalties they closed the city gates behind them, sealing out the wider world. But their city could not live with its gates barred, and whether they liked it or not, whether they admitted it or not, the Strasburghers were part of a greater society. In fact, in the course of the sixteenth century economic and political change made them more and more susceptible to external influences, and Strasbourg, like the other imperial cities, experienced a slow decline before the gathering power of the German princes. The cities were at their zenith when the Protestant reformation began and were able, for a while, to shape their own responses to it. Yet even in the early sixteenth century the Strasburghers had to respond to change rather than initiate it. There is no evidence to suggest that, left to their own devices, they would have found any solution to the late medieval religious crisis, for during the first two decades of the sixteenth century no one in the city was producing effective proposals for change. New ideas were needed to catalyze discontent and produce reform. These ideas came to Strasbourg from outside, as did many of their leading advocates. The Strasburghers naturalized both foreigners and foreign ideas to make their reformation; in short order they also became exporters of ideas, institutions, and the personnel to man them. The local reformation was molded by this constant interaction with the outside world. The movement of ideas was one side of this interaction, and demographic realities, trade patterns, diplomatic maneuvers, and the impact of regional, imperial, and continental wars were others. The absence or alteration of any of these forces would have produced a different reformation in Strasbourg.

Matthis Zell was already in Strasbourg when the reformation began, but Wolfgang Capito, Caspar Hedio, and Martin Bucer were immigrants, and all four men took their initial lead from another outsider, Martin Luther. Their colleagues and successors in the Church Assemblies presided over by Johann Marbach and Johann Pappus were also borrowers within their generations. To acknowledge all this is not to argue that Strasbourg was ever the cultural borrower, always the imitator of outside developments, never a force in its own right. The Strasburghers exerted a reciprocal influence of their own, and on many fronts.[1] Bucer, Hedio, and Marbach, for example, were all seconded to other territories where they contributed in varying degrees to other reformations.[2] In the early years of the reformation Strasbourg's intellectuals and printers set themselves the task of translating religious texts into Latin and French to facilitate their export, and Strasbourg thus had a role to play in the wider diffusion of the German reformation.[3] The three years Jean Calvin spent in the city marked him permanently, and through him the Strasbourg church helped form the Genevan church and its multiple offshoots.[4] Bucer took his experiences with him into exile, and the Anglican reformation thus gained a Strasbourg savor.[5] Strasbourg had its greatest regional influence through its school system, after the magistrates and local intellectuals managed to attract Jean Sturm in 1538. The *Gymnasium* he founded grew into an academy with the right to grant degrees and in 1621 became a university.[6]

Scholars have long been aware of the role of prominent immigrants

[1]Livet et al., *Strasbourg au coeur religieux,* book 5.

[2]Hastings Eells, *Martin Bucer* (New Haven, 1931), chaps. 11, 19, 21, 23; *BDS*, 4, 7; Charles G. A. Schmidt, ed., *Der Antheil der Strassburger an der Reformation in Churpfalz: Drei Schriften Johann Marbachs* (Strasbourg, 1856).

[3]Rodolphe Peter, "Les premiers ouvrages français imprimés à Strasbourg," *Bulletin de la société des amis du vieux-Strasbourg,* 2 (1974), 73–108; William Grayburn Moore, *La réforme allemande et la littérature française: Recherches sur la notoriété de Luther en France* (Strasbourg, 1930).

[4]Jacques Pannier, *Calvin à Strasbourg,* Cahiers de la Revue d'histoire et de philosophie religieuses, 12 (1925); Livet el al., *Strasbourg au coeur religieux,* book 4.

[5]Basil Hall, "Bucer et l'Angleterre," in Livet et al., *Strasbourg au coeur religieux,* pp. 401–30.

[6]Anton Schindling, *Humanistische Hochschule;* Chrisman, *Lay Culture,* pp. 46–47.

like Bucer and Sturm in the making of the city's reformation. Less attention has been given to the mass of anonymous men and women who were drawn to the city to make their living or to escape persecution. Strasbourg was a normal early modern city where deaths exceeded births; merely to survive, it needed to assimilate outsiders.[7] Much of the city's hinterland was Catholic, and the inward flow of Catholic peasants helped to keep the old faith alive within the walls. Migrants from the countryside, whether nominally Catholic or nominally Protestant, also imported superstitious notions and reinforced practices that the local clergy were attempting to stamp out, such as fortune-telling.

Just as demographic realities forced the city to open its gates to immigrants whether Lutheran or not, economic realities influenced the pace and direction of change. Quite simply, Strasbourg had to trade to live.[8] Grain and meat had to be imported to feed the city's people. Merchants had to tap the hinterland for the products—grain and wine in particular—on which their export trade was largely based, for Strasbourg was more of an entrepôt than a producing center. The great merchants traded into Catholic and Calvinist as well as Lutheran lands.[9] Even the lesser merchants who operated principally within the Rhine valley had to cross denominational boundaries. Any attempt to limit commerce to exchanges with the Lutherans, or even with the Protestants in general, would have crippled the city's economy. The prosperity of the city's people depended on a wider trade, and so did the regime's, for the magistrates relied on customs duties to help balance their budget.[10] Catholic and Calvinist merchants had to be allowed into the city and could not be harassed for their heresies, lest their rulers turn to reprisals against Strasbourg's merchants. Every attempt to impose a hardline Lutheran intolerance foundered on this rock because the wealthy families who controlled Strasbourg never forgot that their wealth and its prosperity depended on commerce. At the opposite end of the social scale, the city's poor were unlikely to think in terms of Strasbourg's place in the international economy of the sixteenth century, although its fluctuations controlled their livelihood.

[7]Kintz, La société, pp. 109–10.
[8]Ibid., chaps. 7–10; François Joseph Fuchs, "L'immigration artisanale à Strasbourg de 1544 à 1565," in Artisans et ouvriers d'Alsace (Strasbourg, 1965), pp. 155–97. Chrisman notes that 88 percent of Strasbourg's printers were immigrants (Lay Culture, p. 13).
[9]Kintz, La société, chap. 11.
[10]Crämer, Verfassung, pp. 128–33.

In the three great crises of the century—the mid-twenties, mid-century, and the late eighties and early nineties—economic grievances blended with religious loyalties in their challenges to the oligarchs. The complex political geography of Alsace and the fluctuating rhythms of trade forced a certain consciousness of the outside world on every Strasburgher. Even those who did not venture outside the gates could not avoid rubbing elbows with strangers. Immigrant families with novel ideas settled in their neighborhoods, and foreign mercenaries descended on their taverns. Twice a year, at Christmas and just after St. John's day, the city played host to trade fairs. The early summer fair attracted so many foreigners that the intramural population jumped 10 percent during that fortnight.[11] These contacts with outsiders broadened the Strasburghers' sense of how things could be done and forced upon them a practical tolerance of diversity. This in turn made it harder for the clergy to impose a single notion of truth and a single way to behave on their parishioners.

Regional and international relations set limits to Strasbourg's freedom to control its religious evolution, because the men who made the city's policies had to act with a weather eye on the demands of their neighbors. Most of their immediate neighbors were Catholic; at the height of Protestant expansion in Alsace around 1585 only one-third of the territory had converted.[12] Upper Alsace—essentially everything south of Colmar—belonged to the Habsburgs and remained Catholic. In lower Alsace the greatest landholder was the bishop of Strasbourg. He numbered many Strasburghers among his vassals, and the city, along with the other territorial powers, sent deputies to the Landtag over which he presided. Fifty-three times between 1528 and 1616 deputies from upper and lower Alsace assembled in joint session to deal with common economic, social, and military problems.[13] The need to work together against common menaces—poor harvests, bad money, vagabonds, the threats of foreign invasion—compelled the Alsatian authorities, including the magistrates of Strasbourg, to set aside their religious differences. At the same time it left the Alsatians vulnerable to pressure from one another. The "long-standing good relations" between one territory and another

---

[11]François Joseph Fuchs, "Les relations commerciales entre Nuremberg et Strasbourg au XVe et XVIe siècles," in *Hommage à Dürer: Strasbourg et Nuremberg dans la première moitié du XVIe siècle* (Strasbourg, 1972), p. 80 and n. 14.
[12]Dollinger, ed., *Histoire de l'Alsace*, pp. 233–35.
[13]Ibid., pp. 222–23. The surviving reports are in AMS AA, 1982–87.

could be invoked in requests to moderate religious intolerance, with the underlying threat that good relations could not last if concessions were not forthcoming.[14]

What was true for Strasbourg in Alsace was also true on a wider scale. In the course of the sixteenth century the Strasburghers repeatedly found themselves caught between the demands of the Lutheran Saxons and the Reformed Swiss, and forced to balance the claims to sovereignty lodged by the Catholic superpowers, France and the Empire. In their efforts to retain their own independence the magistrates continually had to play off their neighbors against each other, and this diplomatic balancing act put severe constraints on their freedom to act unilaterally in religious matters even within their own walls. The three greatest crises of the century—the Peasants' War, the Catholic restoration at mid-century, and the Bishops' War of the nineties—all had their origins elsewhere. These confrontations stripped away the myths of civic independence and unity. Outsiders dictated choices, while the magistrates turned on each other, and the people split into factions. The usual pattern of a loose lay combination of magistrates and commons against the designs of the preachers faded before alliances of preachers and lay zealots. Radicalism surfaced and the oligarchs' control wavered.

The diplomatic links between Strasbourg and the outside world and the effects of the larger patterns of imperial history on the city's reformation prior to 1555 are well known. A good part of the city's surviving diplomatic correspondence has long been available in print, and historians have used it in analyzing the city's religious development in the first half of the century.[15] It is clear that the Peasants' War frightened the city council into making concessions to the evangelicals, while the thorough repression of the rebels which followed pushed demands for sweeping social and political change underground.[16] It is also certain that the need to secure protection against Charles V and the threat of counter-reformation by force of arms had a great deal to do with Strasbourg's shift in sacramental theology in the later 1520s. The delicate maneuvers that led to Strasbourg's ac-

[14]For example, RP 1580, ff. 240r–241r and 259v–260r, on representations made to Obernai.

[15]*PC.*

[16]Jean Rott, "Artisanat et mouvements sociaux à Strasbourg autour de 1525," in *Artisans et ouvriers d'Alsace* (Strasbourg, 1965) and "La guerre des paysans et la ville de Strasbourg," in *La guerre des paysans, 1525: Etudes alsatiques,* ed. Alphonse Wollbrett (Saverne, 1975), pp. 137–70; Brady, *Ruling Class,* chap. 6.

ceptance into the Schmalkaldic League and to the signing of the
Wittenberg Concord, which clinched the city's new allegiance to
Lutheran theology, were part of a larger scheme masterminded by
Strasbourg's greatest magistrate-diplomat, Jacob Sturm. Sturm
sought protection for his city and hoped, wrongly, to find it in the
shelter of the Lutheran princes.[17]

When the princes crumbled before Charles V in 1546–47, the magistrates struggled to make a peace that would protect the city's
church, but many of their subjects openly questioned the oligarchs'
loyalty to the Protestant cause. The marketplaces boiled with rumors
that the rich were ready to sell out the city's religion to protect their
fortunes.[18] A sullen, frightened, and nearly rebellious crowd gathered day after day by the city hall, refusing all orders to disperse.
Their fears and hopes alike were stirred by the preachers, who cried
out from their pulpits against concessions to the emperor. The clergy
demanded that Strasbourg fight to the last florin and the last man.
Rather than abandon their reformation, the Strasburghers must complete it and trust in God to protect them. Only the most sincere and
most thorough moral regeneration could save them from the destruction they so deserved for their failings. Penance and subjection to the
Gospel were now needed more than ever to win back God's favor and
save the city from the imperial tyrant.

As defeat became inevitable the clergy raised their pitch. In the
parishes they organized their partisans into fellowships to begin the
work of discipline the Senate and XXI had so long blocked and to
fortify the faithful against the onslaught of Antichrist. The streets
teemed with subversive talk against the magistrates as the potent cry
for social reformation again threatened to sweep away the dikes the
Senate and XXI had built to contain it during the Peasants' War.
Once more the balance of power in the city between rich and poor
was in peril, and this time the clergy were not taking the side of the
oligarchs. The armies of the Schmalkaldic League were still in the
field on the night Philips Ingolt, a magistrate and one of the city's
richest men, cowered under his covers, listening to the voices of a
group of burghers on their way home from a tavern:

[17]Thomas A. Brady, Jr., "Jacob Sturm of Strasbourg (1489–1553) and the Political
Security of German Protestantism, 1526–1532" (Ph.D. diss. University of Chicago, 1968);
"Jacob Sturm of Strasbourg and the Lutherans at the Diet of Augsburg (1530)," *Church
History*, 42 (1973), 183–202; *Ruling Class*, chap. 7.
[18]Brady, *Ruling Class*, chap. 8, captures the emotions and the class conflict that charac-
terized the crisis.

"The preachers say we must punish the evildoers."
"Who should be punished?"
"Adulterers, drunks, usurers, blasphemers. . . ."
"What? Drunks? Then they'll have to punish me!"
"No, no. The usurers. The Prechters. The Ingolts. They are a scandal to God and to the world!"[19]

Echoes of the Peasants' War and of Münster were heard anew in the city.[20] Rather than see the emperor's Interim imposed in Strasbourg, the clergy and their most stalwart supporters would die with swords in hand. Even some of the well-off became caught up in the spirit of apocalypse. As Felix Armbruster, a member of the Senate and XXI, put it, "I will stick by God and the Gospel and if I must fall, better by the hand of man than that of God."[21] Unity within the regime was broken and the solidarity of magistrates and commons had vanished.

Fortunately for the magistrates, Charles V's strength had been exaggerated, and his direct intervention in Strasbourg's affairs proved to be limited.[22] He did not maul its constitution as he did those of the Swabian cities. Instead he acted with some moderation toward Strasbourg, since the king of France had offered the city his military and financial support. Strasbourg's rulers lived in mortal fear of French conquest, but this did not prevent them from flirting with the Valois kings to exploit the emperor's nervousness about his western frontier.[23] If Strasbourg fell to the French it was unlikely that the Habsburgs could long preserve anything in Alsace, not even their family lands in the south. In the end Charles V managed only to force the Senate and XXI to negotiate a new religious settlement with Erasmus von Limburg, the bishop of Strasbourg.

The Senate and XXI saved itself from popular revolution by saving its church. This involved serious losses for the Church Assembly. Martin Bucer was sent into exile, along with Paul Fagius, a young hardliner, and the magistrates chose Caspar Hedio, a much more conciliatory pastor, to be Bucer's successor as president of the Church Assembly. They broke the parish fellowship movement.

---

[19]RP 1546, ff. 456v–457v.
[20]RP 1546, ff. 257v, 399r–400r, 530v–531v; RP 1548, f. 21r.
[21]Quoted by Brady, *Ruling Class*, p. 267.
[22]Jean-Daniel Pariset, *Les relations entre la France et l'Allemagne au milieu du XVIe siècle* (Strasbourg, 1981) analyzes the relationship between Charles V and the German territories in detail.
[23]Pariset, *Les relations*, is excellent for events between 1529 and 1559.

They managed to negotiate a treaty with the bishop which transferred only three parish churches back to the Catholics, preserving
the other four (and the St. Thomas chapter) for the Protestants. The
burghers were slow to accept this, but gradually tensions ebbed and
the talk of rebellion ceased.[24] The radical laity who called for continued resistance to the emperor had often combined hatred for the
wealthy ruling class with religious zeal, but the real center of their
bitterness had been fear for the survival of their church. Once it
seemed safe again, they drifted back into acceptance of the oligarchs'
right to rule.

Outside Strasbourg the Lutheran princes rallied. By 1555 they had
grown strong enough to put an end to Charles's hopes of restoring
imperial authority over them and of imposing a compromise settlement to the religious question. The princes emerged from the
Augsburg Reichstag with the unqualified right to impose either Catholicism or Lutheranism on their subjects. For the Protestant princes
this meant security in their own territories and power over their
churches, provided only that they accept the Augsburg Confession.
The Religious Peace of Augsburg left them free to concentrate on
territorial aggrandizement and the enhancement of their power over
their subjects.

The Peace endured and determined the course of the German reformation for the rest of the century. By tying the legitimacy of Protestantism to the acceptance of the Augsburg Confession, it added a
political dimension to the arguments over the proper interpretation of
that document. Along with the Catholic reformation in Alsace and
the wars in France and the Netherlands, the theological strife to the
east and south was the key to the working out of Strasbourg's religious evolution in the later sixteenth century. Curiously, historians
have paid little attention to the effects of the Religious Peace on
Strasbourg.[25] The Peace has usually been presented as a wall dividing
the first and second halves of the century and marking the end of the
reformation, but it was much more of a bridge than a wall. Its clauses
dealing with the imperial cities ensured that the old rivalries of Catholics and Protestants, Saxons and Swiss, so familiar to the Strasburghers by the end of the 1520s, would continue to bedevil their lives
for four more decades after 1555. The terms of the Peace of Augsburg

[24]See Chapter 5, section 2, below.
[25]Two exceptions are Weyrauch, *Konfessionelle Krise,* and Herman Tüchle, "The Peace
of Augsburg: New Order or Lull in the Fighting,"in *Government in Reformation Europe,* ed.
Henry J. Cohn (New York, 1971), pp. 145–65.

simultaneously bound Strasbourg to the Lutheran theologians and turned it toward the Calvinist warriors. Rather than marking the end of Strasbourg's reformation, the Peace prolonged it; without it the Strasburghers might have found a lasting answer to the religious questions of the late fifteenth century well before the dawn of the seventeenth.

The Religious Peace of Augsburg gave Protestant cities like Strasbourg nothing of the internal security it promised the Lutheran princes. Catholicism had been tolerated here when the Peace was signed, and therefore the city must continue to tolerate it.[26] Strasbourg was thus much more vulnerable to the Catholic resurgence of the later sixteenth century than were the Lutheran princes. The first restoration of Catholicism here collapsed in 1559 when the magistrates temporarily removed their protection from the priests, voiding the treaty they had made with Bishop Erasmus. A few well-timed attacks by the burghers on the priests convinced the Catholic clergy to abandon the cathedral and the two St. Peters, which soon reverted to the Lutherans. Once again there was no public celebration of the Catholic religion in the city, only private observances.[27] This state of affairs provided no guarantee against a second revival of the old church, since imperial law was there to assist the Catholics in Strasbourg if their leaders chose to employ it. There was no particular reason to think that the princes who had failed the city between 1546 and 1555 would be any more help now if the Catholics acted to secure their rights. Under Bishop Johann von Manderscheid the old church did begin to move in the diocesan lands ringing the city.

Manderscheid was elected bishop by the cathedral chapter in 1569.[28] He was no saint of the Catholic reformation, but he was a fine administrator and a careerist with an eye to the main chance. From the beginning he recognized that he was in a stronger position as a Catholic bishop than as the ruler of a Protestantized, secularized diocese. Manderscheid reformed the episcopal finances, giving himself the funds for effective action in his bishopric.[29] He used his own rights of presentation, and the influence of his relatives in the cathe-

---

[26]Karl Brandi, *Der Augsburger Religionsfriede vom 25 September 1555: Kritische Ausgabe des Textes* (Munich, 1896), article 14, p. 35.

[27]See Chapter 5, section 2, below.

[28]Karl Hahn, *Die kirchlichen Reformbestrebungen des strassburger Bischofs Johann von Manderscheid, 1569–1592: Ein Beitrag zur Geschichte der Gegenreformation* (Strasbourg, 1913).

[29]Information on the episcopal finances is scanty, but see René-Pierre Levresse, "L'officialité épiscopale de Strasbourg de ses origines à son transfert à Molsheim (1248–1597)" (Doctorat d'Université, Strasbourg, 1972), p. 168.

dral chapter, to appoint practicing Catholics to the canonries there and in the other Catholic chapters of New and Old St. Peter.[30] He began to conduct regular inspections in his rural territories.[31] He brought in members of the Society of Jesus to found a college in Molsheim, so that there was at last a Catholic institution in Alsace to compete with the Strasbourg academy.[32] Whatever his motives, Manderscheid had taken up the usual tools of the Catholic reformation and was beginning to make them work.

Signs of Catholic revival were soon visible to the Strasburghers. The Senate and XXI began to note "innovations in the Bishopric," evidence that Manderscheid intended to revive episcopal prerogatives, particularly those that could be made lucrative.[33] Jesuits began to appear in the city itself, and the Catholic laity came out of hiding again. The Peace, after all, protected their right to attend mass, and so, now, did their bishop. For nearly a decade after his election Manderscheid refused to swear the usual reciprocal oaths by which the magistrates and their bishops agreed to respect each other's rights and privileges. The city lawyers held the bishop's oath to be a de facto ratification of the reformation, both of the religious changes and of the secularization of church property. Until Manderscheid took that oath, the "main business" of doing away with the masses still celebrated in the city's religious houses had to be postponed. Even after the bishop and the Senate and XXI came to terms in 1578, the magistrates dared not act. There was always the danger that if they did, Manderscheid would invoke the Religious Peace and appeal to the *Reichskammergericht* to place Strasbourg under the imperial ban for violating it. This was a serious threat. As the Senate and XXI soberly concluded, if this happened no Strasburgher would dare venture outside the protection of the city walls, no outsiders would risk entering the outlawed city, commerce would be ruined, "and the Bishop would have the last laugh."[34]

What was going on in and around Strasbourg was disturbing in isolation and thoroughly unsettling in the context of the larger struggle between Catholics and Protestants, a rivalry of more than imperi-

[30]Hahn, *Manderscheid*, pp. 27–35, 78–79; RP 1590, ff. 97v–100v.
[31]Karl Hahn, "Visitationen und Visitationsberichte aus dem Bistum Strassburg in der zweiten Hälfte des 16ten Jahrhunderts," *ZGO*, n.F. 26 (1911), 204–49, 501–43, 573–98.
[32]Karl Hahn, "Das Aufkommen der Jesuiten in der Diözese Strassburg und die Gründung des jesuiten Kollegs in Molsheim," *ZGO*, n.F. 25 (1910), 246–94.
[33]RP 1577, ff. 627v–628r; RP 1579, ff. 452v, 478r.
[34]Hahn, *Manderscheid*, pp. 9–15. The quoted passage is from RP 1578, ff. 237v–240r.

al scope. Ever since the summer of 1565, when the French regent, Catherine de Medici, had held talks at Bayonne with the Duke of Alba, Spain's great anti-Protestant crusader, the Protestant centers had seethed with rumors about an international Catholic conspiracy against them. In March 1567 the council of XIII had discussed the "Papist League against the Lutherans," said to include the pope, Emperor Maximilian II, Philip II, the king of Portugal, and the dukes of Bavaria and Savoy. In the XIII's view these rulers intended to draw the French crown into their intrigues and then to launch a coordinated assault on both the German Lutherans and the French Huguenots.[35] News of the St. Batholomew's massacres five years later convinced the magistrates that a general war and an attack on their own city were imminent.[36]

Living so near the imperial frontier, the Strasburghers felt peculiarly vulnerable to invasion. Catholic territory surrounded them on the west bank of the Rhine, and the Catholics had a foothold in their city, reinforcing their sense of vulnerability. In the view of the Senate and XXI the Lutheran princes were hopelessly complacent about the Catholic menace. To the magistrates of Strasbourg the very survival of Protestantism was at stake and anything that could be done to weaken Catholicism must be done. The Senate and XXI turned to the Calvinists, to Johann Casimir in the Palatinate, to the Huguenots in France, and to the Swiss. They would assist any force that promised to tie down the Catholic powers and to keep them away from Strasbourg. Their own clergy and the Lutheran theologians and princes east of the Rhine might think that the Calvinists were as great a menace to the Lutheran church as were the Catholics, but the Senate and XXI could not afford to be so fastidious. The fiasco of the Schmalkaldic War had not soured the magistrates on the use of force to protect the faith. They supported the Protestants fighting in France, and in the last decade of the century put troops of their own into the field to fight on the side of Calvinists against Catholics in Alsace.

Strasbourg had a long-standing and multifaceted interest in Lorraine and France. In the 1520s it began to admit evangelical refugees from these territories, and the city's printers shipped back evangelical tracts in return. By the 1540s the magistrates were joining their counterparts in Basel to appeal directly to Francis I for mercy toward the "poor persecuted Christians" in his kingdom. They took a particular

[35]RP 1567, ff. 99v–100r; RP 1576, f. 605r-v.
[36]RP 1572, ff. 755v–766r, 790r–796r.

interest in the imperial city of Metz, which the Lutheran princes surrendered to Henry II in 1552. This interest led them, early on, to identify the Guise family as a sinister force determined to crush Protestantism wherever it showed itself.[37] The city's involvement in events over the Vosges was based on more than religion alone. Strasburghers traded in France, particularly in Lyons in the first half of the century, and the Prechter firm had important commercial relations with Lorraine. Several of the larger local concerns were in the habit of advancing money to the French crown; by 1562 Charles IX owed Georg Obrecht and Israel Minckel the resounding sum of 2,142,188 *livres tournois*. French-speaking merchants were regular visitors to Strasbourg's annual trade fairs. French professors dominated the local law faculty, and young men, whether aspiring merchants or students of the law, regularly took part of their training in France.[38]

For its part the French crown had good reason to yearn for an outpost, or at least a sympathetic regime, on the Rhine. Educated Strasburghers were well aware of how dangerous this interest was to their independence, yet the city's rulers continued to court disaster by meddling in the religious affairs of Lorraine and France. The refugees they admitted might endanger the city's German character, but the city's rulers nevertheless assisted them. The Senate and XXI would not surrender French Protestants to the "tyranny" of the Guise family and Catherine de Medici. To do so would increase the strength of Strasbourg's own enemies by bolstering the power of the pope in northern Europe and furthering the dark designs of the Spanish monarchy. The magistrates couched their admission of French refugees in terms of "Christian mercy" and "charity"; in fact, a good dose of self-interest was involved, for the Huguenots were doing their fighting for them.

When the situation in France degenerated into war in 1562 Strasbourg unhesitatingly committed itself to the cause of Protestantism, brushing over the Huguenots' Calvinism. In a series of crucial decisions taken that August, the magistrates set their city on the long road to war at home thirty years later.[39] As the years and the wars wore

[37]The appeals to Francis I can be followed in *PC*. On the Guise family, see Pariset, *Les relations;* RP 1543, f. 124r-v; and PC 3, no. 368.

[38]Kintz, *La société*, pp. 373–74, 380–86. For the Prechters, see also RP 1551, f. 33r-v, and RP 1575, ff. 135r-v, 318v–319r. J. Duquesne, *Les débuts de l'enseignement du droit à Strasbourg au XVIe siècle* (Strasbourg, 1923), pp. 7–8.

[39]RP 1562, ff. 259v–260v, 263v–264v.

on, the magistrates financed mercenaries, allowed recruiting and arms sales in their territory, and made loan after loan to the Huguenot captains despite their record of regular defaults.[40] Charles IX protested and they rebuffed him. When the emperor complained about the rebel alliances forming in Strasbourg (for the city was a frequent rendezvous of English, Dutch, French, and German agents) he too received short shrift.[41]

Aiding the Huguenots and the Dutch brought Strasbourg and the whole Alsatian plain into real danger. The Guisard duc d'Aumale came down out of the Vosges in the winter of 1568–69 and made a bloody swoop through the countryside. He paused outside Strasbourg to warn the magistrates that harboring French refugees and sheltering the Prince of Orange were decidedly unfriendly acts. The Senate and XXI prudently decided to "request" that Orange leave, and for a while sent away all the able-bodied male refugees lest Aumale choose to mistake them for Huguenot troops and attack the city to get at them. Burghers as well as peasants suffered from the pillaging of the mercenaries hired by both sides, and vented their wrath against the Huguenots as well as against the Guise troops. Even in Strasbourg the Prince of Condé's men were unwelcome. They brawled in the taverns, and their constant interest in the fortifications exacerbated fears that sooner or later they would try to take control of the city. The dangers in Alsace were great enough to bring the bishop and the magistrates together in common defense plans.[42]

Still the Senate and XXI refused to accept neutrality. They twice received Condé, in 1574 and 1575. On both occasions he appealed for more support in the name of the violated feudal rights of the Princes

[40]RP 1562, ff. 322r–323r, 330r–v. RP 1568, ff. 429r–430r, and RP 1569, ff. 467r–468r, a loan of 20,000 florins to Duke Wolfgang for an expedition into France. RP 1575, ff. 243v–244v, a loan to the Vidame of Chartres through Elector Palatine Friedrich; ff. 463v–464v, another loan to the Elector himself; ff. 620v–622r, 662v–663r, a loan to Condé and Charles de Montmorency. On Johann Casimir's debts to the foundation of Unser Frauen Haus, RP 1576, ff. 19r–v, 46r–v. In addition, the Huguenots were raising private money; RP 1579, f. 508v, lists some of Condé's creditors, who included several magistrates. As Jean-Pierre Kintz observes, "La politique de soutien à la cause protestante a représenté un gouffre pour le capitalisme strasbourgeois" (*La société*, p. 377).

[41]King Charles's letter: RP 1574, ff. 343v–344r, 349r. For one of the imperial protests, see RP 1574, ff. 635v–636r, and AMS AA 670/59.

[42]RP 1568, ff. 496v, 499v–500r, 501r; RP 1569, ff. 88v–89r, and AMS II/84b/70; Alcuin Hollaender, "Wilhelm von Oranien und Strassburg, 1568 und 1569," ZGO, n.F. 21 (1906), 50–98. Condé's men: RP 1574, ff. 375r–v, 385r–386r; RP 1575, ff. 519v–520v. Joint projects with the bishop: AMS AA 1982, 1984–87.

of the Blood. The magistrates' spokesmen agreed to help, but in the name of the defense of the Protestant religion. By now a minority in the Senate and XXI had become convinced that helping the Huguenots was not the best way to accomplish that. The committee set up to deal with Condé's request illustrated the divisions. Two of its five members urged the Senate and XXI to refuse any new loans. The other three argued that since Condé was battling "popery" and "tyranny" there could be nothing more praiseworthy than to help him. The Senate and XXI followed the lead of the majority.[43] The magistrates had again chosen the cause of Protestant solidarity despite the risks of losing the money they lent, of being drawn into foreign wars, and of having to trust the French—and despite the growing popular opposition to their policy.

From relatively innocent beginnings, printing up propaganda for peddlers to take over the Vosges, the people of Strasbourg had moved into the most brutal realms of international confrontation. Their city did not have the resources in money, in manpower, or even, it would turn out, in conviction to carry off this challenge to the Guise family and the Habsburgs. The alarms grew progressively worse. After the St. Bartholomew's massacres the city feared general war, but that scare passed fairly swiftly.[44] In 1579, however, with a Guisard army prowling in the plain, there was no rest in the city for more than a month, and then no sooner had one threat ebbed than another replaced it.[45] The magistrates themselves were increasingly at odds about the wisdom of supporting Calvinists outside Strasbourg to protect Lutheranism within it, but these debates in the seventies were mild compared to the raging arguments of the 1580s and 1590s, when the wars really came home to Alsace.

The final crisis began down-river in Cologne among the canons of that city's cathedral chapter, and before it was over the Strasburghers had fought a war to transfer control of the bishopric of Strasbourg from the Catholics to the Protestants.[46] In 1583 Pope Gregory XIII excommunicated Cologne's Calvinist canons and their Catholic peers

[43] RP 1574, ff. 388v–391r; RP 1575, ff. 722v–724v, 728v–730r.
[44] RP 1572, ff. 755v–766r.
[45] See RP 1579, passim in October, and f. 656r-v, for news of troops mustering in Lorraine and of plots against Sélestat and Colmar in December.
[46] Aloys Meister, *Der strassburger Kapitelstreit, 1583–1592: Ein Beitrag zur Geschichte der Gegenreformation* (Strasbourg, 1899), and "Akten zum Schisma im Strassburger Domkapitel, 1583–1592," *BSCMHA*, n.s. 19 (1899), 328–59; Eduard Gfrörer, *Strassburger Kapitelstreit und bischöflicher Krieg im Spiegel der elsässischen Flugschriften-Literatur, 1569–1618* (Strasbourg, 1906).

promptly excluded them from the chapter, thus depriving them of their revenues. The excommunicated canons retreated up the Rhine to Strasbourg where they also held canonries, but here again the Catholics excluded them. The Senate and XXI braced for trouble, "since each side has supporters among the burghers."[47] The Protestant canons appealed to the magistrates, playing on their fears that the Catholics were preparing to reintroduce public masses, as was their right under the Peace. Within months the dispute moved from legal arguments about the pope's power to excommunicate and the provisions of the Religious Peace to battles over the enormous revenues controlled by the cathedral chapter and the rights of Protestant nobles to share in the ecclesiastical spoils. At bottom the "chapter strife" here as in Cologne had only the remotest connection with religion. The Senate and XXI, which was unable to stay out of it, nevertheless sought to justify its support for the excommunicated nobles on the familiar grounds of Protestant solidarity.

Local efforts to negotiate a compromise failed. By 1586–87, soldiers hired by both sides were roaming the countryside, seeking to secure villages and their revenues for their respective masters. At the same time mercenaries on their way to France, recruited by both the Catholic League and Henry of Navarre, swarmed through Alsace and compounded the pillaging. Strasbourg had supplied Navarre's men with money, provisions, powder, and guns, and had given them shelter. The peasants were infuriated by the plundering and heartily cursed the Strasburghers for their losses.[48] Citizens with property in the plain shared their outrage. Songs against the magistrates were on many lips.[49] In the public baths one burgher was heard to growl, "Their Graces brought these guests down upon us."[50] Still the Senate and XXI pressed on.

The Senate and XXI had already begun to look for allies to help it should the recurrent raiding in the plain escalate into war. The magistrates first extended diplomatic feelers to Zurich in 1576, but little had been accomplished before the "Thieves' War" of 1586–87.[51] The

[47]RP 1584, ff. 155v–156r, 160r.
[48]Aid to Navarre's troops: RP July–August 1587, e.g., f. 380v; "Bawren wöllen m.h. burger auch zu thodtschlagen," RP 1587, f. 460v.
[49]Songs: RP 1587, ff. 463v, 467r; Rodolphe Reuss, *Zwei Lieder über den Diebskrieg oder Durchzug des navarrischen Kriegsvolkes im Elsass (1587) mit historischer Einleitung und ungedruckten Beilagen* (Strasbourg, 1874).
[50]RP 1587, ff. 479v–480v.
[51]The Strasbourg shooting match of 1576 provided a stage for these overtures: Ville de Strasbourg, *Zurich-Strasbourg* (Strasbourg, 1976). In 1584 the Senate and XXI stepped up the courtship: RP 1584, ff. 501r-v, 625r-v.

magistrates' plans were not a perfect secret, and their project met with noisy criticism from burghers who disliked the Swiss on principle or condemned them as Calvinist heretics. The complaints in the streets mirrored divisions in the councils, where two factions were emerging. Both sought to defend Lutheranism in Strasbourg, but they disagreed on tactics. The war party argued that only a pan-Protestant alliance could beat back the Holy League (by which they meant not just the French Catholic League, but also the Habsburgs, the pope, and the Jesuits) which was conspiring to impose its Tridentine tyranny on the whole of Europe.[52] The peace party considered the Calvinists to be as great a threat as the Catholics. Its members argued that Strasbourg's church could best be protected not by soldiers, but by the repression of dissent at home and the condemnation of theological error. The peace party's sympathies were obviously with the Church Assembly; like the clergy, its members considered the Formula of Concord a better defense of the faith than guns could ever be.[53] In the eighties the war party remained the dominant faction, and in 1588 Strasbourg signed a treaty with Zurich, Bern, and Basel.[54]

Meanwhile the canons' battles continued on their own paths, with neither side gaining any lasting advantage. Frightened by the news that more Guisard troops were loose in the plain, the Senate and XXI voted new subsidies to Navarre's forces, hoping they could throw the Lorrainers out of Alsace.[55] More important, late in 1591 the magistrates made a formal treaty with the Protestant canons. Like the 1588 pact, this one was unpopular, but the Senate and XXI supported it lest "everything be handed over to the papists." Forty-seven magistrates were present for the final debate, ten voted against the treaty, two abstained, and thirty-five approved it. Six days later the Schöffen ratified it, thus giving it a veneer of public support.[56]

So matters stood in April 1592, when Bishop Johann von Manderscheid died without having nominated a successor. The Senate

[52]RP 1587, ff. 536r–537r, 544v–545r; XV 1588, ff. 185r–186r; XV 1592, ff. 102v–104v, 109v–110r. The labels "war party" and "peace party" are Alfred Widmaier's; see *Friedrich Prechter und der strassburger Kapitelstreit* (Strasbourg, 1910), pp. 5–7.
[53]RP 1588, ff. 604v–606r; AMS VI/701a/8; AST 100, unnumbered piece concerning Michael Lichtensteiger, f. 2v.
[54]RP 1588, f. 230r. Copies in AMS AA 1847. The agreement guaranteed the city access to Swiss mercenaries, provided it paid for them.
[55]RP 1589, ff. 642v–643v, 644r, 645v–646r.
[56]RP 1591, ff. 536v–538v, 584v–585v, 595v–596r. This is one of the rare cases where the RP record the actual split in voting. For the text of the treaty, see AMS AA 1621.

and XXI, fearful that the bishopric would be sequestered to the profit of the Habsburgs, reaffirmed its commitment to the Calvinist canons.[57] It authorized the XIII to write to Zurich, Bern, and the Palatinate for help, and to hire troops. Strasbourg prepared for war to preserve its "freedoms, privileges, possessions, and all that we have so far managed to hold through the worst perils."[58] Double elections to replace Manderscheid, one by the Catholics and one by the Calvinists, were to be expected, and Strasbourg intended to be ready to back the Protestant "bishop." The Calvinists met and chose a minor, Johann Georg von Brandenburg; the Catholics elected a Guise, Charles de Lorraine, cardinal of Metz. Open war broke out between the rivals.

The Bishops' War was an unmitigated disaster for Strasbourg.[59] Its troops lost battle after battle. Wherever the burghers came together, they criticized the oligarchs. The hospital filled to overflowing with the wounded. Rumors flew that Stettmeister Friedrich Prechter connived with the Lorrainers, and that many of his colleagues also supported the Catholics. Ammeister Nicolas Fuchs and XIIIer Josias Rihel heard themselves accused of betraying the city by involving it in this ruinous war on behalf of a handful of greedy, foreign, Calvinist nobles. By July money was growing scarce, and in October the city treasury was empty. The Senate and XXI appealed for emergency contributions from all its subjects. Henry IV offered help; the Saxons promised aid; the city secretary set off on a fund-raising tour—but it was hopeless. Large-scale warfare was beyond the resources of any city, and the result was inevitable. Late in 1593 Strasbourg accepted a truce.[60] The Catholics had won.

The magistrates had lost much in the Bishops' War. Strasbourg had temporarily bankrupted itself. The burghers, who had become incensed with the oligarchs, branded some of them Calvinists and others "lackies of the priests," and apparently saw all of them as blind to the city's real interests. The councils of XIII and XV had quarreled violently over the conduct of the war, led by their standard-bearers, Fuchs and Prechter, and these broils were public knowledge.[61] The

[57]RP 1592, ff. 168v–169v.
[58]RP 1592, ff. 182r–184r.
[59]Oskar Ziegler, *Die Politik der Stadt Strassburg im bischöflichen Kriege* (Strasbourg, 1906).
[60]Text in Rodolphe Reuss, *Die Beschreibung des bischöflichen Krieges, anno 1592* (Strasbourg, 1878), pp. 127–37.
[61]XV 1592, ff. 83v–84r, 102v–104r, 109v–110r; Widmaier, *Friedrich Prechter*. Elias Baldus, *Straszburgischer Augustus* (Strasbourg, 1592), a six-page news account of the war, refers to the divisions in the councils.

regime gained nothing to offset its losses. The Catholic party in the city had grown stronger, and the magistrates soon began to quarrel with the Calvinist canons about debts and patronage rights over benefices.[62] To crown it all, the city faced a series of lawsuits in the imperial courts, brought by the Carthusian monks and the nuns of St. Nicolas-in-undis (whose houses the magistrates had closed in preparation for the war) and by Friedrich Prechter, who had been stripped of his offices in the aftermath of the war.[63]

The chapter crisis and the Bishops' War strained relations between the Church Assembly and the Senate and XXI. The magistrates, faced with mounting popular hostility to their policy of supporting the Calvinist canons, wanted more support than they got from their preachers, from whom they requested sermons to remind the commons of their duty to their secular rulers. The preachers complied— after all, the Senate and XXI had been established by God—but they had serious reservations about the competence of rulers who always seemed to be putting secular interests ahead of spiritual ones. From the late eighties through the middle nineties they considered the magistrates' course to be particularly imprudent.[64]

The Church Assembly had never been happy with the magistrates' conviction that Lutheranism within Strasbourg could best be protected by collaboration with Calvinists outside it. For a generation or more they had monitored the magistrates' diplomacy with increasing uneasiness.[65] In 1572 Johann Marbach had pointed out to the Senate and XXI that money advanced to the Huguenots was spent on soldiers, not preachers, and that this was a dubious way to advance the faith. Marbach was alarmed by the pillaging in the countryside, and saw little reason to make Alsatians, Protestant or Catholic, suffer murder and robbery for the sake of the heretic French rebels.[66] Usually the preachers' public attacks on the magistrates' foreign policy were oblique; they hammered away at the errors of Calvinist theology in their books and sermons. At times they were more direct: in 1576 the Senate and XXI had to tell them to mind their tongues and not criticize the Swiss, with whom the magistrates were seeking an

---

[62]AMS II/106b/11 (1597); RP 1595, ff. 303v–304r, 313v–314v; RP 1596, ff. 97v–98r, 102v–103r.

[63]RP 1594, ff. 153r-v, 194r-v, on the Charterhouse; AMS II/6/1–5, 14, and II/8/5, on St. Nicolas. Widmaier, *Friedrich Prechter,* p. 62.

[64]BNUS ms. 998, pp. 6–11 (1589), 43–45 (1592); RP 1595, ff. 495v–496r.

[65]AST 67/2, f. 43v (1566); 67/3, ff. 47r–48r (1567); 67/4, ff. 32r, 37r, 38r, 70r (1568).

[66]AST 64/6, ff. 44r–45r.

alliance.[67] In 1587, during the negotiation of that pact, the clergy again spoke out, and the magistrates again ordered them to keep silent. The Church Assembly was most unhappy about the whole business and replied that it must reserve the right to defend true doctrine. Then, on the eve of the final ratification of the treaty, Johann Pappus backed down, promising that the clergy would lead public prayers for the success of the alliance, and that the Senate and XXI would have no cause to complain about the wording of those prayers.[68]

The preachers' own position was embarrassing.[69] They could hardly support the Catholic canons, but the Calvinists were no better. The Calvinists bragged that when they had finished with the Catholics they would take on the Lutherans; "so we see we have two enemies," said the preachers. At the magistrates' request Pappus preached a sermon on the qualities of a good bishop to the Protestant canons before they proceeded to the election of their new "bishop." The canons' choice of a young boy underlined their lack of interest in religion, and the preachers could only conclude that the Devil was at his work. They were unsure of what to say to their congregations about this scandal, and decided to recommend resignation and penance. Acting as spokesman for the clergy, Pappus published a *Report* which justified the election, blamed the war on the Catholics, and glossed over the Protestant canons' Calvinism. Having thus discharged their unpleasant duty to support their secular masters, the clergy retreated into their own interests. While they urged obedience to the Senate and XXI, they also attacked Calvinists, contributing to the unrest in the city. They knew the magistrates were divided and made few overtures to them. What the Church Assembly wanted was an end to this war, which they thought had been provoked by worldly nobles seeking secular gain. Burghers, magistrates, and the church could not hope to profit from the victory of either side, and the best course was to get out of the struggle.

The Church Assembly was more circumspect in its opposition to the magistrates in this crisis than it had been in the late forties, but

---

[67]RP 1576, ff. 262r–263r; AST 84/91 (1588).

[68]RP 1587, f. 589r; AST 84/103; BNUS ms. 998, pp. 3–5; RP 1588, f. 227r-v.

[69]For what follows, see Pappus, *Ein christliche Predigt* (Strasbourg, 1592) and *Kurtzer und beständiger Bericht* (Strasbourg, 1592); Wilhelm Horning, ed., "Auszug aus einer Copie des Protokoll-buches des Strassburger Kirchen-convents, 1588–1618," *Beiträge zur Kirchengeschichte des Elsasses vom 16–19 Jahrhundert* 5 (1885), Appendix, pp. 31, 43; RP 1592, f. 532v; RP 1593, f. 87v; AST 169, ff. 39v–40r; BNUS ms. 998, pp. 43–45, 63, 100, 131–32.

every burgher with ears knew that the preachers disapproved of the Senate and XXI's conduct. Many of them had absorbed the anti-Calvinism of their pastors and now doubted that the oligarchs really had the best interests of the city or of its church uppermost in their minds. Indeed, more and more of them felt that their masters were either faithless or heretical. Slanders against individual magistrates circulated, as well as threats to turn out the whole regime.[70] In the 1580s and 1590s the bond between subjects and magistrates nearly broke. These were bad years for the city's economy, as war strained public finances and hampered trade, while poor harvests drove up the cost of living and work was hard to come by. Artisans and laborers who had trouble making ends meet blamed their rulers; they claimed that the oligarchs showed no charity and the city courts no mercy toward the poor. The clergy contributed to this ill will by attacking the magistrates' personal business dealings, as well as by stirring up denominational hatreds.[71]

The magistrates' overly ambitious foreign policy had brought marauding armies to the city gates, pulled Strasbourg into a losing war, and divided both the councils and their people. Some burghers suspected the oligarchs of trying to undermine the Schöffen; there were even rumors that they intended to abolish the guilds.[72] These attacks surfaced again and again in handwritten pasquils, printed propaganda, and conversations in the taverns, baths, and marketplaces. The magistrates issued mandates against libel and slander, warning the people that these charges could produce "nothing but division, bitterness, and the destruction of trust between rulers and burghers," but the burghers continued to speculate, complain, and threaten.[73] As Pappus said of his congregation, "You can't shut them up."[74]

The Bishops' War was the last campaign for the magistrates born between the beginning of the reformation and the Religious Peace. Death was now overtaking them, and the generation that succeeded them made a revolution in foreign policy, accepting the demands of their clergy and lay subjects for peace. The old élan was gone. The Strasburghers had grown sick of war and had learned that they could no longer afford to wage it. Their city would never again embark on a crusade for the faith or for the nobles of France or the Empire, nor

[70]RP 1581, ff. 181v–182v; 1587, f. 557r; 1595, ff. 495v–496r, 496v–497r, 501r–v.
[71]RP 1581, ff. 181v–182v; 1585, ff. 353v–354v; 1587, f. 589r; AST 84/103.
[72]RP 1587, f. 557r; 1597, f. 556r–v.
[73]AMS R5, ff. 166r–167r, 178v–179r, mandates of 1590 and 1592.
[74]Horning, "Auszug," p. 43.

would it struggle any longer to ignore the conflicting Saxon and Swiss theologies. In 1598 the Senate and XXI finally bowed to the Church Assembly and ratified the Formula of Concord. Once again Strasbourg had thrown in its lot with the Saxon Lutherans.

In the first half of the sixteenth century Strasbourg defied its emperor and made itself one of the most influential of the Protestant cities. In the second half of the century it pursued a foreign policy more in line with that of German-speaking Calvinists than that of German Lutherans. That policy grew out of the terms of the Religious Peace of 1555 and out of the magistrates' sensitivity both to their frontier position and to the Catholic resurgence they saw around them. The means they chose to protect their Lutheran church had outraged first their clergy and then the rest of their subjects. To carry out this foreign policy they had had to hold their city at a remove from orthodox Lutheran opinion as it had emerged east of the Rhine in the latter part of the century, for they dared not risk joining the other Lutheran powers to condemn the Calvinist doctrines of their military allies.

The magistrates' foreign policy dictated many of the choices made in domestic policy. For example, the rapprochements with the Saxons carried out in the 1530s and late 1590s brought the local church back into line with the Lutheran mainstream, guiding what was taught and practiced within the walls. The contrary currents of the decades of war between the late 1540s and early 1590s, when the city's clergy tried and failed to keep Strasbourg in lock-step with the other Lutheran churches, likewise arose in part as a result of external pressures.

Events outside the walls and the changing nature of Strasbourg's position in the wider world had a particularly strong influence on the internal development of orthodoxy and on the city's treatment of dissenters. In the early years of the reformation the magistrates could act with a fair degree of independence, as their conversion to Protestantism against the emperor's will and their initial treatment of both sectarians and Catholics demonstrated. Even the first generation of magistrates had needed foreign allies and had had to make concessions to them. In the second generation the demands of both allies and enemies grew more pressing, and that pressure largely explains what happened to the city's Catholic and Calvinist minorities after mid-century. The third generation proved to be the most vulnerable of all to the outside world, as its members' attitudes toward dissent and orthodoxy demonstrated.

CHAPTER FIVE

Dissent

Strasbourg's reformation had begun with a series of choices as conservative Catholic reformers, humanists, evangelicals, social radicals, and spiritualists competed for the Strasburghers' support. The Catholic reformers, along with Catholic defenders of the status quo, lost in the city but kept much of the diocese, and eventually the Catholic reformation took hold in these territories. The humanists split and went on to contribute to both the Catholic and the Protestant reformations. Within Strasbourg the evangelical party emerged victorious, and within it the Lutherans carried the day. Zwinglian tendencies in the Strasbourg reformation were submerged but not eradicated by 1536. The radicals never pulled themselves together as a coherent force within the walls, and after the defeat of the peasants in 1525 only the Anabaptists remained to speak for change in the sociopolitical order. The spiritualist vision survived, for example among the followers of Caspar Schwenckfeld. Throughout the sixteenth century Strasburghers needed to make no special effort to come into contact with the Lutherans' rivals; indeed, it would have been almost impossible for a resident of the city to avoid meeting dissidents and hearing about heterodox religious ideas.

A minority of Strasburghers rejected the established Lutheran church in favor of one or another of its competitors. It was a source of constant displeasure to the Lutheran clergy to come across Anabaptists and Schwenckfelders, Catholics, and Calvinists in their parishes. The dissidents were never more than a small minority but in the eyes of the clergy these men and women posed a threat out of all proportion to their numbers. The clergy regularly lumped all their opponents together and advocated the same treatment for all of them. At a minimum, heretics must be silenced; if they persisted in their errors and tried to spread them, they should be exiled. The early preachers recognized in principle that heretics might be put to death, but neither they nor their successors ever urged the magistrates to slaughter their flesh-and-blood opponents. The clergy's position was thus reasonably moderate, and the magistrates tended to enforce that minimum of coercion for which the clergy would settle. The preachers often spoke as if the magistrates did nothing to police dissent. In fact the Senate and XXI did act, but the magistrates moved at their own speed, in their own way, and for their own reasons. Instead of lumping all the dissidents together, they differentiated the main groups—sectarians, Catholics, and Calvinists—and also made distinctions within the groups themselves. Their policies toward Catholics and Calvinists showed striking similarities, and also overlapped somewhat with their treatment of the Schwenckfelders. The Anabaptists received special attention and anomalous treatment.

The Senate and XXI policed dissent, but not consistently. Policy varied depending on the group, the moment, and the individual with whom the magistrates were dealing. Behind the contradictory decisions, however, there was a certain unity of purpose. The magistrates rejected the clergy's egalitarian notion that all forms of dissent could be viewed in the same way. Instead they shaped a flexible set of policies which reflected six general principles. Two of these principles dealt with the ideas of orthodoxy and uniformity; two grew out of the traditions of local jurisprudence; and two were superior principles that regularly took precedence over other concerns in all the magistrates' decisions.

The magistrates established a commitment to orthodoxy and uniformity by insisting that nothing could be taught, preached, or published in Strasbourg except "the pure word of God." They permitted no public criticism of the doctrines or personnel of the established church to go unchallenged. On the other hand, the magistrates specifically and consistently refused to be party to the forcing of anyone's conscience. They did not order adults to attend the services of the Lutheran church, and they did not normally compel Strasburghers to declare under oath that they believed in the Lutheran definitions of Christianity. Those who did not accept the established church were to keep silent; if they spoke out and refused to accept correction, there was no place for them in Strasbourg. The clergy could live with these principles, for to a large extent they shared them.

Local judicial practice had no sympathy for the sort of summary justice encouraged by the imperial legislation against dissidents. Instead, in Strasbourg the time-honored rule that no one was to be judged without a hearing prevailed. The city was not unique in insisting that heretics be allowed to explain their case; the Catholic authorities in Horb had adhered to the same principle in the celebrated trial of an Anabaptist leader, Michael Sattler.[1] The magistrates of Strasbourg also made an effort to try each case on its merits. Their mandates laid down general policies, but the members of the Senate and XXI reserved the right to bend their own rules. As a result, the actual treatment of heretics often differed from the procedures spelled out in the law. The preachers had no quarrel with the first of these principles; if anything, they were more willing than the magistrates to hear out their critics, the better to refute them. They were much less happy with deviations from the letter of the law, since these were invariably in the direction of clemency.

The two superior principles governing the policing of dissent were political rather than religious or judicial. The magistrates refused to allow the clergy an independent power base any larger than the one their pulpits inevitably gave them. Therefore the Senate and XXI would allow no clerical inquisition in the city.[2] Such an institution would have gone against the whole tenor of their religious legislation prior to 1598, all of which aimed at securing and preserving magisterial supremacy. Rather than suffer a renaissance of the church courts, the magistrates resolved to defend the unity of their church themselves. This permitted them to respect their single most important conviction: nothing was to be done that would jeopardize Strasbourg's peace and prosperity (and they regarded their own dominance as a basic part of this), or that would compromise the city's survival as an independent polity. On this level the potential for conflict between the clergy and the magistrates was strong and obvious.

---

[1]The imperial mandate of 1529 against the Anabaptists provided for immediate execution. Horst Schraepler, *Die rechtliche Behandlung der Täufer in der deutschen Schweiz, Südwestdeutschland, und Hessen, 1525–1618* (Tübingen, 1957), pp. 21–22, and 38–42 on Sattler.

[2]The word "inquisition" was current in Strasbourg as a synonym for thorough investigation. The magistrates explicitly rejected the idea of a *religious* inquisition at least twice: RP 1567, f. 453v, apropos of Anabaptists; and again apropos of Calvinists, RP 1577, ff. 96r–99r.

When the magistrates exercised their prerogative to bend their own laws it was usually out of respect for this supreme goal of protecting their city's peace, prosperity, and independence. The Catholics had powerful patrons outside the city walls, and after 1555 the Religious Peace of Augsburg guaranteed their right to practice their faith within the walls. Pressure on Catholics was dangerous because it could provoke imperial reprisals. The Calvinists professed doctrines held by Strasbourg's major military allies in the second half of the century, and blunt condemnation of Calvinists could endanger this network of support. Moreover, since Strasbourg lived by trade, rash actions against either Catholics or Calvinists were impolitic on economic grounds as well. The sectarians were without foreign protectors, but they had some defenders within the city. A too brutal treatment of the sectarians might provoke criticism from these Strasburghers, and perhaps lead to domestic disorder. Caution was in order on all fronts, and understandably the magistrates proceeded slowly.

The Anabaptists and Schwenckfelders monopolized attention in the 1530s and 1540s. The presence of Catholics in the city once again became a live issue in the late 1540s and remained a worry for the rest of the century, while the Calvinists rose to prominence in the 1560s after the wars in France began to flood Strasbourg with refugees. The sections that follow contain some description of the kinds of people who were involved in the dissident groups, but the main focus is on what the magistrates chose to do with dissenters and how the orthodox laity felt about them. A key aspect of the debate on dissent is, of course, the theological views that led the Lutheran clergy to condemn these three groups. Since very few Strasburghers outside the clergy showed any interest in this side of the matter, it receives little attention here.

1. *The Sectarian Challenge*

During the first generation of the reformation some Strasburghers chose to follow radical leaders like Melchior Hofmann and Caspar Schwenckfeld.[3] The combined assaults of the clergy and the magis-

---

[3]The relevant texts have been splendidly edited through 1535 by Jean Rott and Manfred Krebs, *TAE*. This edition is based on materials collected by Johann Adam; I am most grateful to Jean Rott for allowing me to see the remainder of Adam's transcriptions, which extend into the seventeenth century. Few documents have been published for the later period, but see T. W. Roehrich, "Zur Geschichte der strassburgischen Widertäufer in den

The People's Reformation

trates in the 1520s and 1530s failed to wipe out these dissident groups. In 1557 the magistrates had twenty-six suspects to interrogate, one of the largest totals since 1529.[4] Nearly twenty years later, the assistant pastor of St. Aurelia reported several hundred people gathered in the woods outside the city.[5] Information about local sectarians becomes rarer as the century advances, but Strasbourg was never without its sectarians.

The clergy affected to treat the Schwenckfelders, the Anabaptists, and the followers of idiosyncratic individual "prophets" as part of a single group, but there was no all-embracing sectarian community in Strasbourg to correspond to the Catholics or the Calvinists. The two main subgroups, the Schwenckfelders and the Anabaptists, had little in common. The Schwenckfelders distanced themselves from the Anabaptists in their doctrines, for they were spiritualists while the Anabaptists leaned to Biblical literalism. The Schwenckfelders had no quarrel with the existence of secular governments, provided they did not interfere in the church, but some Anabaptists denied the legitimacy of any coercion of Christians. The Schwenckfelders had no intention of organizing a church of their own, but the Anabaptists certainly did. In the shadows of the magistrates' church they put together their own congregations, burying their theological differences in an evolving consensus that left the Swiss Brethren dominant and excluded other dissenters.[6] Their substitution of believers' baptism for infant baptism symbolized their will to create a disciplined, gathered church, more Christian than the parishes of sinners presided over by the establishment. Social position as well as doctrine divided the Anabaptists and Schwenckfelders, for the latter recruited themselves almost exclusively from the city's privileged classes while

---

Jahren 1527 bis 1543," *Zeitschrift für die historische Theologie*, 30 (1860), 1–121. For the Schwenckfelders see also *Corpus Schwenckfeldianorum*, ed. Chester David Hartranft et al., 19 vols. (Leipzig, 1907–61). The secondary literature is voluminous. See in particular George H. Williams, *The Radical Reformation* (London, 1962); Chrisman, *Strasbourg*, chap. 11; and Marc Lienhard, "Les autorités civiles et les anabaptistes: Attitudes du magistrat de Strasbourg (1526–1532), " in *Origins and Characteristics of Anabaptism/Les débuts et les caractéristiques de l'anabaptisme*, ed. Marc Lienhard (The Hague, 1977), pp. 196–215. On the synod, Wendel, *L'Eglise*.

[4]*TAE*, vol. 1, no. 175 (1529); AMS I/14, "Widerteufferbuch 1556–1573," ff. 10r–27r, (1557).

[5]AST 76 (1576). Compare AST 176, ff. 379v–380v (1545). Both accounts are summarized by Claus-Peter Clasen, *Anabaptism: A Social History* (Ithaca, 1972), pp. 93–94.

[6]Williams, *Radical Reformation*, chap. 31; Claus-Peter Clasen, "Anabaptist Sects in the Sixteenth Century," *Mennonite Quarterly Review*, 46 (1972), 259–60.

Dissent

the Anabaptists drew their strength mostly from the artisanal classes. Yet the Anabaptists and Schwenckfelders were linked by the fact that both challenged the established church's claim to monopolize doctrinal truth. Each group offered the Strasburghers an alternative vision of the reformation, and neither accepted the role the Lutherans assigned to the clergy and to Scripture.

In formulating their response to the sectarian challenge, the magistrates of Strasbourg chose to ignore both the imperial authorities and the opinions of the leading Lutheran theologians. Imperial law bound all territorial governments to execute practicing Anabaptists and to confiscate their property. Failure to do so could bring a territory under the imperial ban. Strasbourg promulgated the imperial mandates of 1528 and 1529 but left both as dead letters.[7] Similarly, the Senate and XXI rejected Luther's and Melanchthon's arguments that sectarians should be put to death as blasphemers.[8]

The magistrates also acted independently of their own clergy's advice. The local preachers' opposition to the sects had been slow to crystallize, but after a synod held in 1533 their collective position was clear: the sectarians' doctrines were wrong; they threatened the church and the civil authorities; they must be eliminated. The Senate and XXI concurred, but the clergy and the magistrates disagreed on how to purge Strasbourg of the sectarians. The clergy wanted to refute their rivals through public disputations; after 1526 the magistrates refused to allow this, for they had no desire to publicize sectarian ideas.[9] The Senate and XXI also ordered the preachers to be "mild" in their sermons and published condemnations, of which few were written after the mid-thirties.[10] The magistrates did allow the clergy to talk privately with men and women suspected of sectarianism. The records of these meetings show that the clergy devoted long hours to these attempts at conversion but with little success, particularly in the case of leaders.[11] After mid-century the

---

[7]*TAE*, vol. 1, no. 120 (1528); and RP 1548, ff. 83r-v, 511r, 512r.
[8]Schraepler, *Behandlung*, pp. 24–27; and John S. Oyer, *Lutheran Reformers against the Anabaptists: Luther, Melanchthon, and Menius and the Anabaptists of Central Germany* (The Hague, 1964).
[9]*TAE*, vol. 1, no. 65.
[10]RP 1552, ff. 43v, 54r; 1556, ff. 98v–99r.
[11] AMS I/14. Of 96 sectarians known to have been interrogated between 1536 and 1573, only nine converted. A further six may have taken instruction. None of the fifteen were leaders. The clergy undoubtedly swayed more than fifteen people in nearly forty years, but the proportion of one in six is probably accurate.

clergy directed their denunciations of sectarians primarily against the Schwenckfelders, for by this time Anabaptism was a waning force, and the pastors were now more worried about the appeal of Schwenckfeld's spiritualist views to the upper classes.[12] The magistrates showed little sign of sharing this concern.

The Senate and XXI did not need theological advice to see that the early Anabaptists' attitudes to secular government were a menace. It had begun to expel individuals as early as 1526, and by 1528 exile had become the usual penalty for Anabaptist activity.[13] Meanwhile, in 1527 the magistrates had issued a general mandate warning their subjects to shun the sects.[14] It was renewed in 1530 when the Senate and XXI set up a standing committee of five magistrates, the *Wiedertäuferherren*, to investigate and interrogate suspects.[15] Sectarians could now avoid exile only by converting and swearing a special oath (*Urphed*) to obey the magistrates.[16] Seven years later the magistrates ordered their subjects to report sectarians to the authorities and charged the Schöffen of each guild to oversee this.[17] The next general mandate, issued in 1538, publicly proclaimed the penalties in use in Strasbourg against sectarians: exile for the obdurate; imprisonment for those who returned, with mutilation for a second offense, and drowning for a third.[18] The last mandate against the sects, issued in 1540, threatened those who refused to convert with corporal or capital punishment, and promised the same fate to anyone sheltering Anabaptists.[19]

These laws made no attempt to define the exact nature or full range

---

[12]The clergy argued that the Schwenckfelders, like the Calvinists who were now emerging as their most serious rivals for Protestant support, undermined the authority of the ministry. See AST 180, ff. 576r–634r, for Marbach's sermons against the Schwenckfelders preached in 1556. See also his *Christlicher und warhaffter Underricht* (Strasbourg, 1565), pp. 20, 73–74; *Drey christlichen Predigen* (Strasbourg, 1565), p. 83; *Christlicher Underricht* (Strasbourg, 1567), p. 37. All three are directed primarily against the Calvinists.

[13]*TAE*, vol. 1, nos. 52, 64 (1526), and no. 155 (1528).

[14]*TAE*, vol. 1, no. 92.

[15]*TAE*, vol. 1, nos. 222, 235. The committee was not disbanded until 1590 (RP f. 7v). Its records (AMS I/14) are extant only for 1556–73.

[16]*TAE*, vol. 1, no. 155. The Urphed exists in two versions, one for burghers and one for foreigners, both from 1538 (AST 176, ff. 373v–374v). It was subsequently modified (RP 1540, ff. 123v–125r, 162v–163r, and RP 1556, f. 193r-v), but copies of the revised versions are not extant. The latter revision was intended to cover the Schwenckfelders and was the magistrates' only real response to the preachers' increasing animosity to that group.

[17]AMS R4, f. 139r (1537).

[18]Text: Roehrich, "Zur Geschichte," pp. 109–12.

[19]Text, ibid., pp. 118–19.

of sectarian ideas. Apparently the magistrates had noticed what the clergy would not: every detailed condemnation of error, like every definite formulation of orthodoxy, created more argument back and forth. While the clergy thought that increasingly precise formulations would clarify the truth and win over the errant, the magistrates thought the result would be increased division. Instead of explaining the sectarians' errors, the Senate and XXI preferred to insist on the social and political consequences of their theologies, namely the destruction of "the unanimously accepted Christian order," as they put it in 1527. This allowed the magistrates, in all their general mandates, to argue that they were acting to police secular rather than spiritual offenses. The initial mandate stressed the Anabaptists' rejection of temporal authority and branded them a threat to public order. The same points were made in 1538 and illustrated then by reference to the horrible events of a few years before, when radical Anabaptists had seized control of Münster and conducted a reign of terror in that city. In the 1538 mandate the magistrates explicitly denied that they were punishing people "for not believing what we want them to believe." Dissidents were punished for rejecting oaths or for violating orders of exile, the Senate and XXI affirmed.

Denying that they were engaging in religious persecution was part of the magistrates' attempt to shape public opinion, as were the repeated warnings that the sectarians only seemed pious. The Senate and XXI's uneasiness about popular reactions to the sects and to the laws against them was most obvious in the magistrates' careful defense of the increasing severity of their laws. In 1538 they called all their previous measures "mild" and admitted that mildness had failed. Two years later they again justified harsher measures by pointing to the failure of their previous moderation. They had, they claimed, tried to win back lost souls through kindness, but now their patience was exhausted.

In their public statements and private memoranda the members of the Senate and XXI had laid down a clear program for the repression of the sects. That clarity is deceptive. In application, the magistrates' program turned into a murky mass of inconsistencies, for their motives and actions were more complicated than they were prepared to admit to their subjects. In practice they did both more and less than they claimed to do.

According to their official statements, what particularly disturbed the magistrates about the sectarians was the threat they posed to civil order. Yet the local dissidents were divided on the question of the legitimacy of the secular powers, and the magistrates' judgments in individual cases did not always reflect that division. They condemned Caspar Schwenckfeld's ideas at the synod in 1533, although Schwenckfeld did not attack secular authority *per se*.[20] They exiled some of the Silesian's followers.[21] They expelled Anabaptists like Wendling Haman, who had renewed his burgher's oath each year and had done all his civic duties despite twenty years of activity in sectarian circles.[22] As they admitted to Veit von Helfenstein, they were after something more than secular obedience: "We have no quarrel with your behavior as a burgher, only with your beliefs."[23] On the other hand, some Anabaptists who refused to carry out even the most elementary of a citizen's duties were treated with surprising patience. Michael Meckel was in trouble for almost a decade, and several times made unauthorized returns from exile, but there is no record of his having been punished for this.[24]

The magistrates' indulgence was most marked in the case of the Schwenckfelders. It was common knowledge in the city that Doctor Johann Winter von Andernach's wife, Felicitas Scher, was a disciple of the Silesian, as were her two sisters and their father, Junker Peter Scher. According to the final report on the inspection of the urban parishes in 1554, Andernach himself rented a house to a group of Anabaptists. Nothing was done to any of the Andernach-Scher family. Peter Scher had prominent connections in imperial circles; when he died in 1557, Ammeister Matthis Pfarrer urged his fellow magistrates to attend the funeral. Andernach was one of the most respected doctors of his day and the personal physician of the powerful family of Jacob Sturm. The magistrates went out of their way to keep him in Strasbourg.[25] Katherine Zell, the feisty widow of pastor Matthis Zell, was one of the city's principal distributors of Schwenckfeldian literature. In 1557 she published *A Letter to All the Citizens of Stras-*

[20]Williams, *Radical Reformation*, pp. 291–92. *Corpus Schwenckfeldianorum*, vol. 4, nos. 125, 140, 141, 143, all from 1533. I am grateful to R. Emmet McLaughlin for drawing the latter passages to my attention.

[21]Alexander Berner was exiled in 1535 (*TAE*, vol. 2, no. 660).

[22]RP 1560, ff. 449r–450v, 452r; AMS I/14, f. 13v (1557); RP 1557, ff. 462r–v, 466v.

[23]AMS I/14, f. 21r–v (1557).

[24]RP 1573, ff. 29v–30r; Lorna Jane Abray, "La vie d'un anabaptiste strasbourgeois au 16e siècle: Michael Meckel," *RHPR*, 57 (1977), 195–207.

[25]Jacob Bernays, "Zur Biographie Johann Winters von Andernach," *ZGO*, n.F. 16 (1901), 28–57; RP 1545, f. 192v; RP 1563, ff. 531v–532v, 536v–537r; RP 1557, f. 402r.

bourg, in which she upbraided her late husband's colleagues for their attacks on Schwenckfeld and the Anabaptists. Mindful of her great popularity with the common people, the Senate and XXI treated her with kid gloves.[26] The strange career of the local Schwenckfelders, in theory subject to exile as pernicious heretics and in practice usually treated as respected citizens, reached its peak of paradox late in the century. In 1590 Michael Theurer, a devoted collector of books by and about Caspar Schwenckfeld, found himself appointed by his colleagues in the Senate and XXI to sit on the city's Board of Censors.[27]

The threats of corporal and capital punishment laid down in the general mandates of 1538 and 1540 remained empty warnings. The normal pattern of events in Strasbourg was identification or denunciation of a suspect, then interrogation and instruction, followed by conversion or expulsion. The clergy accomplished most of the work of identifying sectarians; the Strasburghers did not denounce their neighbors. Through the Wiedertäuferherren the magistrates made long drawn-out attempts to instruct and convert sectarian dissidents. They rarely imprisoned suspects, for the obvious reason that it cost money to lock up, guard, and feed prisoners. In only two cases, those of the notorious Melchior Hofmann and the obscure Veit Barthel, did the Senate and XXI resort to long-term detention; the latter case was an accident.[28] The usual punishment for recalcitrant sectarians was exile, and the magistrates did not enforce the clauses in the imperial legislation which demanded confiscation of sectarian property.[29] Some Anabaptists who returned from exile did suffer the statutory spell on bread and water.[30] There is no record of the magistrates

---

[26]*Ein Brieff an die gantze Burgerschafft* (Strasbourg, 1557); RP 1558, ff. 164v, 165v, 169r.

[27]RP 1590, f. 208v. In 1594 he was co-opted by the council of XV, whose members were well aware of his religious beliefs. See AST 77/1 for the postmortem inventory of his Schwenckfeldiana, drawn up in 1603.

[28]Roehrich, "Zur Geschichte," and Friedrich Otto zur Linden, *Melchior Hofmann, ein Prophet der Widertäufer* (Haarlem, 1885) reproduce some of the documents. Barthel was arrested in Strasbourg for his attacks on Duke George of Saxony (AMS AA 479, ff. 64r–65v). Convinced that he would not get a fair trial from the Saxons, the Senate and XXI refused to extradite him. He died, probably in the spring of 1554, a victim of protective custody.

[29]As their lawyers pointed out, since they ignored the rest of the imperial laws, there was no reason to scruple over their property clauses. On one occasion the Senate and XXI did take over the operations of an Anabaptist's mill, holding it in trust for Wilhelm Blum's heirs and providing Blum with an annual pension in compensation. RP 1539, f. 193r; RP 1544, f. 121r; RP 1546, ff. 505r, 507v; RP 1548, ff. 36v, 56r, 83r–v; RP 1553, ff. 392v–393r.

[30]RP 1558, ff. 546v–547r.

mutilating or executing anyone.[31] The magistrates had privately rejected the use of capital punishment for sectarian activity in 1528 and, mandates to the contrary, they never wavered from this decision in practice.[32]

All the extant evidence points to a most erratic policing of sectarian dissent in Strasbourg. The Senate and XXI did not observe its own laws to the letter, and there is no obvious pattern to the deviations. For all that, the magistrates did not act capriciously; they had several reasons to diverge from their stated intentions and practices.

The Schwenckfelders always enjoyed a protected status because of their social position. With the passage of time, the city's Anabaptist community changed in its composition, encouraging the magistrates to alter their attitude toward it. The Anabaptists who first came to the regime's attention were foreigners, as the 1527 mandate suggested. By the late 1530s and the early 1540s the movement had been naturalized. More and more of the men and women the Senate and XXI interrogated turned out to be citizens or long-time residents. Hans Hermels had lived in the city for "thirty years without a complaint against him" before he was questioned in 1557; Nicolas Fuchs had been a burgher for ten years.[33] Along with assimilation came another change; the early Anabaptists had rarely owned real property, but from the 1530s on Anabaptists of some substance began to crop up, although the extant data do not permit any sophisticated reconstruction of their social position. While they moved in less prestigious circles than the Schwenckfelders, it is clear that the proportion of people the magistrates had to acknowledge as respectable was on the increase.[34] When the magistrates interrogated these suspects they confronted people with a settled place in local society.

Certainly their neighbors raised no outcry against the sectarians. As the magistrates noted in 1538, many Strasburghers regarded the dissidents as pious fellow Christians. Faced with this widespread sympathy for the sectarians, the magistrates could ill afford to create martyrs. When the dreaded revolution did not materialize, when the sectarians showed themselves to be law-abiding, and as their num-

---

[31]Claus Frey was executed in 1534, but for the secular offense of bigamy, not for his theological views. *TAE,* vol. 2, no. 573.

[32]*TAE,* vol. 1, no. 154.

[33]AMS I/14, ff. 17v–19r, 13r–v.

[34]Hans Betz: RP 1540, f. 165v. Claus Braunstein: AMS I/14, ff. 32r–33r (1564). Wilhelm Blum: see note 29, above. Wendling Schied's *Zinsbriefe:* AMS KS 35[ii], f. 66v (1538); KS 43[i], f. 37r–v (1540); and KS 46[i], unfoliated, 4 December 1542.

bers decreased, the magistrates themselves began to accept the dissidents as individual eccentrics who could safely be tolerated. Abraham Held, who served five terms on the Wiedertäuferherren, employed an Anabaptist family on his rural property in the 1570s.[35]

The decades of attempts to destroy the sects had involved the magistrates in more than ordinary police work. Their original fear of the subversive potential of the sects had led them to try to stamp them out, and by the middle 1530s they found themselves having to establish the line dividing truth from error. Their frequent attacks of private and corporate leniency demonstrate that they found this role uncomfortable. As three of them observed in 1576, after talking with a man they recognized to be a pious Christian following his conscience, "There are some questions which human beings cannot resolve."[36] It would have been easier to turn the job of dealing with sectarians over to the clergy, who were much more confident about what was true and what was false. Indeed, the clergy did do most of the talking in the Wiedertäuferherren sessions, even if they were never officially more than advisers. But the Senate and XXI chose to protect the principle of the lay supremacy, and the magistrates themselves presided over this local equivalent of heresy trials until the effort to convert the sectarians was abandoned in 1590.[37]

Although the sectarians never amounted to anything but a small minority among the city's population, their history reveals important patterns in the Strasburghers' reformation. Their very existence was a sign of lay rebelliousness against the preachers' claim to monopolize Christian truth, for in every decade some people abandoned the established church for the sects. The survival of the Anabaptists and the Schwenckfelders underlined the impotence of both spiritual and secular authorities to control what the Strasburghers thought. It was not just the sectarians who spoke for lay independence of mind. The supposedly orthodox majority among the common people remained untroubled by the rebels; the ordinary Strasburgher was more likely to accept than to reject the dissidents, despite the preachers' warnings. The magistrates, for their part, had sound reason to police the sects, but from the beginning they did so in their own way and

[35]Christian Wolff, "Une liste nominative des habitants de Schiltigheim en 1575," *Bulletin du cercle généalogique d'Alsace*, 15 (1971), 47. The pastor who drew up the list was incensed by Held's hypocrisy.
[36]RP 1576, ff. 785v–786r, concerning Hans Georg Schied.
[37]RP 1590, f. 7v.

scarcely in perfect obedience to the preachers' demands for rigor. The clash between clerical urgency and magisterial caution in the middle and late decades of the century demonstrated a gap between the two authorities' understanding of the clarity of Scripture and the dangers of dissent. However, despite this uneasiness about the boundaries of orthodoxy, the Senate and XXI did act against sectarians, harassing dissidents and driving people away. In exiling sectarians because of their religious beliefs the magistrates showed that their commitment to the unity of the church was not a matter of simple lip service.

2. The Catholic Menace

Anabaptists and Schwenckfelders merely challenged the Lutheran church's attempt to monopolize religious life in Strasbourg; for a time in the middle sixteenth century the city's Catholic minority had some hope of seeing the Lutheran church destroyed. In the aftermath of the Schmalkaldic War, Strasbourg was forced into a treaty with Bishop Erasmus von Limburg which returned the cathedral, Old St. Peter, and New St. Peter to the Catholics. Signed in 1549, the treaty permitted the exercise of the Protestant faith in the four remaining parish churches, but the Lutherans were warned that they would have to answer to the emperor if they chose to continue their services.[38] The magistrates' church had lost, and never recovered, its claim to exclusive legality. In the general gloom it was feared that the treaty would be no more than a first step toward the day when the Catholics drove the Lutherans out of the city altogether. Still the magistrates knew that if much had been lost, the essential had been saved. Strasbourg would have to join the ranks of the cities where the Catholic and Protestant faiths were forced to coexist, but at least the Protestant services could continue in their old form.[39]

What was vital in Strasbourg at this juncture was to convince the Protestant burghers to accept the restoration of Catholic services. The Senate and XXI explained to its subjects that it had allowed this only to preserve peace with the emperor and the pope. It noted that

[38]*PC*, vol. 4, no. 931. Weyrauch, *Konfessionelle Krise*, and Adam, *Kirchengeschichte*, discuss the restoration in more detail than is possible here.
[39]There was precedent elsewhere. See R. W. Scribner, "Civic Unity and the Reformation in Erfurt," *Past & Present*, 66 (1975), 56, and Paul-E. Martin, *Trois cas de pluralisme confessionel aux XVIe et XVIIe siècles: Genève-Savoie-France* (Geneva, 1961), pp. 14–15.

the Catholics were to have the use of only three of the city's churches; there would be vespers and the mass, but neither processions nor holy water. There were enough churches for all in Strasbourg, the magistrates argued, and the burghers should bear this new arrangement with resignation. The situation was desperate, for Strasbourg stood alone now that the Schmalkaldic League had dissolved and the princes all had become either turncoats or prisoners. Eventually God might send a better solution to the crisis, but the magistrates had labored day and night and so far had not found it.[40] Daniel Specklin, the layman who recorded this appeal in his chronicle, noted that the burghers were not disposed to agree. The Catholic services, which resumed in February 1550 after a twenty-one-year absence, were repeatedly disrupted by Protestants who came to gawk and taunt. The Ammeister intervened, arrests were made, and guards were posted. Eventually an uneasy peace prevailed and the Catholic services went on.[41]

By all accounts these services had little attraction for most Strasburghers. In 1551 Conrad Hubert, Bucer's former secretary and a clergyman himself, noted that "very few" had fallen to the papists. Two years later he wrote to Ambrosius Blaurer that about two hundred people attended the Catholic services. While this is perhaps a low figure, there is some evidence to suggest that at mid-century Strasbourg may have had more sectarians than Catholics within its walls.[42] The plain fact was that people were afraid to go to mass even if they did want to, as Bishop Erasmus protested to the emperor.[43] The priests were in great and continual danger, he complained. The Protestant pastors tried to isolate the Catholics by refusing to marry Protestants who acted as godparents for their Catholic friends, of by refusing communion or burial to people who attended the Catholic

---

[40]Daniel Specklin, "Les collectanées de Daniel Specklin," ed. Rodolphe Reuss, *BSCMHA*, n.s. 13 (1888), no. 2390; *PC*, vol. 5, no. 5 (1550).
[41]Adam, *Kirchengeschichte*, chap. 20, and Weyrauch, *Konfessionelle Krise*, chap. 4; Specklin, "Collectanées," no. 2391; Sebald Büheler, Jr., "La chronique strasbourgeoise de Sébald Büheler," ed. Léon Dacheux, *BSCMHA*, n.s. 13 (1888), nos. 318–20, 324; *PC*, vol. 5, nos. 6–9, 12–13, 16–21, 23–24, 26, 30.
[42]Wilhelm Horning, ed., *Briefe von strassburger Reformatoren, ihren Mitarbeitern und Freunden über die Einführung des "Interims" in Strassburg (1548–1554)* (Strasbourg, 1887), pp. 43–44; Traugott Schiess, ed., *Briefwechsel der Brüder Ambrosius und Thomas Blaurer, 1509–1548*, 3 vols. (Freiburg im Breisgau, 1908–12), vol. 3, no. 1855 (1553). Paulus, *Gewissensfreiheit*, p. 71, quotes a letter from Strasbourg in 1558: "Multi sunt hic Svenckfeldici, plures Anabaptistae, plurimi Sacramentarii, nec pauci Papistae."
[43]*PC*, vol. 5, no. 149 (1551).

services. The city alms cut off the dole to Catholics and Protestants boycotted Catholic shops.

The victims of this upsurge of hostility were the survivors of more than twenty years of underground religious life, drawn from all of the city's classes.[44] Catholic nobles, including branches of magisterial families like the Wurmsers, the Wetzels von Marsilien, and the Wolffs von Renchen, retained priests to look after their households.[45] The merchant fraction of the ruling class also included Catholic families, like the Brauns, who would produce both a senator and an abbess in the latter half of the century. Then there were the families of professional men, of lawyers and notaries in the episcopal service, of doctors, and of apothecaries.[46] Katherine Zell insisted in 1557 that the Catholics were "lost souls . . . and a few bad old women who had worked for priests and students in their youth." The parish registers identify some of these "lost souls": fishermen, hod-carriers, boatmen, and gardeners. Artisans and the servants of priests, of canons, and of episcopal employees were regularly spotted going to mass at the convent of the Knights of St. John in the latter half of the century.[47]

It had not been easy to practice Catholicism in Strasbourg after the reformation began. The mass had been restricted to the chapels of the chapter churches in 1525, and in 1529 it was entirely suppressed. Most of the convents in the city had closed; only the Teutonic Knights, the Knights of St. John, the Carthusians, the Dominican women's houses of St. Nicholas-in-undis, St. Margaret, and the Penitents of St. Mary Magdalene remained, and the nuns were periodically obliged to listen to Protestant preachers.[48] A year and a half

---

[44]The most recent account of Catholic survival is François Joseph Fuchs, "Les catholiques strasbourgeois de 1529 à 1681," *Archives de l'église d'Alsace,* n.s. 22 (1975), 142–69.

[45]RP 1543, f. 438r; and Brady, *Ruling Class,* pp. 223–24. On the Wetzel family, RP 1545, f. 519r-v, and AST 19/86. On Junker Ludwig Wolff von Renchen, AMS N104, ff. 61v–64v (1552).

[46]On the Brauns, AMS, Tables généalogiques. Adam Mechler, a notary and a Catholic like his father, continued to work even after the episcopal notaries had been ordered out of business (AMS R6, f. 141r [1587]). He drew up a marriage contract for Wilhelm Gutjahr, "oculist and surgeon" (KS 283, 1 October 1594). On the apothecary Hans Jacob Rapp, see AMS N132, p. 168; RP 1566, f. 494v; and KS 146^i, f. 1r. I am grateful to Stephen Nelson for explaining the workings of the KS to me and for identifying Rapp.

[47]Zell, *Ein Brieff,* sig. B iii verso. AMS N26, pp. 421–22, Diebolt Vix, 1564; N26, p. 452, Jacob Reytzel, 1564; N28, f. 46v, Adolf Weber, 1576; N30c, f. 9r, Georg Spener, 1591. On the services at the Knights of St. John, see notes 66 and 67, below.

[48]See Joseph Fridolin Vierling, *Das Ringen um die letzten dem Katholizismus treuen Klöster Strassburgs* (Strasbourg, 1914).

after the mass was abolished the Senate and XXI made it illegal, on pain of a hefty £5 fine, for burghers or residents to attend services in the convents, or to go out into the neighboring villages to hear mass. In 1537 they outlawed the practice of going to the villages to be married by a priest, on pain of the same fine. They also punished burghers who sought out priests to baptize their children.[49] Until the aftermath of the Schmalkaldic War there was no wavering in the magistrates' public opposition to Catholic practices.

Despite this legislation, some Catholic burghers managed to practice their religion. There were reports of masses being celebrated in the city, as well as of residents going to the villages, and a few citizens managed to find priests inside the walls to baptize their children. Even some members of the regime "ate the Pope's bread" at Easter. Between the abolition of the mass in 1529 and the Schmalkaldic War crisis there had been few signs of popular hostility to the Catholic laity in Strasbourg. The war, the fear of the subversive potential of even a tiny Catholic fifth column, and then the horrifying realization that Catholicism might return to the city in force, changed all that.[50]

The underground persistence of Catholicism in Strasbourg had always appalled the Protestant clergy. Now at mid-century the Catholics' tenacity was rewarded: the mass was again publicly celebrated in the cathedral itself, and the work of Bucer's generation had been undone. Johann Marbach writhed at these reversals. Fortified by the conviction that a large number of the burghers supported him, Marbach led the Church Assembly into a double campaign, partly against the Catholics, but chiefly against the magistrates who had allowed the sinister Catholic pomp to return.[51] The treaty the magistrates had made with the bishop was, in the clergy's view, an act of corporate cowardice worse than personal apostasy. The magistrates were telling the burghers that gross theological error—for such was the foundation of the mass in the preachers' view—was not dan-

---

[49]Anti-Catholic legislation, Brant, "Annales," *BSCMHA*, n.s. 19 (1899), no. 4882, 1530; repeated 1531, AMS R4, f. 103r, and possibly again, RP 1542, f. 108v. AST 84/33, 1537. On baptisms, RP 1540, f. 194r.

[50]Masses: RP 1543, ff. 438r, 438v, 581r; RP 1542, f. 108v. Baptisms: RP 1540, f. 194r; RP 1542, ff. 448v–449r; AST 84/39. RP 1540, f. 118r-v, "Das etlich im Rath sitzen, die das Baptz brot essen," and another item from the same agenda, "Das etlich hern des Regiments dise Karwoch zu Eschau zum Sacrament gehen"; Eschau was a Catholic village. See also RP 1543, f. 438r, no. 3, and 1548, ff. 402v–403v. On the subversive potential of local Catholics, see RP 1546, f. 398v, concerning meetings the innkeeper "zum Nesselbach" held late at night in his back rooms.

[51]Adam, *Kirchengeschichte*, chaps. 20–21, provides more detail than is possible here.

gerous enough to the Strasburghers' salvation to warrant suppressing it. That was tantamount to saying that the truth did not matter. The magistrates had insulted the honor of God and imperiled the souls in their care because temporal concerns had made them into cowards who bowed to the emperor rather than to Christ. The magistrates had sinned and the clergy intended to correct them.[52]

The magistrates put quite a different construction on their treaty.[53] They, too, hated and feared the consequences of the Catholic restoration, but they knew that it would be suicidal madness to defy the victorious emperor, for such a course of action could only lead to the total eradication of the city's Protestant church. They had managed to save four parishes at a time when emperor and bishop seemed likely to recapture every church in the city. They knew that for thirty years they had done everything humanly possible to protect the faith, and they saw their treaty not as an act of apostasy but as a rampart against iniquity built solely by their diplomatic skill. After all, they told each other, "There is a great difference between the meaning of the little word "tolerate' and the idea of taking something to be right."[54] They had worked out a compromise that allowed true religion to survive, and in doing so they had followed the lead of "the most famous of theologians," Philipp Melanchthon. The clergy owed them gratitude and support, not criticism and insults.

In the middle 1550s relations between the Senate and XXI and the Church Assembly reached their low point for the whole century. Preachers and magistrates accused each other of lying. When the pastors charged the magistrates with an unprecedented neglect of duty and threatened to resign en masse, the magistrates replied that this would only leave their flocks at the mercy of the papist wolves. The clergy demanded immediate suppression of the mass; they assumed that God would protect the righteous. The Senate and XXI reminded them of the way in which the imperial forces had manhandled Constance; the Lord did not always rescue the reckless. The preachers threatened to mount their pulpits and rouse the commons, but before the magistrates could reply the preachers backed down. That would be rebellion; they would not do it. Probably they remembered that they had tried this tactic and failed with it in 1547–48.

[52]AST 87/43 and AST 87/49 (1554); AST 87/50 (1555), RP 1555, unpaginated material from 12 January. See also Weyrauch, *Konfessionelle Krise,* pp. 165–77.
[53]AST 87/44, 87/47, 87/48 (1554); RP 1554, ff. 406v–407r.
[54]AST 87/47, f. 8v.

Somehow in those grim months the oligarchs had survived, and it was Martin Bucer who had gone abroad to perish. The burghers meanwhile had come to terms with the new routines, although they loathed the pope and his minions. Like their preachers and their magistrates, they were powerless.

In the end the people, the clergy, and the Senate and XXI all made concessions. The burghers swallowed their wrath and ignored the Roman rituals, while the preachers stayed at their posts and restrained themselves from preaching rebellion. The magistrates, for their part, promised to take action against the nuns, always wrongly regarded as the old church's weakest members. They bought time, arguing that the crucial Reichstag of 1555 would give good Protestants room to act.[55]

What happened at the Augsburg Reichstag of 1555 was not the liberation for which the Strasburghers yearned. The Religious Peace obliged them to allow both Catholic and Protestant services, a blow against which the city councils would protest to no avail.[56] Despite the way it hobbled the Protestants in Strasbourg, the Peace betrayed the weakness of the Catholic powers. Instead of sweeping back over Germany, they had had to settle for a ratification of the status quo. The expedient moment for which the magistrates had prayed had at last arrived. They could now begin to chip away at the treaty they had signed in 1549.

The magistrates proceeded against the Catholic establishment in the 1550s in the same way they had acted in the 1520s. The clergy wanted them to begin with the essence, the suppression of the mass. The Senate and XXI instead tested the waters by probing the external support for Strasbourg's convents. They ordered the nuns to take in no more novices, a ban the nuns ignored, but which the outside authorities left unchallenged.[57] Then they restored their Marriage Court, a secular tribunal that had been mothballed in 1550.[58] No response again. Finally they found a cunning method to put an end to the masses in the cathedral and the two St. Peters, without risking a formal statute against them.

The tenth anniversary of the treaty between Strasbourg and Bishop

[55] AST 87/50 (1555), and RP 1555 for 12 January; RP 1555, f. 61v (18 February); AST 87/51, 18 November 1555.

[56] Karl Brandi, *Der Augsburger Religionsfriede*, article 14, p. 35. Strasbourg's protests: *PC*, vol. 5, no. 510, and Appendix, pp. 654–56; AST 166, pp. 128–69.

[57] Adam, *Kirchengeschichte*, pp. 290–92; RP 1555, ff. 144v–145r.

[58] RP 1550, ff. 30v–31r; RP 1556, f. 253r.

Erasmus came in 1559. Traditionally, these *Schwirmbriefe* lasted only a decade and were then renegotiated. Now the magistrates temporarily refused to renew a clause in the 1549 treaty that guaranteed protection to the Catholic priests, hoping in this way to ease them out of the churches. A new wave of violence against the priests broke out, thoroughly intimidating them, and they refused to conduct their services. The three churches transferred to the priests in 1549 all stood empty for some time, as the Senate and XXI prudently waited to make sure their ploy would provoke no reprisals. When all continued peacefully, the magistrates allowed the Church Assembly to repossess the buildings.[59] What they had done was a clear violation of the Peace of Augsburg, but it had worked.

The suppression of the public celebration of the mass satisfied those burghers who had grumbled against the magistrates since 1546. Once again the city's rulers were comfortably abreast of the opinion of the majority of their subjects. The clergy continued to see great danger in the remaining convent masses, and clergymen and magistrates both were disturbed by the nascent Catholic revival outside the city. So were many other Strasburghers who monitored events in other territories and feared that war in France and the Netherlands, and the rising Catholic power across the Rhine, would eventually threaten Strasbourg. As long as there were priests and Catholic laity in the city, there was a danger of a new restoration. The old church still had what it had held before the Schmalkaldic War: the convents and the monasteries, now resupplied with religious and able to appeal to the protection of the Peace; the three chapters themselves, slowly becoming more militant; and the changing faces of the faithful. The abolition of the mass in 1529 had not made a Protestant of every Strasburgher then, and the collapse of the restoration did not do so now. Catholic observance went underground again, but it persisted. As the magistrates sourly noted in 1564, "The papists are again holding their secret conventicles, practicing their idolatry, and baptizing their children at home."[60]

Catholics continued to immigrate to Strasbourg, drawn by the hope of making their fortune. The city was easy to enter; it had to be, as it relied on immigration to keep up its population. No formal

---

[59]Adam, *Kirchengeschichte,* pp. 292–95; Weyrauch, *Konfessionelle Krise,* pp. 210 ff. Weyrauch is rightly suspicious about the possibility of clerical or magisterial involvement in these disturbances, although there is no extant evidence of collusion.
[60]RP 1564, f. 178r-v.

religious test was imposed on immigrants, and there was no legal barrier to Catholics buying citizenship or even exercising political rights.[61] Admission of Schultheissenbürger was in the hands of an episcopal employee. The gates of Strasbourg were open to men and women who were willing to forgo the free exercise of their faith in the hope of improving their lot in the world. Perhaps they were not abandoning all that much; conditions in the villages were deplorable. The shortage of priests and the ignorance of the rural clergy combined to ensure that Catholic religious life was not much better developed in the episcopal villages than in Protestant Strasbourg.[62]

While some of the immigrants may have found their faith strengthened by exposure to the Lutheran challenge, the majority probably drifted into the Protestant church. Given the conditions in the countryside, few of them could have had a very firm understanding of their religion, and this left them vulnerable to assimilation. There was no formal process of conversion since the magistrates did not attempt to spy out and then convert or expel Catholics, as they did Anabaptists. Before 1549, those who came to their attention for practicing their faith were fined and let go. After 1555, when the Lutheran clergy came across Catholics, they could do little more than encourage them to come to the parish churches.[63] A certain pressure to convert did exist, and the dangers of parading Catholic sympathies during the restoration period have already been evoked. It was possible to remain Catholic in Strasbourg, but it was easier to slide into conformity. The boatman Adam Thoma, who declared himself willing to take instruction in the Lutheran faith, cannot have been alone.[64] Had the flow of Catholic immigrants been choked off, the lay community would have disappeared within a generation. As it was, new arrivals made up for losses.

Many of the burghers had balked at the Catholic restoration that the magistrates had been compelled to enforce. The initial outbursts

[61]AMS Bürgerbuch, grants by marriage, col. 483, Bastian Wagner vom Hall inn Saxenn, goldschmidt, 1580; Fuchs, "Les Catholiques," p. 163 and n. 104a. Grants by purchase, col. 128, Adam Mechler (1568); on the family, see note 46, above.
[62]Karl Hahn, *Manderscheid,* p. 59, and "Visitationen und Visitationsberichte."
[63]After the Religious Peace the magistrates must have had to resign themselves to reprimanding the delinquent rather than fining them: RP 1564, f. 116r, on Meister Jorg der Scherer; AMS N26, p. 451 (1564), on Jacob Reytzel, a hod-carrier from Sélestat, who was apparently getting no special religious instruction beyond being told to come to St. Wilhelm and to take communion.
[64]AMS N29b, f. 43r (1583).

of violence had eventually died down, although the Catholic services were disrupted once or twice again before the terminal flare-up in 1559. As far as the record shows, the magistrates never had to intervene to protect the Catholic laity from violence, only the priests. Indeed, the Schöffen of *Zur Lucerne* three times sent Adolff Braun to sit in the Senate, although he was certainly a Catholic. Popular hostility was directed more against the priests than against the laity, and more against the Catholic powers outside the city than against the local figures. This hostility was kept alive by the steady repetition of anti-Catholic sermons, by the frightening revival of Catholicism in the Empire, and by the pro-Huguenot propaganda that poured off the Strasbourg presses. The chief pamphleteer was Johann Fischart, a master satirist who related the French wars to the Strasburghers, translated resistance tracts, and mocked the new order of "Jesuwider." Fischart taught his generation to identify Roman Catholicism with tyranny and its stalwarts, the blood-thirsty Guise family and the unscrupulous Philip II.[65]

While most Strasburghers continued to reject Catholicism as both a false and a foreign religion, not all resisted the appeal of the counterreformation, which began to make itself felt in the diocese of Strasbourg after Johann von Manderscheid became bishop in 1569. Jesuits began to appear in the city, and some people took to going to the house of the Knights of St. John to hear anti-Lutheran sermons.[66] Clandestine baptisms increased, and some burghers managed to receive extreme unction. In 1579 watchmen posted by the magistrates counted sixty-three people going into the monastery to attend mass one Sunday. Fears of the political dangers of the Catholic presence revived. In 1570 the magistrates had to investigate rumors that 1,800 pikes were stored in a house in the Krutenau district, and that somehow the nuns of St. Nicolas, whose convent was in that quarter, were involved.[67]

[65]*Nacht Rab oder Nebelkraeh* (Strasbourg, 1570); *Binenkorb desz heyl. roemischen Imenschwarms* (Strasbourg, 1580); *Ordenliche Beschreibung* (Strasbourg, 1588); *Ausschreiben . . . der ubelfridigten Ständ inn Frankreich* (Strasbourg, n.d.). Chrisman, *Lay Culture*, pp. 246–47, 264–69.

[66]Jesuits: RP 1570, ff. 320r–321v; RP 1576, ff. 404r–405v; RP 1577, ff. 577v, 578v–579r, 648r–v; AST 72/12. Knights: RP 1570, f. 553r–v, and 1571, ff. 534v, 748r–749r.

[67]On baptisms and extreme unction, RP 1574, ff. 102r–103v; on the masses, RP 1578, ff. 246r–247r. Later reports vary between a dozen and fifty to sixty in attendance. RP 1579, f. 196r–v claims that more than two hundred and fifty did their Easter duty that year. On the pikes, RP 1570, ff. 605r–606r. The magistrates decided to investigate "as secretly as possible," and no other records have survived.

The preachers pressed for the abolition of the convent masses. The magistrates wanted to act, but could find no lever. Their lawyers were unanimous and firm in their interpretation of the Peace: it was binding on Strasbourg and could be changed only by the Reichstag. Johann Nervius went so far as to tell his masters that although they had undoubtedly abolished the mass in the chapter churches out of a Christian zeal, this was nevertheless utterly illegal, and "Your Graces may thank God almighty you got away with it."[68]

Unable to use force, the Senate and XXI embarked on a campaign to bribe, bully, or wheedle the Catholic clergy and religious into excluding the burghers from their services. Appeals to the commander of the Knights of St. John brought no success. He told the magistrates that since he would not refuse food to a hungry man, he certainly would not withhold the consolations of religion. The Penitent sisters were fittingly apologetic, but would not budge. At St. Nicolas the nuns were obstinate and vocal, and the abbess of St. Margaret told the magistrates' delegates, who had apparently leaned a little too far in the direction of threats with her, that the nuns had done nothing to deserve being treated so ungraciously. The Provost of the cathedral chapter, the bishop's brother Eberhard, had people in to mass in his private chapel; when the magistrates objected he told them that, as a count of the empire, he was outside their jurisdiction and would "ring his bells when he pleased."[69]

The magistrates were stymied. The Catholic establishment had powerful friends outside Strasbourg, and could not be coerced. The laity were protected by the Religious Peace. The greatest show of force that the magistrates could make was to post guards around the convents to intimidate the laity. This may have had some effect, for the watchmen were told to make themselves as conspicuous as possible, but as late as 1590, there were reports of one or two hundred people going to the Knights of St. John for mass.[70] Victory in the Bishops' War of 1592 reinforced Catholic loyalties.

Catholicism survived in reformation Strasbourg because of demographic realities that encouraged the immigration of Catholics and because of political realities that tied the magistrates' hands after 1546.

---

[68]Clerical petitions: e.g., AST 87/60 (1572); AST 87/61 (1575); RP 1573, ff. 492v–493r; RP 1574, ff. 102r–103v. On the magistrates' reactions, see also RP 1575, ff. 312r–313v. Nervius's opinion, AST 87/61c, composed in 1574, but not presented until 1575, ff. 4v–5r.

[69]RP 1578, ff. 242r–245r, 261r–263r.

[70]RP 1578, ff. 256v–257r; RP 1590, ff. 580v–581r.

The fate of the Catholics, like that of the sectarians, illustrates the importance of political factors in decisions about the limits of religious toleration. When the sectarians were thought to be a menace to the established power structure the magistrates feared them; in the latter part of the century this fear ebbed. Catholics, on the other hand, became more frightening after mid-century. Magistrates and clergy did not agree on what tactics to use against either group, but as a general rule magisterial policy and popular feelings remained fairly close. There were two exceptions: there is some evidence that lay Strasburghers found the laws against the Anabaptists too severe; and there is considerable evidence, particularly from the late 1540s and early 1550s, that they found the 1549 compromise and the Catholic restoration difficult to accept. In both cases the magistrates moved toward these currents in public feeling by bending their own laws and by breaking imperial law. In dealing with the sectarians they had been able to act with considerable independence; when it came to the Catholics they had much less room to maneuver. Their problems with the Calvinists present a third picture of dissent in Strasbourg, and one that was even more entangled in events outside the city.

3. *The Calvinist Conundrum*

Strasburghers unhappy with the established Lutheran church could turn not just to the sects or to the old church, but also to the Swiss version of the reformation. Very few did. Even when the magistrates and clergy were most concerned about Calvinism, it would have been difficult to assemble as much as a conventicle of German-speaking Calvinists. Yet for most of the second half of the century Strasbourg probably had as many Calvinists as Catholics within its walls, thanks to the Senate and XXI's willingness to admit refugees from religious wars and persecution. The real Calvinists in Strasbourg were a foreign enclave set off from the Strasburghers by language as well as by doctrine. Along with the real Calvinists, however, there were some highly placed men in the regime and in the city's senior school who were regarded by the orthodox Lutherans as at best Genevan fellow travelers and at worst outright Calvinists or Zwinglians. Their existence alarmed the Church Assembly, whose members feared that these "subversives" might succeed in detaching Strasbourg from the Lutheran camp and realigning it with the Swiss.

These fears were not groundless given Strasbourg's history, for the city had been more Zwinglian than Lutheran in the 1520s, and in the second half of the century its aggressive foreign policy linked it to the crusading Calvinist forces in France and the Netherlands.

The clergy's fears must be seen in the context of their city's own past and of the general evolution of religion in the sixteenth century.[71] Strasbourg had submitted its own Tetrapolitan Confession at Augsburg in 1530 to try to bridge the Saxon-Swiss quarrels of the 1520s. Soon after, the city signed Melanchthon's original Augsburg Confession. Melanchthon had felt free to revise his text, and by 1540 there were two versions of the Lutheran confession, the original or *invariata,* which was closer to the Catholic interpretation of the eucharist, and a second, or *variata,* which was closer to the Swiss understanding of that sacrament. Lutheranism was pulling apart and would not be stitched back together for decades. Meanwhile, as the Lutherans tore at each other, both the Swiss and the Catholics enjoyed a resurgence. Caught between their Calvinist and Catholic competitors, Lutherans had an unhappy choice: fight both or ally with one against the other. The magistrates of Strasbourg chose the latter, but their clergy were convinced that the righteous should stand alone.

The Church Assembly had serious and growing misgivings about the magistrates' policy. The city's Zwinglian interlude in the 1520s and its present collaboration with the French Calvinists, together with the ambiguity hanging over "our Augsburg Confession," brought Strasbourg's denominational allegiance into doubt. Locally and from abroad the clergy were challenged to declare themselves: which Augsburg Confession did the city recognize? Was it claiming allegiance to the Lutheran confession simply to come under the protection of the Religious Peace? The Church Assembly could easily prove its own sincerity; its members regularly and repeatedly declared for the *Augustana invariata* of 1530. The magistrates' position was problematic since they saw advantages in the very ambiguities the clergy deplored. Meanwhile several professors in Jean Sturm's school, including the rector himself, defended the Tetrapolitan Confession and made interpretations of the Augsburg Confession which

---

[71]Karl Brandi, *Gegenreformation und Religionskriege,* vol. 2. of his *Deutsche Reformation und Gegenreformation* (Leipzig, 1930); Mark U. Edwards, *Luther and the False Brethren* (Stanford, 1975). The Formula of Concord, written to settle the arguments, is still the best guide to the substance of the controversies: Theodore G. Tappert, trans. and ed., *The Book of Concord* (Philadelphia, 1959), pp. 463–636.

stretched it to cover the Swiss Protestants. Outside the circle of intellectuals and magistrates, few Strasburghers took much notice of the controversies before the late 1570s.

The first open sign of trouble within the intellectual community came in 1561 when church president Johann Marbach and one of his clergymen, Melchior Speccer, clashed with academy professors Jean Sturm and Girolamo Zanchi over predestination and over the city's confessional history.[72] The magistrates were loath to take up the reading and evaluation of the wheelbarrow-load of charges and countercharges that the two sides hurled at each other, and unloaded the task on their lawyers, who received it with heartfelt dismay. Bernhard Botzheim, one of the unlucky lawyers, pointed out to them in exasperation that it would not be amiss for at least a few of them to read at least some of the memoranda involved.[73] The urgent thing, in his eyes, was that the quarrel not be settled without the magistrates. It must not be left to Johann Marbach alone, and as if by right as church president, to establish doctrinal norms for Strasbourg, he warned. He noted as well the danger that the city might, through this dispute, be drawn into the doctrinal battles raging in Saxony.

Zanchi and Sturm had taken the position that the Wittenberg-trained Marbach was trying to jettison Martin Bucer's heritage, symbolized by the Tetrapolitan Confession, in order to impose a foreign Lutheranism on Strasbourg.[74] Marbach, who always presented himself as Bucer's protégé, denied this accusation and countered it with his own version of the city's past.[75] The *Tetrapolitana*, he began, had not been accepted by the Augsburg Reichstag and was therefore void. Strasbourg had signed the unaltered Augsburg Confession to secure its admission to the Schmalkaldic League. Bucer had submitted to Luther in the Wittenberg Concord of 1536. Thereafter, Strasbourg had declared its allegiance to the unaltered Augsburg Confession at a variety of theological conferences: at Trent in 1551, at Frankfurt in 1558, and most recently at Naumburg in 1561. Strasbourg had long been Lutheran, but Zanchi and Sturm were "good Zwinglians and Calvinists" whose ideas were as distant from the real Augsburg Confession as earth from heaven. Marbach objected to the way Sturm, Zanchi, and Bucer's former secretary, Conrad Hubert, had published

[72]James M. Kittelson, "Marbach vs. Zanchi: The Resolution of Controversy in Late Reformation Strasbourg," *Sixteenth Century Journal*, 8 (1977), 31–44 demonstrates in opposition to earlier studies that the dispute did revolve around matters of substance.
[73] AST 55/3; see also city lawyer Jacob Hermann's opinion, AST 55/2.
[74]For example, AST 54/7, ff. 510r–519r.
[75]AST 52/2, f. 24r-v; AST 54/12, ff. 637v–638v.

old manuscripts of Bucer's, all written before 1536, all annulled by the Wittenberg Concord, and all misrepresenting Bucer as an unregenerate "sacramentarian." The magistrates had better settle this dispute and put an end to his adversaries' antics, Marbach concluded. If not, he would resign so that the whole Empire could see that Strasbourg indeed had little real attachment to the Augsburg Confession.

Strasbourg could not afford to be separated from the churches of the Augsburg Confession, and the Senate and XXI knew it. No one agreed anymore about what that document meant, or indeed on which version of it was authoritative, but it was the one Protestant text enshrined in the Religious Peace. To protect their position under the Peace, the magistrates had to silence the continuing controversy between their pastors and their professors. The council of XIII brought in four theologians (Jacob Andreae of Tübingen, Cunman Flinsbach of Zweibrücken, Simon Sulzer and Ulrich Coccius of Basel) to join four lawyers and four magistrates in resolving the feud. While this committee was at work, the Senate and XXI pronounced its verdict on the rival confessional histories the two sides had defined. Given the terms of the Peace, the result was inevitable: "The Senate and XXI signed the *Augustana* in 1561, with reservations on nothing but ceremonies. By this Confession and by the Wittenberg Concord we wish to take our stand. We wish to hear no more about the Tetrapolitan Confession, whether praise of it or criticism."[76] The decision was a trifle ambiguous, thanks to the reference to the Wittenberg Concord, which had equated the Tetrapolitan and Augsburg Confessions, but clearly the Senate and XXI was finding for Marbach and against Sturm and Zanchi.

The verdict was not made public to the burghers, but it was passed on to the XIII's committee, which managed to work out a doctrinal formula acceptable to both sides. The formula came before the Senate and XXI, which approved it and forwarded the text to the pastors and professors. Zanchi signed it, although reluctantly, and so did the Lutheran clergy. Peace seemed to have been restored, but even so, when the Senate and XXI heard that Zanchi had received a call to Chiavenna, it was happy to allow him to break his contract with the school and return to Italy.[77]

The magistrates had been slow to resolve this controversy and for a

[76]RP 1563, ff. 75v–76.
[77]Jean Calvin, *Calvini opera quae supersunt omnia*, ed., Wilhelm Baum et al., 59 vols. (Braunschweig, 1863–1900), vol. 19, no. 3919. Zanchi's departure, RP 1563, ff. 352v–353r.

year and a half the bickering between the clergy and the professors had been public knowledge. They had had to farm out the doctrinal questions to foreign theologians, for they were in no sense capable of understanding them, but at least they had made sure that the quarrel was settled in such a way that Strasbourg remained under the mantle of the Religious Peace. They had avoided having to fire Sturm or Zanchi, either of whom could have been counted upon to send criticism of the regime flying across Europe had he been dismissed. They had averted the even graver scandal of seeing the president of their Church Assembly resign in anger. Moreover, they had heeded Botzheim's advice and made sure that the settlement came under their sponsorship. The committee that worked out the Strasbourg Concord was a committee of the council of XIII, and the Concord itself had been ratified by the Senate and XXI before it had been signed by the disputing parties. The magistrates had also avoided condemning any opinions whatsoever, which they hoped would deprive theologians outside the city of any excuse to revive the controversy. The Senate and XXI was relieved to see the affair so well settled. Fourteen years later its members would still be congratulating themselves on their dexterity.[78]

No matter how clever the magistrates' settlement of the Marbach-Zanchi dispute had been, they had been slow to act, and what was worse, their settlement did not put an end to the rivalry between Marbach and Sturm. The long months of debate had exposed to their people, indeed to the whole Empire, disunity in Strasbourg, and not just the strife between the pastors and the professors. Melchior Speccer was rumored to have preached that the city now had "a tripartite council: one group doesn't pray at all, the second sticks to the sectarians [that is, to the Calvinists, in this case], and the third, which does pray, has no influence."[79] Whether or not Speccer said this, there was some truth in it, and the division he suggested would persist until the end of the century. Some magistrates were more concerned with this world than the next (did not pray, in Speccer's exaggerated phrase), others insisted on keeping up good relations with Calvinists outside the city, and those who accepted the clergy's view that Calvinism was a menace everywhere long remained a minority. Nevertheless, the Senate and XXI was beginning to move against Calvinism within the city.

[78]RP 1577, ff. 725v–732v.
[79]RP 1563, f. 365r.

Calvinist services were conducted in the city's refugee parish. Strasbourg had begun to take in refugees, particularly French people, in the 1520s, as had Basel and other cities. Martin Bucer and his fellows had welcomed these allies against the Catholics and made Strasbourg a major center for the production of Protestant propaganda for export over the Vosges.[80] A few Italians, like Zanchi, straggled in from time to time, and during the 1550s some Marian exiles came to Strasbourg from England, but the refugees were usually French-speaking. Jean Calvin, who himself came here as an exile from Geneva (1539–1541), organized a parish for his fellows within the city's established church.[81] Until the 1560s the refugee church remained small, but then the religious wars began to pour waves of Huguenots into the city. Most came only for the duration of hostilities, then returned home when a truce was proclaimed, possibly to reappear when the fighting began again in their districts.

The refugees ranged from the truly powerful, like the families of great nobles, to the very humble for whom the Senate and XXI had to provide both food and shelter at public expense.[82] Little direct evidence survives about the way ordinary Strasburghers responded to the strangers who came to live among them. All but a few of the refugees were ordered to live with burghers so that the behavior of these foreigners could be scrutinized by loyal eyes, but no comment on how either the exiles or their hosts felt about this domestic contact survives. Separated by language from the local population, the refugees seem to have kept to themselves as much as possible. Still, the official welcome extended to them was enough to make Strasbourg's name a byword for charity in the war-torn regions of France and the Netherlands from the 1540s to the 1580s.[83] Some of the refugees obtained permission to register with the guilds and exercise their

---

[80]See Chapter 4, note 3, above.

[81]Pannier, *Calvin à Strasbourg.* The most accurate account of the refugee church's troubled existence is Jean Rott, "L'Eglise des réfugiés de langue française à Strasbourg au XVIe siècle: Aperçu de son histoire, en particulier de ses crises à partir de 1541," *BSHPF,* 122 (1976), 525–50.

[82]The principal lists are AMS R26, f. 123r-v (1553); AMS III/271/12 (1553); AMS III/64/1 (1559–83); AMS II/84b/56 (1562). The lists are incomplete. On food and shelter, RP 1566, ff. 212v, 214r, and RP 1568, ff. 321r–323r. Roger Zuber, "Les Champenois réfugiés à Strasbourg et l'église réformée de Châlons: Echanges intellectuels et vie religieuse, 1560–1590," *Mémoires de la société d'agriculture, commerce, sciences et arts du département de la Marne,* 79 (1964), 31–55.

[83]See, for example, Philippe Denis, "La correspondance d'Hubert de Bapasme, réfugié lillois à Strasbourg (1545–1547)," *BSHPF,* 124 (1978), 84–112; and note 84, below.

trades. This did not at first provoke complaints. In the last quarter of the century, as the local economy deteriorated, there were complaints about foreigners in general, but the refugees were not singled out. A few local women married refugees, although the magistrates discouraged this as it made citizens of the Huguenots. Now and then a master interceded with the Senate and XXI to allow a refugee in his employ to settle permanently. By and large, people in Strasbourg seem to have responded to the plight of persecuted Protestants from over the Vosges or down the Rhine with considerable sympathy.[84]

An undercurrent of fear limited and colored this sympathy, causing the magistrates to monitor the rising number of refugees with increasing concern. Most were French, and throughout the century the Valois monarchs coveted Strasbourg. The city's willingness to harbor French "criminals" might increase the French crown's interest in the place. There was also the fear that spies could infiltrate the city in the guise of refugees, or that the French, even the Huguenots, might prove to be a dangerous fifth column if the Valois ever did lay siege to the city. Henry II had seriously considered doing just that after the Schmalkaldic League had whetted his appetite by handing Metz over to him. Even before the confessional allegiance of the refugees became a problem, the Senate and XXI had decided to limit their numbers "to ensure that there aren't too many foreigners here."[85] The magistrates wanted to help the victims of persecution in other territories, but they recognized the dangers they ran in doing so. In 1566 they decided to review their policies toward refugees "so that this will remain a German city," and "because such people have given us much grief in the past."[86] By now the French were coming in droves, so that in 1566 alone, the cost of aiding them was £437 and more than 776 *viertel* of grain. The next year the Senate and XXI laid down stringent new conditions for the admission of refugees. No more than two hundred were to be admitted; they were to be taxed; all were to register with the

---

[84]AMS II/64/1, ff. 13v–14r gives the conditions under which refugees were allowed to stay in the city. Reputation for charity: RP 1571, f. 1015r-v, and RP 1572, f. 905v. However, a special collection of funds to aid the refugees, held in some parish churches early in 1573, produced only £45.3.4: RP 1573, ff. 15v–16v. A month later the regular collection for poor schoolboys produced £126.3.5: RP 1573, f. 48r. See RP 1562, f. 378r-v, and RP 1568, f. 398v on the right to work. For complaints about foreign competition see Kintz, *La société*, pp. 494–496. Marriages, RP 1566, f. 53v; RP 1567, f. 120v. Intercessions, RP 1568, f. 407r-v; RP 1570, ff. 173v–174r.
[85]RP 1557, ff. 53r–54r; AMS II/93/5.
[86]RP 1566, ff. 31v, 212v, 214r.

Chancellory.[87] The quota would be breached, for the magistrates prized charity, but they kept wary eyes on the guests that circumstances forced upon them.

The refugees were a problem in themselves, and their church was becoming a real irritant. There were rarely any troubles between the preachers and their congregations in the German parishes, but as the refugee parish grew it became fractious. Twice, in 1555 and again in 1559, the Senate and XXI was pulled into the arguments, and on both occasions it dismissed the pastors to settle the problems.[88] When Jean Calvin passed through the city in 1556 the magistrates refused to allow him to preach in the parish, "because he has another opinion on the Lord's Supper than we do, and is suspected by the adherents of the Augsburg Confession."[89] When they dismissed two refugee pastors in succession they knew full well that those pastors shared Calvin's views on the eucharist, and that those ideas were not protected by the Peace, but they acted only to restore order in the refugee parish, not to purge it of its Calvinist theology.

In the 1550s the Lutheran clergy themselves were still willing to tolerate the views of the refugee pastors provided that the refugee ministers subscribe to the Augsburg Confession and not attack the Lutheran interpretation of the Lord's Supper. In 1559, for example, they accepted the appointment of Guillaume Holbrac to care for the refugees, although he was "aller dings Calvinisch" in his eucharistic theology. Johann Marbach, Johann Lenglin, and Johann Flinner advised the magistrates to go ahead and hire Holbrac since it would be impossible to find a French-speaking pastor who accepted the Lutheran position on the eucharist. Holbrac at least seemed orthodox on other points.[90]

There were a number of reasons why the Church Assembly chose compromise at this time. In the first place, its members were much more concerned in the 1550s with obtaining a reversal of the Catholic restoration. The city inspection in 1554 had turned up a large number of sectarians. Since the magistrates were willing now to crack down on these people (partly to distract the clergy from the Catholics), the

[87]RP 1568, ff. 321r–323r, on the cost of aiding the refugees in 1566; RP 1567, ff. 632v–633v.
[88]RP 1555, ff. 117v–118v, 126r–127r, 139v–140r, 153v; RP 1559, ff. 389v–393r and passim through 402v.
[89]RP 1556, ff. 406v–407r.
[90]RP 1553, ff. 383v–385r; RP 1559, f. 533r–v.

Church Assembly was eager to profit from the magistrates' cooperative spirit.[91] In the fifties the French parish was still quite small and the Genevan faith was only beginning to reveal its power to spread. For the moment the Calvinists in Strasbourg could be dealt with in fits and starts, although it would be otherwise after the early sixties. Finally, there was still some hope that the Swiss might be converted. In the eyes of the Church Assembly their former colleague Jean Calvin had been orthodox while he had been in Strasbourg; they held that his sacramentarian errors had come over him only after his departure. His lieutenant, Theodore de Beza, twice came into Germany to see if the long schism between the Swiss and the Lutherans could be ended. Heinrich Bullinger, in Zurich, was skeptical about this effort, and so was Johann Marbach. Marbach was already speculating with his colleague Hartmann Beyer in Frankfurt about how both cities could rid themselves of their refugee congregations, but as long as there was hope of reconciliation Marbach did not openly sabotage the efforts.[92]

The quarrel between the Church Assembly and professors Sturm and Zanchi helped push the Lutheran clergy into a hardened attitude. Before long the Lutheran pastors had defined Sturm and his supporters, along with the refugees, as a new opposition that had taken its place in the sack with the "papists and Anabaptists and others who condemn our church."[93] The French pastor Guillaume Holbrac had enraged them by his support for Zanchi and had offended the magistrates by refusing to sign their formula of consensus; even worse, his church was becoming a magnet for refugees. When the Church Assembly complained that his sermons disturbed the city's peace, the Senate and XXI promptly fired Holbrac and closed his church.[94]

The elders of the French church, who included Christopher Mont, Elizabeth I's diplomatic agent in the Rhine Valley, appealed to the magistrates for a reprieve.[95] They called for a common front against the Catholics, whose hearts would undoubtedly be warmed by the decision to close the refugee church. They warned that its parishioners, left without a pastor, might drift into sectarianism. The

[91]RP 1554, f. 294b verso; RP 1556, ff. 108r–109r, 245r-v.

[92]Marbach, *Christlicher und warhaffter Underricht* (Strasbourg, 1565), p. 28 on Calvin. Paul-F. Geisendorf, *Théodore de Bèze* (Geneva, 1949), pp. 82–85, 89–92, 95. Marbach's letter: *Calvini opera,* vol. 15, no. 2294 (1555).

[93]AST 84/114, f. 721r-v (1563).

[94]RP 1563, f. 329r; AMS II/84b/54.

[95]RP 1563, ff. 343r–344r; AMS II/84b/51.

Senate and XXI spent five years in a rather desultory search for a French-speaking Lutheran pastor and, not unnaturally, failed to find one. In 1568 the magistrates decided to relent—a little. The French would now be allowed to hold prayer meetings and hear sermons, but under no circumstances were they to celebrate the sacraments.[96]

The Senate and XXI refused to issue any official condemnation of Calvinist doctrines, but it did allow the clergy some leeway to write against them. In 1565 Johann Marbach prepared a treatise on the Lord's Supper, and although the magistrates forced him to alter it lest the bluntness of his attacks offend the Swiss and other neighbors, censoring Marbach's work did not prevent trouble. The Calvinists in the Palatinate had a special grudge against him because of his attacks on Zanchi and because of his collaboration with their Lutheran prince, the late Ottheinrich. Books against Marbach found their way to Strasbourg from the Frankfurt fair, and finally the Senate and XXI agreed to let him reply.[97] They also permitted his colleague Isaac Kessler to publish a work on the eucharist, and then authorized the publication in Strasbourg of a booklet in which David Chytraeus set out to demonstrate how Genevan doctrine contradicted the Augsburg Confession.[98] In 1567 they even allowed Marbach to dedicate a new anti-Calvinist work to them and rewarded him with twenty-five *gulden* for the compliment.[99]

The clergy remained unsatisfied. All this time the members of the Senate and XXI continued to retain Jean Sturm as the rector of their school and were becoming more and more deeply involved in the Huguenot war effort. They had also allowed the refugees to start meeting again. Not until 1577 did the magistrates make another move against the refugees, prompted as usual by a mixture of religious and secular motives. Early in 1577 the XIII spoke up.[100] Its members would like to see the French leave, for they were a security risk, and as long as the city tolerated Calvinist preaching, Huguenot refugees would come. "Besides which, their religion is opposed to ours and the cathechism with which they indoctrinate their children is

[96]RP 1568, ff. 560v–561r.

[97]RP 1565, ff. 53v–54r, 55v–56r, referring to the *Christlicher und warhaffter Underricht*. On Marbach's efforts in the Palatinate see Schmidt, *Der Antheil der Strassburger an der Reformation in Churpfalz*.

[98]RP 1565, f. 453r, on Kessler's *Kurtz Examen* (Strasbourg, 1566), and RP 1567, f. 385r, for Chytraeus.

[99]Marbach's reward for the dedication of his *Christlicher Underricht:* RP 1567, f. 490r.

[100] RP 1577, ff. 94r–96r.

Zwinglian." The question, said the XIII, was whether or not to get rid of their preacher and end the prayer meetings "so that fewer Frenchmen will be drawn here." The Senate and XXI struck a committee of senior magistrates to consider the question.

The committee was unable to arrive at a unanimous recommendation, and its presentation to the Senate and XXI set off vigorous debate.[101] The committee first listed the most pressing reasons for halting the French services: they attracted foreigners; there was disagreement about the sacraments between the French and the Germans; the public preaching by the French pastor disturbed Strasbourg's Lutheran neighbors and the city's own people; most of the French understood enough German to attend Lutheran services; giving the French the opportunity to convert could save their souls. Then it turned to the counter-arguments: it would be uncharitable to abandon the refugees in their misery; the Calvinists recognized the Bible as the sole authority in religion and opposed the pope, so that condemning them would increase the persecution of Protestantism; finally, how could Strasbourg suppress the Calvinist meetings when it tolerated papists, whose teachings contradicted the Protestant position at every point, and whose mass was an abomination and the greatest blasphemy against Christ? The committee could see two possible solutions. The Senate and XXI could end the Calvinist meetings and provide the French with a Lutheran pastor to convert them, or it could leave the Calvinists alone until the Catholics could be dealt with as well.

The full Senate and XXI chewed over these proposals for three hours—an unusually lengthy debate—before deciding to ignore the committee's alternatives. The French meetings were to cease and their minister was to be dismissed. Henceforth the French were not to meet even privately in their residences. On the other hand, they were not to be assigned a Lutheran pastor for to do so would bring trouble, as one or another of the Calvinist leaders, perhaps even Beza himself, would surely use this to draw the city's clergy into more disputations. The Senate and XXI concluded: "We may not and ought not make an Inquisition out of this. [The Calvinists] are not to lose their citizenship, nor are they to be forced or dragged into our religion or have burdens placed upon their consciences. If they do not wish to join our church and be saved, they can remain outside it. Further-

[101]RP 1577, ff. 96r–99r.

more, we will not tell them why we have done this, only that we have valid reasons."[102] Meanwhile the standing committee on how to abolish the convent masses was told to get on with its work.

Count Palatine Johann Casimir, whose military adventures in France the magistrates had been subsidizing, urged them to reconsider, and so did the Swiss. A violent debate, lasting the whole day, erupted in the council chambers.[103] In the course of it, the city secretary, Paulus Hochfelder, intervened to defend the refugees. He acknowledged that their presence offended the city's Lutheran neighbors, but he urged the magistrates to put their forefathers' tradition of "Christian love and mercy" above this. Warming to his theme, he launched an account of the city's history very much in the tradition of Sturm and Zanchi. Strasbourg's true confession was the *Tetrapolitana*, as explicated by the Wittenberg Concord. Calvin himself had taught in Strasbourg, and had served the city on diplomatic missions, while Marbach and the Genevans had been as one in their opposition to the Interim. The Huguenots recognized the Augsburg Confession, Hochfelder concluded. They were victims and enemies of tyranny, and as such they should be protected. Hochfelder's speech set off raging arguments round and round the room. One magistrate turned on the corpulent Altammeister Wolfgang Schütterlin and roared, "The big gut's all blown up pregnant with a Zwinglian inside—he'd love to make the whole city Zwinglian!"[104] In the end, the Senate and XXI refused to change its course. Their allies were to be told that Strasbourg would tolerate only one religion, and that the French meetings had been stopped because of "pressing danger."

The banning of all public Calvinist services in Strasbourg was undoubtedly a victory for the Church Assembly. Refugees continued to enter the city, however, and rumors about clandestine conventicles persisted. Repression of Calvinist dissent, like the measures against the Catholics and the sectarians, merely drove people underground, and the Calvinists did not even go entirely out of sight. On Sundays they rode out of the city to attend services elsewhere, in a public demonstration of their rejection of the Church Assembly's teachings.[105]

[102]RP 1577, f. 99r.
[103]Johann Casimir's letter, AMS II/84b/77. The Swiss pleas, RP 1577, ff. 353r–356r, 357r-v.
[104]RP 1577, f. 357r-v. For Schütterlin's belly, see the portrait reproduced by Wilhelm Schadt, "Wolfgang Schütterlin, Ammeister der Stadt Strassburg," *Die Ortenau*, 54 (1974), 257–59. Padding one's paunch was the male fashion of the day.
[105]AST 64/6, f. 44r (1572); RP 1582, ff. 67v–68r; RP 1597, ff. 545r–546v; AST 90/23.

Not until 1597 did the magistrates make the logical last move against the local Calvinists. By this time the anti-Catholic Bishops' War was over and so were the French wars; all but a tiny remnant of the refugees had gone home. In November Ammeister Hans von Hohenburg informed the Senate and XXI that a poster, signed "the Gardeners," had been found, which claimed that many burghers were attending Calvinist services in nearby Bischweiler and that their minister, Johann Gottfridi, was coming into Strasbourg to proselytize. Three days later the Church Assembly lodged a formal complaint against Gottfridi.[106] The Senate and XXI decided to bar him from the city and ordered that its subjects were not to attend his services, sending a message to the guilds in December to publicize this new policy. The magistrates resolved to word the message so "that the weak in faith will not take umbrage and that no one will be put under compulsion in matters of faith. Rather everyone's conscience is to be left free, provided only that people conduct themselves peacefully."[107] With this decision the Senate and XXI closed the long debate on the status of Swiss theology in Strasbourg.

That debate had been conducted almost entirely by the educated elite. Professors and pastors had argued about the city's history and over doctrine, forcing the Senate and XXI to arbitrate their battles. The magistrates remained involved because external events, like the French wars and the doctrinal split between their neighbors in the Empire and Switzerland, made confessional rivalry as much an issue in foreign policy in the latter part of the century as it had been at the time of the formation of the Schmalkaldic League. The theological differences dividing Lutheran and Calvinist intellectuals were not of a nature immediately to arouse the passions of the majority in the laity, so few ordinary Strasburghers took sides in the controversies as long as Calvinism remained the property of academics and foreigners. Eventually a popular anti-Calvinism did develop—witness the Gardeners' placard—but it was as much a by-product of discontent with the magistrates' foreign policy as a product of the Church Assembly's denunciations of the Genevan faith. The rise of this popular anti-Calvinism and the role it played in the evolution of the city's reformation properly belong in the next chapter.

For the clergy the Calvinists were an unusually difficult problem.

---

[106]RP 1597, ff. 542v–543r, 545r–546v; AST 90/23.

[107]RP 1597, ff. 592r–593r; AST 103, unnumbered text of what was read from the pulpits; and AST 84/112, ff. 703r–704r.

The Catholics certainly never claimed to be Protestant; they were an external enemy even when they were physically present in the city. The secretarians also dissociated themselves from the established order, and certainly the magistrates never took their wishes into account in shaping official policy. The Calvinists were quite another matter. In the latter half of the century they were the dynamic face of Protestantism in western Europe, and they made gains at the expense of the Lutherans as well as of the Catholics. They had a potential to mine from within by presenting themselves as the true heirs of the first generation. Claiming allegiance to the Augsburg Confession, but reading it in a way that the Lutherans could not accept, they threatened to subvert the Lutheran reformation. The danger was all the greater since so many of the laity regarded the defense of fine points of doctrine as hair-splitting that ought to be eschewed in the interest of Protestant solidarity.

For the magistrates as well, Calvinism presented more difficulties than either sectarianism or Catholicism. The willingness of the intellectuals to engage in technical controversy was a problem in itself. In dealing with the sectarians, the Senate and XXI had been able to sidestep theological debate by concentrating on the secular consequences of sectarian doctrines. The majority of magistrates had concluded that Catholicism was a false religion at a time when the evangelicals were putting their case in broad terms a layman could follow; their successors had never had to reconsider this decision. There was no such easy way to avoid theology in assessing the Calvinists. The magistrates could not comprehend the arguments spun by the two sides, and bit by bit they were forced into accepting their clergy's expertise, with all the consequences that could entail for the lay supremacy. Nevertheless, as long as sound foreign policy required collaboration with Calvinists abroad, the Senate and XXI refused to issue any condemnation of Calvinist doctrine in its own name.

4. Conclusion

From the 1520s through the 1590s and beyond, the city of Strasbourg had its heretics, condemned by the clergy and controlled by the magistrates. In the twenties the evangelical clergy had thrust upon the magistrates the right to evaluate what was and was not good doctrine. The first two generations of magistrates exercised this authority reluctantly, since they knew themselves to be anything but expert in theology. They were even more reluctant to return to the clergy the right to declare doctrines to be binding on their city. The power to ratify theological statements in the city's name was one they always kept for themselves. They recognized the Tetrapolitan Confession and then the Augsburg Confession, presided over the creation of a formula of consensus in 1563, and their sons would at last commit Strasbourg to the Formula of Concord in 1598. These statements were all the work of theologians, not magistrates, but only the magistrates could make them official definitions of what the Strasbourg church upheld. In the public statements on orthodoxy and error which they wrote themselves, the magistrates stuck to broad and vague comments. The pattern set in the twenties and thirties in their response to the sects held good later for the Catholics and Calvinists as well. "The less said the better" remained their rule of thumb.

The magistrates proclaimed that their established church taught the pure word of God and that their city belonged in the Lutheran fold, yet they refused to force their subjects to be Lutheran or even to attend the Lutheran church. Since the 1520s the Senate and XXI had always insisted that what its subjects thought was their own business. Only in the cases of Anabaptists and Catholic nuns did the magistrates compromise this principle by attempting to convert dissidents. In Strasbourg the regime never forced religious beliefs on the mass of the adult population.

While the Senate and XXI left the Strasburghers free to think what they pleased, it did not let them act as they pleased. It had no scruples about policing behavior by suppressing rival churches. The magistrates broke up the Anabaptist meetings in the city and ordered their burghers to stay away from meetings outside the walls. They proceeded in the same way against the Catholics and eventually against the Calvinists. First they banned services within their own territory (in 1529 and 1563 respectively) and then they forbade their subjects to participate in these services elsewhere (1531 and 1597). Despite this, some Strasburghers always rejected the established church in favor of one of its rivals. The magistrates' fears about the power an "inquisition" would give to their clergy restrained them from any attempt to eradicate all vestiges of dissent. They could live with contained minorities of heretics.

There was thus a broad pattern to the policing of dissent in Strasbourg. It was done by the lay authorities, not by the clergy acting on their own initiative. Heresy was controlled, but not eliminated, by choking off alternatives to the established church. The magistrates paid much more than lip service to the unity of the church, but they never satisfied the clergy's demands for a complete repression of dissent. They learned to tolerate individual Anabaptists and Schwenckfelders; they suffered a partial Catholic restoration; they made alliances with foreign Calvinists even as they slowly destroyed the local Calvinist parish. All these actions were anathema to the clergy, who believed that nothing should be allowed to interfere with the defense of the faith, but the magistrates had to balance the unity and dominance of the church against concern for the city's internal peace and its external security.

In normal times the lay Strasburghers judged their fellows by neighborliness rather than by the orthodoxy of their beliefs. The clergy were never bloodthirsty, but they viewed dissent more harshly than did the laity, for they cared more for doctrinal purity. By and large, the magistrates' policies were in keeping with lay rather than with clerical sentiments. Their subjects accepted the sectarians faster than they did, and the magistrates could not at first afford to share the anti-Catholicism or the anti-Calvinism of their people. In each case the Senate and XXI eventually swung round to positions which, if they did not entirely please the clergy, were palatable to the rest of its subjects.

The clergy regarded the suppression of their rivals as a vital part of their work to reform Strasbourg, yet it was not the whole of their struggle to defend the doctrines of the Augsburg Confession. Silencing the opposition was important, but so was their campaign to explain and proclaim religious truth.

CHAPTER SIX

The Triumph of Lutheran Orthodoxy

The reformation had begun with a search for doctrinal truth. Between 1520 and 1597 the victorious Lutherans had managed to push their rivals underground in Strasbourg, even if heretics remained in the city, while outside Strasbourg Lutheran theologians slowly and painfully arrived at a lasting definition of their faith. By 1580, eighty-six Lutheran territories had ratified the definition of orthodoxy embodied in the Formula of Concord, but Strasbourg's magistrates obstinately refused to sign the Formula. For most of the century the Church Assembly confronted a Senate and XXI determined to prevent any revival of the old clerical powers and a population bent on thinking for itself.Increasingly the clergy resented this lay intransigence, whether it came in the form of an obscure dissenter refusing to respect their church, Rector Jean Sturm's conviction that he understood the early reformation better than did the original preachers' successors, or the magistrates' refusal to bow to their pastors' theological authority by accepting the Formula of Concord. In the last third of the century, as the clergy strove to reestablish the clerical monopoly on religious decision making, the campaign for the Formula became the centerpiece of their effort to complete Strasbourg's reformation. In a sense, they had come full circle and returned to the premise of the early reformers: first define true doctrine.

Late in 1570, Jacob Andreae, who seven years earlier had won the magistrates' good will by helping to draft the consensus that halted the quarrel among Johann Marbach, Girolamo Zanchi, and Jean

Sturm, wrote to the Senate and XXI about his latest pacification efforts. At the urging of the volatile Saxon elector and of his own prince, Duke Ludwig of Württemberg, Andreae had taken on the onerous chore of trying to patch up the schisms among Luther's heirs. He and his fellow theologians had now arrived at a draft set of articles of agreement, and Andreae wished to submit them for Strasbourg's approval. The Senate and XXI resolved to thank Andreae, but it assigned no one to read the articles. The magistrates' lack of enthusiasm brought the president of the Church Assembly to their chambers, for the clergy approved Andreae's project. Citing Strasbourg's long tradition of seeking the unity of the churches, Marbach asked to be sent to the Maulbronn colloquy to participate in the discussion of Andreae's draft.[1]

A committee struck by the Senate and XXI to consider Marbach's request reported a month later.[2] Past attempts to solve these theological disputes, the committee noted, had resulted only in increased bitterness. Andreae's project was unlikely to bring unity, but all too likely to produce street fighting (an allusion to rioting in Saxony and the Palatinate and an accurate prediction of what was to come in Strasbourg). Strasbourg had enjoyed more peace than its neighbors, and it would be better not to trouble the local unity by getting involved in these Saxon quarrels. The committee regretted that the clergy had signed Andreae's draft on their own authority. It was the members' unanimous conviction that the Strasburghers should continue to live together in the pure appreciation of God's word, isolated from all the foreign, damaging discord. This was the same advice Bernhard Botzheim had offered in 1563 when the local intellectual community had split, setting pastors and professors against each other. It was advice that continued to sit well with magistrates who were convinced that theological precision was more trouble than it was worth, particularly if there were any risk that the common people would be inflamed by the arguments of their superiors. The Senate and XXI accepted the advice of its committee, and for nearly thirty years the magistrates would have nothing to do with Jacob Andreae's project.

The magistrates' refusal to back the prototype of the Formula of Concord unsettled the clergy, who did not appreciate this rejection of their theological judgment. Once again the Senate and XXI had put

[1]RP 1570, ff. 785v–786r, 908r–912r.
[2]RP 1570, ff. 985v–987v.

secular before spiritual interests. On the heels of this rejection came another blow, a reduction of the clergy's power in the city's senior school. The old ill will between Jean Sturm and Johann Marbach, more or less dormant since 1563, now awoke again. The clergy lobbied to get Sturm removed from his office of rector, arguing that as a "Calvinist" he was a pernicious influence. They had the support of Heinrich von Mülnheim, a XIIIer and a member of the school board, but Mülnheim was unable to carry the Senate and XXI, which voted its confidence in Sturm in 1570 and two years later moved to diminish Marbach's authority in the school.[3]

During this new duel between rector and president, Sturm had brought up foreign policy by raising the question of the French Protestants. He demanded to know how Marbach could dare criticize him for putting his personal fortune on the line to defend the true understanding of Scripture through three horrible wars in France.[4] Marbach was incensed by this claim. His opponents pretended to know more about the Augsburg Confession than he did because they defended it inside and outside the Empire at greater risk than he had ever taken for it? Travesty! His opponents connived against that confession day and night. Sturm welcomed refugees who had no more respect for the Lutheran church than for that of the papists. They preferred to trek off to services at Markirch or in the Palatinate rather than to take communion with the Lutherans. This was the religion on which Sturm spent his money, and his fortune went to pay for atrocities. The French troops came into Alsace and plundered the homes of the country clergy. They ransacked the pastors' libraries and whenever they found books with Luther's name or picture, they ripped out the pages, tore them up, and trampled them, even the Bibles, underfoot. Sturm's money financed "murder, robbery, theft, and all manner of injustice against friend and foe alike."[5]

Sturm had provoked Marbach to compromise himself, for the Senate and XXI was as deeply committed to the Huguenots as was the rector, and Sturm's contacts were highly useful to the magistrates in their diplomatic endeavors. His school, which was renowned in Europe, drew students from across the continent. The Senate and

[3]Many of the relevant documents are in Marcel Fournier and Charles Engel, eds., *L'université de Strasbourg et les académies protestantes françaises* (Paris, 1894), nos. 2054–56, 2058, 2060–61. See also RP 1570, ff. 76v–77r, 130r-v, 191v–192r, 195v–196r; RP 1572, ff. 300v–302v, 322r–326r, 352v–355r.
[4]AST 64/3 (1572), f. 28v. Jean Rott, "Le recteur strasbourgeois Jean Sturm et les protestants français," *Actes du colloque l'amiral de Coligny et son temps* (Paris, 1974), pp. 407–25.
[5]AST 64/6, (1572).

XXI was not about to dismiss him when such a decision would set his friends' tongues wagging to convince influential men from London to Prague that Johann Marbach, not the Senate and XXI, ruled in Strasbourg. Sturm was becoming a symbol of the lay supremacy, and rather than let Marbach replace him, the Senate and XXI reasserted its own control.

The Church Assembly protested these moves to diminish its leader. Dr. Marbach, "our loyal superintendent," had been deeply wounded by the magistrates' actions, said the clergy. Worse, the Senate and XXI's decision to restrict Marbach's power in the school would cause rejoicing not only among Marbach's personal enemies, but also "among the common, public enemies of truth, such as the papists, Anabaptists, Schwenckfelders, Calvinists, and other epicurean blasphemers."[6] The protest backfired. A council committee noted that Marbach had never been appointed "superintendent" and that his status ought to be clarified. God, it argued, had appointed the lay magistrates to police the church. Marbach had gathered too much power into his own hands and had provoked dangerous disputes over the Augsburg Confession, so that the magistrates' reputation and authority were at stake. The Church Assembly must be told that the magistrates alone were the superintendents of the church and intended to administer it for the honor of God. The members of the Senate and XXI agreed, so the whole affair ended in a clear rejection of the clergy's attempt to increase its authority.[7]

Some four years later the lay superintendents once again had to confront the question of Lutheran orthodoxy and, as in 1570, they took their stand on solidly secular grounds. In the early autumn of 1577 Duke Ludwig sent his court preacher, Lucas Osiander, to explain the evolution of the Concord project since Strasbourg's initial rejection of it. Osiander brought with him the latest results, the Bergen Book of doctrine. He received a slightly warmer welcome than had Andreae, since this time the Senate and XXI agreed to discuss the proposal and struck a committee to read the text.[8]

Six weeks later Johann Carl Lorcher, recently a driving force behind the suppression of the Calvinist refugees' prayer meetings, introduced the committee's report in the worst possible terms.[9] He had read only part of this Bergen Book; it was so long and involved that a

[6]Fournier and Engel, *L'université,* no. 2070 (1573).
[7]RP 1573, ff. 878r–881v, minutes for early January 1574.
[8]RP 1577, ff. 535v–537v.
[9]RP 1577, ff. 722v–723v, 725v–732r.

man could spend a year on it and never sort it out. Better to keep the thing under lock and key, he growled, as it would only cause trouble if the common people got wind of it and set to arguing about religion. Duke Ludwig, he added sarcastically, had gotten mixed up in this looking for prestige, and Andreae only wanted money. His fellow committee members summarized the content of the proposed Book, reviewing the long history of the Lutheran controversies and pointing out that this Bergen Book had sections on "what is damned as heretical, false, and erroneous," whereas damning the opposition had never been Strasbourg's practice. Instead, they noted smugly, the Strasburghers had concentrated on building up the true church. Strasbourg, they concluded, had settled these quarrels quite satisfactorily in 1563 and without condemning anyone. The committee also challenged the accuracy of the Book's historical account of the relationship between Luther and the Swiss. Its members recommended that the Senate and XXI reject the Book: they could see no advantage to signing it, as it could be relied upon to bring even more bitterness into the church and into political affairs.

Ammeister Jacob von Molsheim, a partisan of the Book, called on each magistrate in turn and for once the minutes give some indication of individual replies. Sebastian Mieg and Heinrich von Mülnheim agreed with Lorcher: bury it. David Geiger and Barthel Keller probably spoke for the majority when they said this matter was over their heads and they hoped their consciences would not be bound to the contents of the Book. Then Altammeister Michael Lichtensteiger demanded that the clergy, "as physicians to our souls and our appointed pastors," be consulted and their opinion followed. Molsheim seconded this proposal, but he and Lichtensteiger won a mere six votes. The great majority rejected the Bergen Book and voted to advise both Duke Ludwig and the Church Assembly of this decision "as politely as possible."

Stadtadvocat Ludwig Gremp, who had close connections to Württemberg, feared this rejection would cause uproar among the theologians and isolate Strasbourg. On the other hand, the Swiss, whom the magistrates had so recently affronted by terminating the refugees' prayer meetings, wrote to thank them for refusing to endorse this public condemnation of Calvinist teaching.[10] At a time when the magistrates were trying to ally themselves with the Swiss, this was a

[10]Gremp, RP 1577, ff. 754v–756r; the Swiss, RP 1578, ff. 30r–32r, and AMS VI/701/9.

hopeful sign. Foreign policy had a place in the magistrates' ruminations over the Bergen Book, but as their debate showed, they had solid reasons for disliking it no matter what their neighbors thought of it. It was long, it was complicated, and they did not understand it. Their fathers had expressed reservations about the Tetrapolitan Confession on those grounds, and the Bergen Book was worse, not better. Worst of all, it was far too likely to create trouble among their subjects.

Over the next years letters for and against what was now called the Formula of Concord poured into the city as its neighbors tried to sway the magistrates.[11] As more and more Lutheran territories signed the Formula, Strasbourg did indeed isolate itself. In the midst of this Jean Sturm once again heaved himself into the debate, setting off another row with the ailing Marbach and his successor Johann Pappus. Sturm wrote against Osiander, while Marbach attacked Daniel Tossanus, a Palatine Calvinist and enemy of the Formula. Both Marbach and Sturm circumvented the Strasbourg censors by publishing their tracts elsewhere, leaving the magistrates to hope in vain that they would stop.[12]

In his polemics Sturm once again defended his old thesis that Strasbourg's confession was the *Tetrapolitana*. He called upon his recollections of the first generation of magistrates and preachers—he had been in the city since 1538—to support his claim that nothing could be more foreign to Strasbourg than this new Lutheran orthodoxy with its condemnations of fellow Protestants. The rector challenged Pappus's reasoning that the "Damnamus" clauses in the Book of Concord should be construed as a work of love which sought to save souls by winning the errant back to the truth. Pappus responded by repeating the version of Strasbourg's history which Marbach had outlined in his battle with Zanchi nearly twenty years before. Although much of the arguing back and forth was done in Latin, neither party could resist the temptation to publish in German as well. The conflict thus moved from the studies of the intellectuals into the chambers of the magistrates and out into the streets.[13]

---

[11]AMS VI/701, 550 folios of copies, 1577–82.

[12]RP 1579, ff. 439v–440r, with the marginal title, "Bücher inn Religionsachen. Streyttbücher. Theologische Bücher. Theologi Schreyben wider eynander. Widereynander schreyben."

[13] Hans Werner Gensichen, *Damnamus: Die Verwerfung von Irrlehre bei Luther und im Luthertum des 16ten Jahrhunderts* (Berlin, 1955) gives a good account of the arguments, pp.

[147]

The People's Reformation

Sturm and Pappus had their seconds. Theodosius Rihel, brother of the XIIIer Josias Rihel, reprinted the text of the Tetrapolitan Confession in 1579. When the Senate and XXI confiscated the edition, printers in Neustadt promptly reissued it.[14] Jacob Andreae entered the fray on Pappus's side. Sturm was a Calvinist, Sturm was a heretic, and Sturm was a liar, said Andreae. Moreover, Sturm was a layman, unqualified to speak about doctrine. "In theology Sturm is untutored. . . . He cannot rightly interpret a single verse of Scripture." Andreae mocked Sturm's incompetence in a German tract directed to the citizens of Strasbourg, in which he seized upon the rector's fatal admission that he had never read the Formula of Concord. Sturm was "an academic and an epicurean" who thought it was enough if two sides could settle on common phrases to explain a disputed doctrine, even if both continued to mean different things by these words. Sturm's theological writings were "so childish and pernicious that anyone with sense can see that the old man has fallen into senility and does not know himself what he is writing." Andreae applauded the fact that Pappus, once Sturm's pupil, used the languages and arts the rector had taught him to put his former teacher in his place.[15]

Andreae had advanced the thesis that Sturm, as a layman, was incompetent to judge matters of doctrine. He was not content to stop there. It was not just Sturm, but all the laity who must keep silent and let the theologians rule on what was true and what was false. This right he denied to "the grammarians, the jurists, the physicians, and the so-called philosophers, who in these days claim to be the reformers of theologians"—in short, to all the educated classes of the laity. He argued that every calling had its sphere of competence which should not be encroached upon by those in other walks of life, applying this maxim in a stern warning to the Strasburghers: "When the

133–43, but without reference to the magistrates' original rejection of Andreae's project. Of the German writings see in particular Sturm, *Communitio oder Erinnerungschrift* (Neustadt, 1581) and Pappus, *Bericht und Warnung . . . an eine christliche Burgerschafft* (Tübingen, 1581).

[14]*Bekandtnus der vier frey und Reichstatt* (Strasbourg, 1579). See RP 1580, ff. 98v–99v, 101r–v, 105v–106r, and AST 75/92, for Rihel's explanation of why he reprinted it. *Confessio oder Bekantnuss* (Neustadt, 1580) contains a preface asserting that this was the official confession of Strasbourg.

[15]*Abfertigung des Vortrabs Johan Sturmii* (Tübingen, 1581); *Kurtz Antwort . . . auff Herrn Johan Sturmii Buch Antipappus Quartus genant* (Dresden, 1581). The quotations are from the former, p. 48, and from the latter, sig. Bi recto and Biv verso.

jurists would be priests and reign over the pulpit, and claim to know better than the loyal pastors what should be taught, and how these teachings should be defended, and how things are to be done, and according to what standard, there will be discord both in God's Church and in the Council Chambers."[16] Under the guise of reprimanding lawyers, Andreae was rebuking magistrates. The rulers of Strasbourg had dared to defy their clergy, and Andreae was calling them to heel. His attitude toward the lay magistrates was far different from the one that had led the Bucers and Zells of the first generation to call upon the laity to judge the truth of their teaching and to urge lay rulers to undertake the reformation of the churches. Andreae harkened back to the elitism of Wolfgang Capito.

Inevitably the battle of the books produced violence in the streets. Pastor Johann Faber preached against the Calvinists, and a group of Sturm's students roughed him up before his parishioners could rescue him.[17] Early in January 1581 gangs of students gathered around the pastors' homes and hurled stones at the windows.[18] Pappus and Sturm continued to write, helped along by Andreae, while the magistrates bickered among themselves. The Lutheran Elector Palatine wrote to accuse Sturm of libel, citing page and paragraph in the Rector's *Antipappus quartus*.[19] Satires and placards appeared in public places. The clergy piously commented on one that it could not be the work of a Lutheran because "no one has ever heard of a Lutheran seeking disturbance, but all the Calvinists ever want is to shed blood."[20] Ammeister Lichtensteiger pleaded with the Senate and XXI to settle the brawling, but nothing was done.[21]

Pappus preached against the papist abominations and against those in the city who mocked the true understanding of the Lord's Supper, a transparent reference to Sturm and his supporters, and an obvious attempt to link anti-Catholicism and anti-Calvinism in order to increase popular animosity toward Sturm. He criticized the magistrates' attempts to impose silence, and urged the councils to show that they could distinguish truth from error by deposing Sturm and

---

[16]*Kurtz Antwort,* sig. C i recto-verso, and the quoted passage, sig. Cii recto.

[17]RP 1580, ff. 398r–399r.

[18]Fournier and Engel, *L'université,* no. 2088; and RP 1580, ff. 645v–646r, minutes for early January 1581.

[19]Fournier and Engel, *L'université,* no. 2089.

[20]RP 1581, ff. 128v–129r, 169v–170r.

[21]RP 1581, f. 144r-v.

signing the Formula of Concord.[22] Pappus was treading on dangerous ground, inciting his parishioners to criticize the magistrates. A new and more radical placard soon turned up in which "sixteen hundred" artisans and day laborers announced that they were ready to storm the city hall to protest high taxes and high prices but also, significantly, to punish the magistrates for their connivance with "the Zwinglians." Their forefathers, they boasted, had known how to force the nobility to do their bidding, and they knew how to deal with merchants.[23] The magistrates blamed popular discontent squarely on the preachers, and ordered the clergy to switch to sermons on Christian love and obedience.[24]

As the situation within the walls deteriorated, pressure from outside increased.[25] A full-scale riot was narrowly averted.[26] Through it all Sturm continued his crusade until finally a majority in the Senate and XXI voted "to suggest" to the rector that he resign, since he had misused his office to create a platform for his polemics. When he still refused to resign the magistrates at last fired him.[27]

Jean Sturm's dismissal in 1581 was a moral victory for the Church Assembly. The magistrates had at last dissociated themselves from the man whom the clergy had come to consider their chief opponent in the city. Yet the preachers won no more than a symbolic victory, since for more than a decade to come something of Sturm's vision of the world guided the majority in the Senate and XXI. Sturm had dared to dream of a general reunion of the Protestant churches. His hopes were reminiscent of those of the first generation of reformers in Strasbourg, and with good reason, for he was a living link to those men. He clung to the Tetrapolitan Confession because that ambiguous document, drafted to bring together the Swiss and the Saxons, might still serve to unite the Germans, the Swiss, the French, the English, and the Netherlanders. The theologians of the second and third generation swept away this dream because their concern was for peace and unity within the Lutheran community rather than for a general rapprochement of all Protestants, most of whom they had

---

[22]AST 100, unnumbered document. The sermon followed on the heels of an ordinance against religious controversy: AMS R4, ff. 126v–127r.

[23]RP 1581, ff. 181v–182v; the reference to forefathers is to the medieval guild revolution against the local nobility.

[24] RP 1581, ff. 183r–185r.

[25]RP 1581, ff. 170v–171v, 180v–181v, 196v–197v, 198r.

[26]RP 1581, ff. 201r, 202v–203r; AMS N29, f. 76r.

[27]Fournier and Engel, *L'université,* no. 2094.

come to regard as no closer to the truth than were the Catholics. The magistrates, for their part, had long ago buried the *Tetrapolitana* and recently outlawed all Calvinist services, although they continued to believe in the need for secular cooperation among the Protestants, since only by fighting together could Lutherans and Calvinists hold off the resurgent Catholic church and its Guise and Habsburg champions. Sturm's disgrace did not lead to a reversal of the city's foreign policy and therefore could not produce acceptance of the Formula of Concord.

Even so, the majority that rejected the Formula and voted for an aggressive foreign policy was slowly eroding, as bit by bit the Senate and XXI broke into factions. With each passing year, more and more of the magistrates had grown up in a Strasbourg whose pastors were wholeheartedly Lutheran and had formed their opinions under the direction of these pastors. A Lutheran orthodox and neutralist faction had begun to coalesce in the Senate and XXI in the 1570s, but that faction was still plagued by private altercations between some of its members and the inconstancy of others. The proponents of vague doctrinal statements and of intervention in France continued to defeat the partisans of precision and neutrality.

Before the Church Assembly could consolidate the victory it had won in destroying Strasbourg's "Calvinist" rector, the chapter crisis blew up, binding the magistrates more tightly than ever to heretical Protestant powers, even as the militants in the council chambers faced more and more opposition. Shortly after the Schöffen had ratified Strasbourg's treaty with Zurich, Bern, and Basel in 1588, the hardliners in the Senate and XXI introduced a draft briefing paper for the Schöffen which linked the local chapter crisis to Catholic machinations against the Protestants everywhere in western Europe. Altammeister Abraham Held, an opponent of the war party and an ally of the clergy, introduced an amendment to tell the Schöffen that the magistrates opposed the presence of all non-Lutherans in the city, including the Calvinists.[28] Several of his colleagues recoiled at this idea. Held's idea was folly in their eyes; what religion a Protestant professed must not be made an issue. Held claimed that he won eighteen votes for his amendment; the secretary counted sixteen, and someone else seventeen. In foul temper the Senate and XXI adjourned to let the XV, which adjudicated questions of procedure, sort

[28]RP 1588, ff. 604v–606r.

things out. Georg Golder, summarizing the clash in the minutes of the XV, characterized the embattled factions as "the Pure" and those "who in part are not considered Pure."[29]

Golder's remark is of more than passing interest for what it tells about the divisions in the Senate and XXI. The "Pure," led by Held, Jacob von Molsheim, and Michael Lichtensteiger, shared the Church Assembly's conviction that the way to defend the true faith was to silence its rivals, something that could best be done by severing contacts with the Calvinists and condemning their theology. The "Damnamus" clauses in the Formula of Concord held no terrors for these men.[30] The war party, which wanted to work with the Calvinists, was naturally suspected of heterodoxy, for these men were not prepared to sacrifice Strasbourg's military security for confessional purity. One or two of them may have had some leanings toward Calvinism; as late as 1595 Josias Rihel refused to say he thought its teachings false.[31] On the other hand, Johann Schenckbecher supported the militants and in his private papers expressly rejected Calvinist doctrinal formulae.[32] In all likelihood Schenckbecher's were the views of most of the men in his faction.

The militants remained the majority. Held's amendment failed, and the Schöffen accepted the war party's arguments.[33] The result of the militants' triumph, as we have seen, was disastrous. Strasbourg put an army into the field to fight for the Calvinist cathedral canons and lost badly. Within the council chambers mud flew in all directions, with the members of the peace party, who were denounced as lovers of Lorraine and lackeys of the clergy, taking the worst of it. Their stronghold, the council of XV, had its power sharply reduced, and two of their leaders, Friedrich Prechter and Bernhard Kageneck, were forced out of office.[34]

By 1594 the war was over and the constitutional crisis that had pitted the XIII against the XV was settling down. The clergy had been uncharacteristically silent during the war and its aftermath, al-

[29]XV 1588, ff. 185r–186r.
[30]For Molsheim, AMS VI/701a/8; for Lichtensteiger, AST 100, unnumbered piece, f. 2v.
[31]AST 326/22.
[32]AST 1655, ff. 163v–168r.
[33]RP 1588, ff. 608r-v, 609v–610r.
[34]On the amendments to the constitution see BNUS ms. 959, and RP 1594, ff. 267r, 269v–270r, 271v–272r. On Prechter, see Widmaier, *Friedrich Prechter*, p. 62; on Kageneck, RP 1594, f. 326r-v.

though certainly their old agonies persisted. As long as the Formula of Concord remained unsigned, there was no guarantee that the Senate and XXI might not resume its ill-considered flirtations with the Calvinists. The Catholics had grown stronger. The clergy's best ally within the regime, the council of XV, had betrayed the cause of orthodoxy in 1594. Desperate to protect its corporate privileges against the assaults of a XIII maddened by military defeat, the XV had co-opted the best lawyer it could find to argue its case—Michael Theurer, the Schwenckfelder.[35] Heresy survived, to the great grief of the Church Assembly. Pastor Johann Thomas on his deathbed mustered what remained of his strength and "began to speak about the Schwenckfelders, the Calvinists, and sacramentarians, and what harm they do our church," but he died without relief.[36] The burghers, like the magistrates, could not be trusted. They might disparage the magistrates' policies and even, in 1595, plot rebellion to turn out their heretical masters, but nevertheless they remained mired in sin. Too much drinking, too much dancing, too much gambling, too much adultery, and no respect for the Sabbath—the common people were a feeble reed.[37]

Despite these troubles, the Church Assembly was accumulating support below the surface. As early as 1590 it had managed to secure the dismissal of a young clergyman, Michael Philipp Beuther, who had refused to sign the Formula of Concord when the senior members of the Church Assembly demanded this submission from him. He had an ingenious argument: since the Senate and XXI had rejected it, he could not accept it without rebelling against the secular powers. The Senate and XXI did not reward his loyalty, preferring to sidestep this opportunity to make trouble with the clergy.[38] This was a straw in the wind, and the burghers' brooding anti-Calvinism was a better and far more useful sign of how the wind was blowing. The Church Assembly could use popular opinion to bring about its long-awaited victory.[39]

---

[35]XV 1593, ff. 22v, 223v–224r, and 1594, ff. 3v–4r, 5v–6r, 8r. For the clergy's reaction, BNUS ms. 998, pp. 37–41.

[36]BNUS 998, p. 105 (1593).

[37]On the near-rebellion in 1595, RP 1595, ff. 495v–496r, 496v–497r, 501r–v; and AMS IV/49/20. On the clergy's continuing grudges against the laity, RP 1594, f. 104r–v; RP 1596, ff. 138v, 195r; and RP 1597, f. 49r–v.

[38]Otto Jung, *Michael Philipp Beuther*, pp. 11–19.

[39]BNUS ms. 998, selections from the lost minutes of the Church Assembly, helps reconstruct their plans in the nineties.

The pastors' timing was good, for by the late nineties much had changed in the Strasburgers' world. In France the wars were over, and most of the refugees had left the city. The Swiss, who had pulled out of the Bishops' War as soon as the magistrates failed to meet their payroll, had few friends left in the Senate and XXI. There was little reason now to court Calvinists, and much to recommend some fence-mending with the Lutherans. Although the 1593 truce was proving durable, there was as yet no peace treaty and thus no security.[40] In the face of continuing Catholic success elsewhere in the Empire, the magistrates felt a need to reassert their solidarity with the Lutheran powers. Military defeat, constitutional crisis, and popular antipathy toward their policies combined to chasten them. In 1597 the members of the Senate and XXI announced to one another that it was "thoroughly necessary that we go along with the clergy in every way, so that the Lord our God will not be moved to rain down more punishment upon us."[41]

Behind this new attitude was a massive change in the membership of the city council, in particular among the senior magistrates. Of the thirty-five men who made up the XXI in 1597, only seven were veterans of the debates over the Formula of Concord in 1577 or of those in 1581 over Jean Sturm's opposition to it. Johann Carl Lorcher and Heinrich Joham, who had supported Sturm, were dead now, and so were two of his chief antagonists, Jacob von Molsheim and Michael Lichtensteiger. In the nineties the turnover rate had become so abnormally high that by the end of the decade barely half the members of the permanent councils had been in office during the Bishops' War. Certainly a few old faces lingered. Hans von Hohenburg, who had protested Sturm's dismissal, and his war party allies Nicolas Fuchs, Wolfgang Schütterlin, and Jacob Kips still sat in the XIII. The old peace party had lost Abraham Held and Hans Auenheim to the grave, but Sebastian Mieg, Georg Jacob Bock, Heinrich Obrecht and Hans Beinheim still hung on. They were a rearguard; the battling second generation had had its day. The overpowering majority in the Senate and XXI in 1597 consisted of men born after the Religious Peace, who thought of themselves and their city as Lutheran. This group had long been waxing in the councils; even the old war party had been "Calvinist" only in its foreign policy. The

---

[40]The final settlement came only in 1604. *Warhafftige und Eygentliche Vertrags Articulen* (Cologne, 1605).

[41]RP 1597, f. 49r-v.

moment had now come for the third generation to review its heritage and to define its future.

The Church Assembly was not unaware of the way the Senate and XXI was changing in the nineties. Nor was it oblivious to the opinions of the population at large. When Johann Pappus launched a flanking attack on the old opposition, he and his fellow pastors expected to carry the day without trouble. The pastors' plan was to achieve ratification of the Formula of Concord by including it in a new Church Ordinance, and to obtain passage of that ordinance by playing on anti-Calvinist sentiment.

The whole affair moved swiftly. Early in November Ammeister Hans von Hohenburg reported to the Senate and XXI the discovery of a poster signed "the Gardeners," which anathematized Paulus Hochfelder, once a mainstay of the old foreign policy and still active in the city's diplomatic service. The former secretary, said the Gardeners, was a Calvinist. Their poster also fingered Michael Theurer of the XV, denouncing him as a Schwenckfelder, and claimed that many burghers were attending Calvinist services in Bischweiler. To all these assaults on the true religion the Gardeners demanded an end.[42] Three days later the Church Assembly petitioned, echoing the Gardeners' complaints and pointing out that the chancellor of Zweibrücken had publicly accused Strasbourg of being Calvinist. The clergy urged the magistrates to promulgate a church ordinance that would tell the world "what religion they confess," since only this could clear both magistrates and clergy of these charges of heresy.[43] The Senate and XXI thanked the clergy for this "loyal submission." They took action against the Calvinists and they asked the clergy to submit a draft church ordinance.[44]

The discovery of another poster from the Gardeners against Calvinists and Schwenckfelders—two groups the clergy had long presented as linked in their errors—hurried the magistrates along.[45] The Elector Palatine wrote to warn that "no regime divided against itself has ever stood for long," urged them to stand by their Confession of 1530, and begged them to protect the religious freedom that had

[42] RP 1597, ff. 542v–543r.
[43] AST 90/23.
[44] RP 1597, ff. 545r–546v.
[45] RP 1597, f. 556r–v. This placard named Hohenburg and Kips, as well as Hochfelder and Theurer. There is no direct evidence to link the clergy to these posters, but the timing is suspicious.

always prevailed in Strasbourg.[46] Too late—the regime had over-
come its divisions and the magistrates had no intention of restricting
religious freedom as they understood it. Margrave Ernst Friedrich
wrote to warn them not to antagonize the Swiss.[47] Too late—the
Swiss had abandoned Strasbourg in the Bishops' War. Domestic
opinion was what counted now.

On the last day of December 1597 the Senate and XXI took up the
tripartite Church Ordinance submitted by their clergy. The first section stated explicitly that new pastors in Strasbourg were examined
for conformity to the Formula of Concord and that the Senate and
XXI did not retain preachers who deviated from it. This statement
was embedded in an account of Strasbourg's church history which
built on the version Johann Marbach had argued against Girolamo
Zanchi in the sixties and against Jean Sturm in the seventies. According to it Strasbourg had been Calvinist (sic) until 1531, when it joined
the Schmalkaldic League, and then Lutheran, particularly after the
Wittenberg Concord of 1536. The committee assigned to read the
draft, only two of whose members had been in the permanent councils when the historical sections of the Formula of Concord had been
rejected in 1577, had gone over this material that very morning and
found it pleasing. Apparently they saw little need to spend much time
on it. The Senate and XXI listened to a reading of the first section,
approved it, and ordered it sent to the printer.[48] There was none of
the delay that followed the submission of synod proposals in 1533
and 1539 and none of the acrimony that had turned discussion of the
city's religious history into pitched battles in the seventies and
eighties. If there was opposition, the secretary, whose sympathies
had been with the so-called Calvinist war party, did not record it.

On January 2 and 4, 1598, the magistrates turned to the rest of the
draft, which covered the liturgy and the duties of the pastors and
included a selection of old mandates, which were not read out to the
Senate and XXI. The committee proposed a few minor changes. The
Senate and XXI then approved this lightly revised draft and dis-
patched the second and third sections to be published.[49] Jost Martin

---

[46]RP 1597, ff. 580r–582r; AST 90/76.

[47]RP 1597, ff. 588r–589r; AST 80/77, 78.

[48]RP 1597, ff. 623v–625v. The committee members were Georg Jacob Bock von
Erleburg, Claus Jacob Wurmser, Heinrich Obrecht, Johann Heinrich Prechter, and Wolfgang Grunenwaldt. Bock and Obrecht had been members of the peace party.

[49]RP 1597, ff. 628r, 629v–630r.

took on the printing, and in March the 375-page *Church Ordinance* came off the presses, complete with the city arms on its title page, and bearing a preface that designated it the approved manual of the Senate and XXI of the Free City of Strasbourg.[50]

The Church Assembly had finally found the opportune moment and the right magistrates to give it what it had long desired. The new Church Ordinance accepted the truth of the clergy's version of the city's history by expressly repudiating the Tetrapolitan Confession of 1530, confirming that Martin Bucer had submitted to Martin Luther in 1536, and insisting that Strasbourg had been faithful to the unaltered Augsburg Confession since 1531. It proclaimed the Formula of Concord to be the correct explanation of that Confession and asserted that the Formula taught nothing new, "but only the same things that the current pastors and their dear predecessors, even Bucer and [his companion in exile Paul] Fagius themselves, had so long taught and preached." The new Ordinance included formal public condemnation of all the Church Assembly's rivals together: the epicureans, the sectarians, the Catholics, and the Calvinists; it even denounced Zanchi and Sturm by name. The Ordinance left no doubt that the city's allegiance was to the orthodox Lutherans.[51] Of course, no mere Church Ordinance could tame the refractory elements in the city's population.[52] But the Protestant dissidents at least were now nothing more than troublesome individuals, incapable of overturning the religious settlement, and as for the Catholics, if the Religious Peace protected them, it also protected the adherents of the Augsburg Confession, to which the city now reaffirmed its allegiance.

The new Church Ordinance built on a whole series of official and unofficial descriptions of the organization and practices of the city's church. It confirmed some very old decisions, already present in the 1534 Church Ordinance: the essentials of pastoral recruitment through election by the parish notables, the importance of baptism and the Lord's Supper, the need to indoctrinate children in their faith, regulations concerning weddings, and the means of policing the country

---

[50]*Kirchenordnung* (Strasbourg, 1598). The preface is dated 14 March 1598; RP 1598, ff. 102r–103r. There was a second printing in 1601 which has a few typographical variants but is otherwise identical to the first edition even in pagination.

[51]*Kirchenordnung*, pp. 12–82; the quoted passage is on pp. 81–82.

[52]For the persistence of dissent see Adam, *Kirchengeschichte* (Strasbourg, 1922), pp. 391–422.

churches by regular inspections. It reprinted some earlier texts *in extenso,* such as the original 1527 condemnation of the sects and a 1534 mandate on the observance of the Sabbath. Traces of decisions taken at synods held in the city in 1533 and 1539 appeared in it, and the 1563 consensus between the pastors and the professors was repeated in full. The sections on liturgy and church organization had grown out of the agenda Marbach had prepared in 1553 and his 1576 description of the Church Assembly, two documents that the magistrates of his day had rejected.[53] The ordinance was nevertheless not entirely a local product, for it also incorporated borrowings from two Württemberg texts of the 1550s.[54] What its authors had done was to draw together the experiences of three generations to give an answer to the questions of the 1520s: this is what we are to believe and this is what we are to do. It was a codification and a monument to the taste of its age, precise, arcane, and verbose.

Like the Wittenberg Concord of 1536, the 1598 text stressed continuity with the past, and in both cases this continuity was suspect. There had been more to the troubles between Wittenberg and Strasbourg in Bucer's day than mutual misunderstanding. Likewise, no matter how many old practices the new ordinance confirmed and no matter how many old texts it reprinted, it was more than a summing up of the past. A reader had only to hold the two church ordinances in hand to catch one major difference between them: the 1598 text was at least ten times the size of the 1534 text. Moreover, for further explanation of their beliefs, it referred the Strasburghers to the Formula of Concord, a document again ten times the length of the Augsburg Confession. Having turned the beautiful early baroque title pages of either the Ordinance or the Formula, the lay Strasburgher would plunge into passages that made little effort to mask the complexities of theology in statements an ordinary man or woman could grasp. Jacob Andreae had said it in 1581: these matters were not within the ken of the laity. The magistrates of the third generation, unlike their fathers and grandfathers, showed no terror at binding their consciences to documents this complex. Perhaps they did it

[53]1534 Church Ordinance, *BDS,* 5:15–41; Synod of 1539, AST 75/52; Marbach's Agenda, AST 200 and a variant copy, AST 201; "Beschrybung der Strassburgischen Kirchen Convents," AST 79/3, ff. 18r–20v.

[54]Adam, *Kirchengeschichte,* p. 358. Nevertheless, the Strasbourg and Württemberg systems differed markedly. For the latter, see James Martin Estes, *Christian Magistrate and State Church: The Reforming Career of Johannes Brenz* (Toronto, 1982), chap. 4.

because they accepted Andreae's arguments that these documents were for the theologians, not the laity.

The descriptions of church government in 1534 and 1598 reflected another important shift in the balance of power between the clergy and the laity. The magistrates had loaded the 1534 Ordinance with devices to keep religious life under lay control. Any Strasburgher who had doubts about what the church taught was to take the problem to a board of five magistrates assisted by two pastors, and if this body could not sort things out the Senate and XXI would take over. Particular stress fell on the powers of the lay church wardens to control the clergy and to discipline parishioners. The office of president of the Church Assembly did not yet exist.

Like the original Church Ordinance the second was issued in the name of the Senate and XXI, although by now a theory of separation of powers had taken hold which undermined the lay supremacy. As the new ordinance remarked, the Strasburghers now believed that there was something wrong with the authorities "when they abandon their own vocation to take over someone else's, for instance when the laity want to be clergymen and rule over the church in a worldly way."[55] The 1598 ordinance made no reference to a lay body explaining doctrine to the confused; the Wiedertäuferherren had been abolished in 1590.[56] Now that settling religious disputes no longer meant hearing out unlettered Anabaptists but instead required the refuting of trained theologians, and now that the norms of orthodoxy were not just Scripture alone, but Scripture, the patristic and conciliar texts (in so far as they agreed with Scripture), the three Creeds, the unaltered Augsburg Confession, and the Formula of Concord, doctrine had become so obviously a matter for specialists that it was unnecessary to say so explicitly.[57]

The new ordinance likewise drew no particular attention to the altered status of the church wardens; indeed it reprinted both the mandate establishing the wardens to police religion and a later mandate confirming the Senate and XXI's resolve to work through them.[58] However, the Ordinance also included a description of the way the Church Assembly disciplined itself and indicated how the clergy had won a role for themselves in the punishment of lay of-

[55]*Kirchenordnung,* pp. 197–98.
[56]RP 1590, f. 7v.
[57]The doctrinal norms are given in the *Kirchenordnung,* pp. 4–11.
[58]Ibid., pp. 318–25, mandates of 1531 and 1539.

fenses. By now the Assembly was pronouncing judgment on sinners and administering public rebukes to hardened sinners.[59] Its president, as the magistrates at last admitted in this Ordinance, did vastly more than preside over meetings. He was the clergy's spokesman and chief censor of his colleagues. He could, if he chose, deal alone with inquiries from foreign churches. The Ordinance confirmed the range of powers acquired by the sixteenth-century presidents without indicating the struggles of the two previous generations of magistrates to limit those powers.[60] All that remained of that effort was the title "president," for Johann Pappus still could not style himself "superintendent." Foreign critics of the new Ordinance recognized the changes and altered the old bugbear of "neues Papsthum" ("new papacy") to "neues Pappusthum" to draw attention to them.[61] Yet the only real innovation was the willingness of the third generation of Strasburghers to put its imprimatur on what had been going on for decades.

To most Strasburghers the Church Ordinance made little difference. The majority, raised in the city, had no quarrel with its contents, most of which they had been hearing in their parish churches since childhood. The hated Calvinists were getting their comeuppance, so the magistrates must have remembered their Christian duty at last. As for all the complications of the Formula of Concord, perhaps it was reassuring to know that the answers to all the tricky questions over which the learned tied themselves in knots were written down somewhere, particularly when it was someone else's responsibility to keep track of them. All that could be left to the professionals. A New Testament and a good clear sermon gave the laity quite enough to think about.[62] Free from the straitjacket of authority in which the clergy had imprisoned themselves, the ordinary Strasburghers could speculate on what interested them and ignore what did not. Those who kept their mouths shut in public could think what they liked, and there was still no law to say an adult had to go to church. The clergy worked hard and lived decently; they created nothing like the scandals the old priests had made. Since they wanted this ordinance, let them have it. The burghers showed no sign of resenting it.

[59]Ibid., pp. 330–36, 194–95. See Chapter 8, below.
[60]*Kirchenordnung*, pp. 282–94, 330.
[61]Adam, *Kirchengeschichte*, p. 368.
[62]Chrisman, *Lay Culture*, pp. 154–55, notes that lay families were more likely to have psalm books or a New Testament than to have a complete Bible.

The magistrates' and commons' acceptance of the great 1598 Church Ordinance had complex roots. The evolution of events outside Strasbourg in the nineties pushed the city into the arms of the Lutherans east of the Rhine. The catastrophes of the decade humbled the magistrates, and they and their lay subjects turned to the clergy for protection from God's manifest wrath. More important still were the clergy's own labors. The acceptance of the Church Ordinance must be recognized as the result of their long and conscientious campaign to bring the magistrates and lay people around to their vision of the reformation. Since the 1520s and 1530s the pastors had pressed for an expansion of their power over the laity, for uniformity in church services, for the condemnation of error, and for the clarification of truth. They had worked away, week in and week out, from their pulpits; they had written books, petitioned magistrates, and taught by example. Their concern to reach the city's youth and working class—children, servants, and apprentices were the only groups the magistrates ordered into church—began to pay dividends by the early eighties, as the disturbances in the streets showed. The people who beat up Johann Faber for criticizing Jean Sturm were Sturm's students, many of them foreigners, and the people who rescued Faber were his own parishioners. The petition of the "sixteen hundred" artisans and laborers in 1581, with its threats against the "Zwinglians," can be taken as another indication of the clergy's penetration of popular values, as can be placards of the Gardeners in 1597. The magistrates were slower to support the Church Assembly, but this is not surprising. Not only were they bearing external pressures in mind, they were much older than the mass of their subjects. In a literal sense they were the "city fathers." A senator might be as young as twenty-five, but the privy councillors who dominated the regime were usually around forty when they joined the still older men already seated in the XV and XIII.[63] Not until the 1590s did privy councillors taught by pastors pushing for the ideals of the second Church Ordinance begin to enter the higher ranks of the regime. When they were there in force—and the turnover in the mid-nineties was without parallel in the sixteenth century—these men speedily granted the Church Assembly much of what it wanted.

Lutheran orthodoxy thus won a satisfying triumph on the official and public level in 1598. The city had, once again, rejoined the

[63]See the preface, note 6, above. Evidence of generational conflict crops up occasionally in the last quarter of the century, for example in the complaints of Daniel Burtsch, a young senator, against the men of the XXI (RP 1589, ff. 640v–641r).

Lutheran mainstream, and it would remain a city with a Lutheran majority until well after its annexation to Catholic France in 1681. For all that, the clergy's campaign to reform Strasbourg was not crowned by total success. The private religion of the Strasburghers, in so far as we can now catch its outline, did not become a copy of the clergy's religion as this was described in the Formula of Concord and the 1598 Church Ordinance. In their beliefs and in their behavior the lay Strasburghers demonstrated their own understanding of the meaning of the reformation.

CHAPTER SEVEN

The Strasburghers' Religion

B y the mid-1530s Strasbourg had become a Protestant city. From the local confessions of faith and church ordinances we can work out what Protestantism meant to the clergy, but the clergy were not representative of the population at large, for even counting the preachers only a handful of people in the city could claim to have mastered orthodox teaching. The majority considered themselves to be "good Protestants," and sources of information about what they meant by this are not scarce, although they are fragmentary; there are no general statements from the laity comparable to the clerical texts. We must try to piece together the laity's religion from a mass of hints and anecdotes, from which we can assemble no more than themes and tendencies.

From the beginning, the lay response to the reformation varied. Some let events roll on without them, ignoring the pastors as once they had ignored the priests. There were parents in Strasbourg who preferred to send their children to unlicensed schoolmasters or schoolmistresses to learn to read and write and count, because the legal parish schools spent too much time on religious instruction.[1] Other families remained loyal to the old church. Still others were caught up in the excitement, like the carpenters who fashioned a portable pulpit for Matthis Zell when the cathedral canons locked him out of Geiler's pulpit, or the men and women who took part in the iconoclastic riots.[2] Some of these people later grew cool toward

[1]AST 372, third foliation, f. 20r-v (1546).
[2]Chrisman, *Strasbourg*, p. 100.

[163]

the new church, for the enthusiasm of the twenties gave way to indifference once the mass was abolished. Among their neighbors were men and women who found sectarian teaching more truthful, or who resisted the Lutheranizing of the Strasbourg church. The majority found an abiding comfort in the new church; in 1547 these men and women filled the square by the city hall, in despair lest their church be taken from them. What united all of them, even the comparatively apathetic, was their insistence on their right to define their own beliefs.

We do the Strasburghers an injustice if we assume that they cared so little for the greatest abstract issues of their day—salvation and morality—that they would accept blindly what the more learned told them, whether the more learned were Catholic priests, Lutheran pastors, Calvinist divines, or sectarian preachers. Just as the peasants of Montaillou in the thirteenth century balanced the rival claims of Catholics and Cathars to construct interpretations of their own, so the Strasburghers in the sixteenth century heard out a welter of conflicting opinions and arrived at their own conclusions.[3] As organized dissent in the city ebbed, the majority's conclusions increasingly reflected their pastors' teachings.

In 1530 an Alsatian nobleman, a Zorn von Plobsheim, wanted to read the Bible. Luther's translation was not complete and apparently he could not obtain one of the older vernacular Bibles. He took what he could from Luther: the Pentateuch, the historical and poetical books, and the Gospel; he purchased a copy of the translation of the Prophets done by the Anabaptists Hans Denck and Ludwig Hetzer; he added the translation of the Apocrypha done by Zwingli's friend Leo Jud. Then, with a fine disregard for the theological differences of his translators, he had the separate parts bound together and sat down to read it all for himself.[4] A generation later Johann Marbach complained about printers in Strasbourg who published hymnals in which they mingled Schwenckfeldian and Anabaptist hymns with Lutheran chorales.[5] Throughout the century the city's residents continued to pick, to mix, and to choose. Daniel Sudermann described his religious evolution: "First I was a Catholic [in Liège]. But soon, in 1558, I went to the Calvinist school. I attended Lutheran services as

---

[3]Emmanuel LeRoy Ladurie, *Montaillou, village d'Occitan* (Paris, 1975).
[4]The Bible is now in the BNUS, R 10087. See Peter, "Les groupes informels," pp. 194–212.
[5]RP 1576, ff. 632r–637v.

well. Heard the Anabaptists. In 1594 I came to understand the truth."[6] Sudermann was forty-four when he came to his truth, the teachings of Caspar Schwenckfeld.

Few Strasburghers set down their experiences even as summarily as did Sudermann. All of them, if they had curiosity and a modicum of courage, could expose themselves to as many ideas as he did without leaving their own territory. Imagine walking through the city on any Sunday in the middle thirty years of the century. In a parish church we find the Lutherans at prayer. Walk down another street and we hear refugees singing Clement Marot's translations of the Psalms. Look quickly and we catch someone slipping off to hear mass. Follow another person and we end up in a forest clearing, listening to someone read Scripture to a gathering of Anabaptists. With good social connections we might gain entry to a private home where Schwenckfeld's ideas are discussed. If it is a fine day we shall certainly see people neglecting all these possibilities to idle in the sunshine of the marketplaces.[7]

A small but significant minority of the population rejected the established church to join one of its rivals. How many dissenters? Impossible to say, for dissent was not limited to confessional differences. The maidservant who made love to the manservant without the pastor's blessing rebelled against official teaching as surely as did the Anabaptist on trial for heresy or their neighbor who preferred a Sunday stroll to a church service. The old woman who did go to church and, leaving it uncomforted, went home to hang herself, had also rejected the official explanation of the meaning of life.[8] This sort of dissent escapes quantification. Of dissenters in the more usual sense of the word we can count a few hundred Catholics, several hundred sectarians, and a few hundred more Calvinists, the latter rarely natives. The combined total is not high when set in the context of three generations in a city of more than 20,000 people, but these people had an impact on the reformation out of all proportion to their numbers.

The majority of Strasburghers, whether they went regularly to church or turned to the clergy only for baptisms, marriages, and

[6]Hans Horning, *Daniel Sudermann als Handschriftensammler: Ein Beitrag zur strassburger Bibliothekgeschichte* (Tübingen, 1956), p. 23. Sudermann worked for the Cathedral canons; he lived in the city from 1585 to 1596 and from 1597 until his death, c. 1631.

[7] It was this latter sort who caught the eye of a clergyman from St. Thomas on an October Sunday in 1552 (AST 84/65).

[8]RP 1572, f. 98v.

funerals, counted themselves members of the established church. These are the people about whose religious lives we know least. Unlike the dissenters, the orthodox did not have occasion to give accounts of their beliefs before record-keeping bodies.[9] The easiest way to approach them is to begin with the external framework the clergy created for their lives. From there we can review evidence about prevalent beliefs not necessarily spelled out in confessions and church ordinances, like superstition and bigotry, then turn to the men who ruled Strasbourg and left in their records our most comprehensive picture of lay values.

The orthodox had no difficulty in meeting whatever need they felt for public worship.[10] Every morning at five o'clock in summer and six o'clock in winter the assistant pastors of the seven parishes held a short early service with prayers and a half-hour exhortation to piety. At eight or nine the cathedral preacher gave a sermon on a Biblical text, working his way through the Testaments according to an annual schedule, and there was another daily service in the cathedral in the late afternoon. On Sunday morning there was an early service in each parish, intended for servants in particular; they could hear the word of God and then return to mind the house while their employers attended the longer second service, or *Amptpredig,* which was the central weekly service in each parish. In the second half of the century it began with an organ recital and hymn singing by the congregation.[11] Standing before the altar, the pastor then led his parishioners in a general confession of sins, reminding them of God's mercy and forgiveness, and reciting other prayers with them. This was followed by more singing before the pastor moved to his pulpit to join the congregation in a silent recitation of the Lord's Prayer. He then announced his text and preached for about an hour. After this came prayers for the well-being of the congregation as a whole and also for particular members, for example, the sick. Another round of

[9]Their neighbors in the rural territories, however, were scrutinized almost annually by visitors representing the Church Assembly and the Senate and XXI. The records of these inspections leave little doubt about the success of Lutheran ideas among the peasants. See James M. Kittelson, "Successes and Failures in the German Reformation: The Report from Strasbourg," *ARG,* 73 (1982), 153–75.

[10]What follows is based on the 1534 and 1598 Church Ordinances, the decisions of the Synod of 1539, and Marbach's Agenda of 1553. See Chapter 6, note 53. For the evolution of the services see Bornert, *La réforme protestante.*

[11]Chrisman, *Lay Culture,* pp. 154–55, 166, notes that hymnals were among the books most likely to be owned by the laity. She argues that it was through the Psalms that the laity absorbed much of their Biblical knowledge.

singing and a blessing completed the service, which ended with a final organ recital. Four times in the year this Amptpredig was given over to a review of parts of the catechism. At noon on Sunday those avid for instruction could take part in a second service at the cathedral and even return there for a third in the early evening. Meanwhile, in the afternoon catechism classes had been held in each parish for the youngsters. Special services of prayer and penance were held every Tuesday, once a month there was a half-holiday for these exercises, and four times a year a full day was given over to them.

The sacraments naturally had a place of their own. Parishioners could take communion every Sunday in the cathedral, fortnightly or monthly in the other parishes, and in all the churches on Easter Sunday, Whitsunday, Christmas Day, and New Year's Day. They were urged to attend a preparatory service the preceding Saturday evening, at which their pastors reminded them of the importance of the sacrament, and went through the long list of those who should exclude themselves or be excluded as unworthy. Those wishing to do so—and the practice was encouraged—could remain for further in-struction and for a voluntary private confession of sin. The other sacrament was baptism, and like the Lord's Supper, it was intended to be communal. A child's father was to arrange it with his pastor in advance, which gave the pastor an opportunity to veto unsuitable godparents. The clergy admonished parents not to pick sponsors on "worldly" grounds (for example, to establish a connection with a powerful family), but to choose pious members of the church who would help to ensure that the child received a Christian education. In an emergency a child could be baptized at home and even in the absence of a clergyman. When this happened the child was to be brought before the congregation later, not for rebaptism, but for the public prayers that acknowledged its membership in the visible church.

Marriage was no sacrament, but it remained a religious as well as a secular act and again a public one. When people whom the pastor did not know presented themselves, he had the right to examine them on their beliefs. Reading out the banns to the rest of the congregation reinforced the social nature of the contract.

Encouraged by their doctors to turn to the clergy for help, the sick and dying readily did so.[12] Pastors came into their homes to offer

[12]This made the clergy particularly vulnerable to death from contagious diseases; see Kintz, *La société*, p. 158.

them the Lord's Supper and to pray with them, and also commended their cases to their congregations for public prayer. Johann Marbach was called to Jacob Sturm's deathbed in 1553; he found the Stettmeister unable to talk, but fully conscious. Marbach stayed with him to the end, reading to him from the Gospel according to Saint John.[13] Funeral services were kept brief and were devoted to strengthening the living. In exceptional cases, when the deceased was an adult whose life the preacher could praise without hypocrisy, a short eulogy might be given. The pastors could, and did, refuse to conduct any service at all for dissidents.

For young Strasburghers the clergy offered a special Sunday service at which girls and boys were drilled on the fundamentals of their faith.[14] The 1534 Church Ordinance specified that they were to learn the articles of faith, the Lord's Prayer, and the Ten Commandments. Many of the pastors of the first generation developed their own catechisms for this purpose. Johann Marbach slowly imposed a slightly modified version of Luther's shorter catechism, not on doctrinal grounds, but because he found children absorbed and retained their lessons best from it. Parents or guardians, masters, and teachers were obliged by law to get their charges to these lessons; the older children and young adults were particularly recalcitrant. Many of the pastors instituted special prizes for diligent students. In 1551 Christoff Kolöffel, who was then eleven, recited his whole catechism before the congregation, along with twenty-eight other youngsters. Each of them got a new Strasbourg penny; children in other parishes might get a little book instead.[15] The city schools emphasized religious training, including instruction in hymn singing. Pious parents could supplement all this with home instruction, and books were available to help them. One local manual recommended that family Bible readings be held four times daily.[16] By the time children were ready to take communion for the first time, the pastors could reasonably expect them to understand the elements of their faith.[17] It is likely that most of the children brought up in the city did, although there was no guarantee that all this indoctrination would remain alive in the child's mind.

---

[13]AST 198, ff. 100r–101r.
[14]Ernst and Adam, *Katechetische Geschichte des Elsasses*.
[15]Kolöffel's recollections, BNUS ms. 847, f. 18r. Nicolas Florus, *Kurtze und einseltige Auslegung des 91 Psalmen* (Strasbourg, 1576), p. 5; AST 198, f. 123v.
[16]*Tischgebete für die Kinder* (Strasbourg, 1557), sig. A iii recto.
[17]Kessler, *Kurtz Examen*, gives a good example of what was expected.

Through sermons, books, private instruction, and catechizing, the clergy devoted endless energy to educating their flocks. Much of the effort may have been wasted initially since many Strasburghers, from the magistrates on down the social scale, remained vague about the tenets of their faith. In 1534 the XVer Peter Sturm told his fellow magistrates that he was too preoccupied with official business to know what he believed, and declined to express any opinion about the Tetrapolitan Confession; his colleagues were equally unsure of themselves.[18] Admittedly a formal confession of faith would be daunting to non-theologians, and Sturm's successors in the second generation regularly expressed a distaste for reading theological arguments.[19] Other Strasburghers showed an equal incomprehension of much simpler material, and comments in the parish registers of the 1560s identify people unable to answer even the most basic questions about their faith. Parishioners turned up who could not recite the Lord's Prayer or the Ten Commandments, and men and women who remembered parts of their catechism in adulthood were evasive when asked about the Lord's Supper.[20] The last phenomenon may be a reflection of the eucharistic controversies and the theologians' own confusions, but after 1536 the clergy in Strasbourg had a simple enough formula to teach the laity: they truly received Christ's true body and true blood. Understanding that formula might cause problems, but surely remembering it should have been no great strain.

The much-praised educational system in Strasbourg obviously had its gaps and failings. One man told his pastor in 1587 that he had never taken communion because his parents had died when he was young and he had had no one to instruct him.[21] Yet this man was probably an oddity among the people raised in the city; by the 1570s clerical complaints about ignorance were already on the wane. Either the massive campaign of indoctrination was working, or the clergy were giving up. The clergy's increasing insistence that theological expertise was theirs alone may suggest that they were lessening their demands on the laity. After all, Martin Luther himself had advised in his *Large Catechism* that the clergy should be satisfied if the unlearned mastered the Creed, the Commandments, and the Lord's Prayer. Geiler von Kaysersberg, another reformer beaten down by lay ob-

---

[18]*TAE*, vol. 2, no. 523.
[19]AST 55/3, f. 26r (1563); RP 1563, ff. 396v–397r.
[20]AMS N26, pp. 309, 393 (1563), and p. 469 (1565).
[21]AMS N30, f. 11v.

duracy, had arrived at the same conclusion a generation before.[22] Nothing suggests that the clergy had given up inculcating these rudiments of the Christian faith, and there was nothing to make them stop complaining if they were failing in this. The laity may not have believed what they were taught, but at least they had come to know what they were supposed to believe.

One old lesson that continued to be pounded home was that of God's power. Both natural and man-made disasters—fires, floods, bad harvests, plagues, wars, defeats—were set down to the operation of God's wrath. For example, Pastor Nicolas Florus, commenting on the Hundred and Thirty-Seventh Psalm ("By the Waters of Babylon"), explained that the Jews had been subjected to the anguish of exile for neglecting their religious duties and that this sort of calamity could be visited on the Germans just as easily. The magistrates sounded similar themes in the preambles to their statutes.[23] Both sets of authorities argued that God operated on a theory of collective responsibility, so that the sins of the few could result in divine punishment for the whole city.[24] When disaster threatened, the first reflex was supposed to be toward prayer and repentance; the greater the danger, the greater was the need for collective atonement and improvement. It was not always forthcoming, as the stream of complaints about frivolous, worldly behavior during the Schmalkaldic War and Interim crisis showed.[25] To balance the fear of God's power, the clergy also emphasized his love for his people. Good harvests, healthy babies, and most of all, the promise of salvation, demonstrated this. Release from danger was to be celebrated by prayers of thanksgiving.[26] Whether individual Strasburghers were more impressed by God's love or by his wrath cannot be known. What is clear is that they believed he intervened directly in their collective and personal lives.

They also believed in the Devil, and some of them were willing to risk their souls by consulting his agents. Strasbourg had its "warsager" or soothsayers who could find lost or stolen objects and who

---

[22]Tappert, trans. and ed., *The Book of Concord*, p. 362; Schmidt, *Histoire littéraire*, 1:423.
[23]*Der CXXXVII Psalm* (Strasbourg, 1587), sig. Bii verso and Biv verso; BNUS ms. 39.894, "Christliche Errinerung eines erbarn Rhats," 1585.
[24]RP 1540, f. 273v; AST 80/39 (1541); RP 1546, f. 618v; RP 1547, ff. 178v–183v; RP 1564, ff. 418v–419r; RP 1566, f. 270v.
[25]For example, RP 1546, ff. 299v, 334v, 393v–394v, 460r, 561r–v; RP 1547, ff. 35r–v, 78v, 248v, 250v, 293r.
[26]RP 1571, f. 1010v, on the news of the Christian victory at Lepanto. Kintz, *La société*, pp. 219–21, on childbirth.

claimed to know what was going on miles away or in the future. One of these was Batt Ott, reputed to have been a priest in the city before the reformation, and in and out of it thereafter, attracting a large clientele, particularly among the country folk who had moved into town. Pastors and magistrates agreed he was involved in the Devil's business. The clergy preached against this kind of divination and banned its practitioners and their clients, while the magistrates threw Ott out and absolutely forbade their subjects to consult anyone like him.[27] Measures like these did not put an end to the thirst for illicit knowledge, particularly about the course of the future, and throughout the century Strasburghers sought out any books of prophecies and "Prognostications" which escaped the censors.[28] The warsager Ott was stopped, but others replaced him, some of whom also claimed to be healers. Their activities shaded into black magic and witchcraft in the authorities' judgment.[29]

Accusations of witchcraft and sorcery begin to occur in the city records in the early 1560s. Peter Aller's wife was thought to be a witch because of her quarrelsome disposition. A woman was burned in 1564—the first execution in a long time, according to the chronicler who recorded it. In 1579 a woman in the Krutenau district was supposed to have laid a spell on her husband, filling his body with chopped straw; she too was burned. Two years later, as a result of neighbors' complaints, the magistrates burned another woman from the same quarter. There were more executions in 1581, 1587, and 1588, around the time Johann Fischart translated and published Jean Bodin's *Demonomania*. In 1593 several people were in prison awaiting judgment on charges of witchcraft.[30] The magistrates did not always believe the evidence submitted to them.[31] They also made some

[27]Specklin, "Collectanées," no. 2364; AMS R3, f. 255v (1537); RP 1544, ff. 334v–335r, 408r, 411r; Kessler, *Kurtz Examen,* sigs. Bvii recto–Bviii verso.

[28]Otto Brunfels, *Almanach . . . von dem xxvj Jar an, bitz zuo Endt der Welt* (Strasbourg, 1526); Anon., *Alle alten Propheceien von keyserlich Maiestat* (Strasbourg, n.d.); Johann Carion, *Practica und Prognostication* (Strasbourg, 1545). The list could be expanded, for example by the inclusion of astrological tracts.

[29]RP 1556, ff. 187v, 189r; RP 1566, f. 528r; AST 67/II, ff. 14v–17v (1566); AST 67/III, ff. 46v–48r (1567); RP 1568, f. 91r.

[30]For Aller's wife, RP 1562, f. 255r–v; Büheler, "La chronique," nos. 415 (1564) and 539, for the second execution in the Krutenau; Specklin, "Collectanées," no. 2504 (1579), Léon Dacheux, ed., "Fragments de diverses vieilles chroniques," *BSCMHA,* n.s. 18 (1898), no. 4078; BNUS ms. 998, pp. 130–31 (1593). Fischart's translation went through three local editions between 1581 and 1591.

[31]For example, RP 1569, f. 777r–v, and RP 1585, f. 336v.

effort to keep stories about the Devil, witches, and magic out of their subjects' hands. In 1533 they refused to allow a printer to bring out a tale about an appearance by the Devil in nearby Schiltigheim. Thirty years later they ordered Diebolt Berger not to print a song about a witch burned in the county of Helffenstein. In 1587 they rejected a book about Faust on the grounds that the young people were already too much interested in the black arts and such a book would only lead more astray.[32]

Official prohibitions did little good when both the magistrates' executions and the clergy's sermons confirmed the reality of the Devil and his works. The sense of malign powers brooding over vulnerable humans is brilliantly evoked in Hans Baldung Grien's spare and haunting print, "The Stable-hand Bewitched." There he lies, toppled on his back, his feet toward us, his face partially concealed, struck down. Behind him the horse in his care half turns its head to eye him uneasily. We look to find the cause of his destruction and there, at the side, peering through the small stable window, is the dreadful face of the crone who ruined him, Satan's agent.[33]

Like the warsager and the witches, strange visionaries and prophets found a following in the city, despite official condemnation. Melchior Hofmann, Clemens Ziegler, Lienhard and Ursula Jost all had connections with the sectarians, but there were also independent figures, such as Martin Steinbach.[34] Steinbach was an illiterate cooper from Sélestat who claimed to be the Holy Ghost, the prophet Elias, and a light of truth. His disclosures were more than a little obscure, even to his followers, yet he did attract both men and women, and according to a chronicler his sect's articles got into print. Pastor Matthis Negelin considered the Steinbachians enough of a problem to write a book against them.

Some Strasburghers thus showed a taste for special revelations, and

---

[32]Brant, "Annales," no. 3579; RP 1563, f. 382v; RP 1587, f. 615v. Stephen Nelson is preparing a study of religion, magic, and science in early modern Strasbourg.

[33]Reproduced in Bernhard, *Hans Baldung Grien*, p. 76. Robert Heitz comments on Baldung's work: "Dans son esprit croupit tout un monde de mythes et de fantasmes, de surnaturel et de magique qui ne demande qu'à se réveiller," *La peinture en Alsace* (Strasbourg, 1975), p. 38. Baldung sat on the Senate in 1545.

[34]For Hofmann, Ziegler, and the Josts, see *TAE*, passim; AST 76/45; and AST 166, pp. 300–303. On Steinbach, RP 1544, f. 176r-v; RP 1545, f. 464r; RP 1549, f. 63v; RP 1551, ff. 263v, 279v–280r; RP 1553, f. 95r; RP 1566, ff. 172v–173r, 263v; AST 45, f. 501v; AST 176, f. 379r-v; AMS I/14, ff. 34v–38v; Specklin, "Collectanées," no. 2450. Reinhard Lutz, *Verzaichnus . . . der kaetzerischen, und verdampten Leer Martin Steinbachs . . .* (Strasbourg, 1566).

there was a widespread fascination with the Biblical prophets and the Apocalypse. The magistrates discouraged sermons on these matters but their preachers went ahead, whether out of their own interest or to pre-empt or refute false exegetes. In 1568 Melchior Speccer published a commentary on Matthew 14 and more particularly on the second coming. It drew a great deal of its color from the Revelation and from the early modern fascination with monstrous and deformed infants.[35] A few years later Johann Marbach took a rather different tack in *On Miracles and Miraculous Signs*.[36] In it Marbach attacked Jesuit propaganda about miracles and exorcisms; the book was addressed to the people of Bavaria and Augsburg, but could also have been used against doubts Catholic migrants to Strasbourg might plant in Lutheran minds. What particularly worried the president was the effect of the Jesuit claim that while Catholics still experienced miracles, the Lutherans had not produced a single one in fifty years. Marbach first hinted broadly and then announced flatly that Father Peter Canisius's success as an exorcist should be attributed to the Devil's collusion. Against this sort of wickedness Marbach flourished the Lutheran miracles: the exposure of Antichrist and the destruction of the papacy; the "wonderful" reception of Luther's teaching; the translation of the Bible. Marbach might have described this as fighting superstition with true religion, but it was perhaps not very effective against the Strasburghers' craving for horrors, supernatural tales, and visible manifestations of God and the Devil.

Heterodoxy and orthodoxy coexisted; indeed they were mutually reinforcing. Burghers who never met a false prophet or a witch—to say nothing of God or the Devil—learned about them from the preachers. The effort to teach correct attitudes by describing and condemning error could backfire when it stimulated curiosity and speculation. This was as true of superstition as it was of heresy. The Strasburghers did have other sources of information (one another, travelers, immigrants, books, pamphlets, and broadsides), but paradoxically the Church Assembly itself was the channel through which many of them learned ideas neither the clergy nor the magistrates wanted them to endorse. Caspar Hedio told a story of a magus who met a peasant hauling wood to the Kreuznach market. The magus ate the peasant, his horse, his cart, and his wood, although on another

---

[35]AST 75/52, f. 761r; Speccer, *Auslegung des Evangelii Matthei am XIV Capitel* (Strasbourg, 1568). The book is clearly intended for a lay audience.
[36]*Von Mirackeln und Wunderzeichen* (Strasbourg, 1571).

occasion he had trouble digesting a man in armor and had to spit him out again. Probably the armor was the whole armor of God, but as the tale has come down to us it sounds as likely to have enhanced the reputation of the Devil's agents as to have fostered trust in God.[37] Superstition and orthodoxy are notoriously hard to separate, and the Strasburghers' religion certainly contained a good dollop of the former.

Historians have made much of the Strasburghers' toleration for those whose views were unorthodox in the confessional sense—the relatively lenient treatment of sectarians, the willingness to allow Catholics to live in the city, and the charity shown to Calvinist refugees.[38] This toleration was real, but limited, since official policy and public opinion tolerated individuals, rather than faiths. The non-Lutheran denominations were all condemned, and the Strasburghers' religion was heavily tinged by this. For many people the confessional debates reduced themselves to automatic attacks on abstract labels like "popery," fed by the century's gift for scurrilous invective on the order of "Jesu-wider."[39] For the illiterate, pictures told the tale. In the early days there were woodcuts depicting the pope as Antichrist, as mercenary, or riding on the seven-headed beast of Revelation in the company of the Great Whore. In 1577 Tobias Stimmer did a woodcut, which also carried verses by Johann Fischart, showing "The Weird and Grotesque Mill" which ground up priests and exposed their kernels: monsters and demons.[40] Lutheran congregations sang battle hymns against the Catholics:

> From false lips does their talk proceed,
> From disunited hearts,
> Their doctrine's empty, baseless creed,
> Which gives the conscience smarts;
> With purgatory, absolution, mass
> And ban, the world misled it has.[41]

[37]Johannes Janssen, *History of the German People at the Close of the Middle Ages,* trans. M. A. Mitchell and A. M. Christie, 16 vols. (London, 1896–1925), 12:365.

[38]See Chap. 3, note 44, above.

[39]For example, Johannes Fischart, *Nacht Rab oder Nebelkraeh* (Strasbourg, 1570).

[40]R. W. Schribner, *For the Sake of Simple Folk: Popular Propaganda in the German Reformation* (Cambridge, 1981), pp. 94, 71, 161, and illustrations 78 and 131.

[41]Janssen, *History of the German People,* 11:290, quoting hymnbooks of 1562 and 1566. Büheler, "La chronique," gives the texts of secular anti-Catholic songs from the Interim crisis, pp. 363–69. The manuscript "Stedel" chronicle in the Musée historique de la ville de Strasbourg gives others: pp. 328–45, 345–46, and a third from 1584, pp. 652–53.

Peter Canisius, who was in Strasbourg around the middle of the century, described a play performed in the Latin school, which dealt with a man made ill by swallowing Catholic ideas, and cured by vomiting up Catholic objects of worship.[42] Catholics were not the only victims of these attacks; the Lutheran clergy habitually referred to Caspar Schwenckfeld as "Stenckfeld."[43] As Katherine Zell noted, what was lacking in all of this was any sense of Christian charity.[44] The Lutheran clergy undoubtedly felt themselves under siege in Strasbourg in the second generation and tried to develop a fortress mentality in their congregations.[45] To some extent it worked. Lambert Daneau, a professor of theology in Geneva en route to Leiden with his family in mid-winter 1582, described his arrival in the city at sundown, in a driving rainstorm. Inn after inn turned him away. When ammeister Michael Lichtensteiger was told of the family's plight he refused to help. Some of Jean Sturm's students finally found an inn where the pastors' writ against the Calvinists did not run, but in the morning Lichtensteiger hauled Daneau in and browbeat him at length.[46] The anti-Catholic and anti-Calvinist demonstrations of, for example, 1559 and 1581 reveal a current in the Strasburghers' religion far removed from toleration, but likewise part of their sense of being Lutheran.[47]

To move deeper into the meaning of Lutheranism for sixteenth-century Strasburghers we need to find a sample of lay people who left a regular record of their reactions to the reformation. The only group that did so were the members of the Senate and XXI. Using them as a sample of the lay majority raises difficulties, because the magistrates were not typical. They were older, better educated, more sophisticated, and wealthier than their subjects, and all were men. Yet the magistrates' opinions, taken in their eighty-year sweep, can serve as a

[42]Janssen, *History of the German People,* 13:182–83.

[43]AST 180/53, ff. 575r–634r, Marbach's six sermons against "Stenckfeld" (1556).

[44]*Ein Brieff,* sig. M ii recto, D iv recto-verso, and E i recto-verso.

[45]AST 100, unnumbered piece (1579), a sermon preached by Johann Liptitz on holding to the true faith.

[46]AST 100, unnumbered piece, "Lambertus Danaeus in Apologia adversus Doct. Jacobum Andreae."

[47]Little has been written about this side of the reformation, but see Nikolaus Paulus, *Protestantismus und Toleranz im 16. Jahrhundert* (Freiburg im Breisgau, 1911) and "La liberté de conscience et les professeurs du séminaire protestant de Strasbourg au 16e siècle," *Revue catholique d'Alsace,* 9 (1890), 108–21, 158–61, 200–212. For another result of intolerance, see the account of the disagreeable last days of St. Nicholas-in-undis in Marie-Théodore de Bussière, *Histoire des religieuses dominicaines du couvent de Sainte Marguerite et Sainte Agnès à Strasbourg* (Strasbourg, 1860).

[175]

guide to the lay understanding of the reformation. In the 1520s the magistrates were outpaced by early converts to the new faith; in the late forties and toward the end of the century they stepped ahead of their subjects by negotiating with Catholics and Calvinists. In each case they worked themselves back closer to popular opinion in about a decade.

Like their subjects, the rulers of Strasbourg were not all Lutheran (see Appendix A). Some, like Ludwig Wolff von Renchen, Adolff Braun, and Wolf Sigismund Wurmser, remained Catholic. Others adopted a Protestant position, but set their own interpretation on it. Jacob Sturm seems to have leaned toward Schwenckfeld, and Michael Theurer made no secret of his admiration for the Silesian. Jacob Wetzel von Marsilien was fascinated by the Anabaptists, but he may well have been Catholic like other members of his family. A very few of the magistrates accused of Calvinism had some inclination to the Genevan faith; Josias Rihel always refused to condemn it. Adolff Braun was never re-elected to the Senate after the discovery that he had circulated a Jesuit attack on Johann Marbach in the city, and Wetzel was dismissed from the XV as a result of difficulties more constitutional than religious. The others had normal, even illustrious, careers. All of them managed to work effectively with their Lutheran colleagues, just as their heterodox subjects managed to coexist with the Lutheran majority.

Again, like their subjects, the magistrates were not all, or not always, consistent. Nicolas Fuchs was a determined advocate of pro-Calvinist foreign policies; Jacob von Molsheim and Michael Lichtensteiger were equally adamant in their support for the Formula of Concord and its condemnation of Calvinism. On the other hand, many of their colleagues slid into contradictions. Johann Carl Lorcher voted against the Calvinists one month and against the Lutherans another. The passage of time changed the opinions of other men, banking the enthusiasm of one and kindling that of another. Claus Kniebis had led the militant evangelical faction in the twenties, but by 1547 he rejected the idea of prolonging the Schmalkaldic War. His contemporary, Martin Betschold, had been slow to accept the Protestant preachers, but in 1546 he urged the passage of two of their most cherished projects, a uniform liturgy and a means to examine parishioners on their beliefs.

Individually and as a corporation, the magistrates of Strasbourg proclaimed themselves to be Christian. Very early, perhaps by 1524 and certainly by 1526, the majority of them had become evangelicals. After 1529, when they abolished the mass, they consistently defended the Protestant cause, committing themselves and their city again and again to the Augsburg Confession. Twice, in 1546 and in 1592, they went to war for it. Between these wars they pursued an aggressive foreign policy that challenged the Habsburg plans for Europe. Defeat in the Schmalkaldic War did not blunt their resolve to fight the Catholic powers where and how they might. Their links with the Huguenots brought them the suspicion of Lutherans east of the Rhine and the constant menace of French siege and conquest. Still they persisted. For the Protestant cause they would risk their autonomy and prosperity.

What was this Protestantism that meant so much to them? It was the accomplishment of God's will, for the magistrates were no less convinced than were their clergy that their own way was God's way. In their public statements they stressed their desire to advance the honor of God, a theme which recurs as the justification for their policies in their 1527 mandate against the sects, in a 1559 address to the guilds, a 1568 blasphemy statute, and the 1597 condemnation of Calvinism.[48] The explanation was no empty rhetorical flourish, but the accurate expression of one of their deepest convictions.

A sincere piety informed the magistrates' discharge of their responsibilities. In 1564 Johann Schenckbecher set down this prayer in his diary: "On the sixteenth of September the Council of XV elected me to replace the late Diebolt Gerfalck on that council. May our beneficent and merciful God grant that I may fill this office for the praise and honor of his holy name, for the succor of many people, and the salvation of my soul."[49] The following year Hans Hammerer said much the same thing to his colleagues on being elected Ammeister: "Since it has pleased God almighty to put me in this office this year, I want to pray to him that he will lend me his divine grace and wisdom, so that I may the better fulfill my task."[50] As they were in the privacy of their chambers, so they were in public. The annual Schwörtag ceremony closed with the oligarchs joining the burghers in a prayer for divine guidance. Every year on the day following the Schwörtag the magistrates invited their subjects to a special church

---

[48] *TAE*, vol. 1, no. 92; AMS IV/48/31; BNUS R22, part 12; AST 84/113.
[49] AST 1655, f. 31r. Compare f. 55v, a similar reaction to his election to the XIII in 1575.
[50] RP 1565, f. 1v.

service where all those present solemnly repeated this appeal.[51] At regular intervals throughout the year they authorized special prayer days to implore God to grant protection to the city. Likewise they called for special public prayers during their most difficult enterprises; Jacob Sturm personally requested such a service before the Catholic-Protestant colloquy at Worms.[52]

The magistrates' religion was not the increasingly convoluted doctrinal edifice the Lutheran clergy in and out of Strasbourg constructed in the sixteenth century. Eventually they approved that edifice, for sooner or later they always bowed to the clergy's technical competence and accepted their theological judgments. But they accepted precise statements of doctrine more because these statements were politically expedient and might settle quarrels than because they thought precision necessary to salvation. Their attitude was rather like that of someone who admires a beautifully detailed topographic map, indicating every feature on the road from one place to another, but who travels that road guided only by a bare sketch on a scrap of paper. It took the framers of the Book of Concord hundreds of pages to lay down the essence of their version of the Christian faith. The magistrates regularly did it in a paragraph.

In 1529, fully nine months after they had abolished the mass, the members of the Senate and XXI summed up the "principle parts of our true Christian faith, necessary to the soul's salvation, as: That Almighty God, out of his love for mankind, sent his beloved only-begotten son, our Lord Jesus Christ, into this world. While truly divine, he took on a human nature. He died for us and rose again for our justification."[53] The magistrates wanted a faith that they themselves could understand. Carl Mieg said it about the Tetrapolitan Confession in 1534: "I hope that as a layman, I won't be trapped into something I don't understand and then forced to confess and believe it." Barthel Keller said it about the Formula of Concord a generation later: "This is over my head and I am reluctant to bind my conscience to it."[54] The Formula was finally accepted by another generation of magistrates, but by then it had been presented by Jacob Andreae as something not for the laity to master. For themselves, the magistrates preferred creeds to confessions.

[51] AST 80/35 (1539); 80/40 (1544).

[52] RP 1540, ff. 378v–380v.

[53] *PC,* vol. 1, no. 682, instructions for the negotiators sent to Schmalkald. Compare no. 718, instructions for delegates to the Augsburg Reichstag of 1530.

[54] *TAE,* vol. 2, no. 523; RP 1577, ff. 725v–732v.

Very few members of the Senate and XXI discussed their personal beliefs before their colleagues, but statements by a Catholic, Adolff Braun, by a possible Calvinist, Josias Rihel, and by the probably Lutheran Wolfgang Schütterlin have survived. Braun said: I subscribe to the Old and New Testaments and to the Apostles', Nicean, and Athanasian Creeds. I was saved by the unique sacrifice of Jesus Christ, the son of God and Man. Of the sacraments I believe what Scripture tells us.[55] Braun was bending over backward to be accommodating. The Protestant Schütterlin, under no such pressure, was scarcely more forthcoming: I learned my catechism here in the St. Lawrence chapel (that is, from Matthis Zell), he began, and I stand by it. I am neither Zwinglian, Calvinist, nor Lutheran, for I follow Christ who saved me. I believe in the teachings of the Christian faith, simple and unbeclouded. I believe that God created me, that Christ saved me, and that the Holy Ghost leads us to the truth. I was baptized in the name of the Trinity. Of the sacraments I believe what every Christian can and should believe from God's Word.[56] Rihel echoed Schütterlin's story: I was born into a Christian, evangelical family and brought up to be the opponent of error. I learned my worthlessness from the Ten Commandments, my salvation and sanctification from the articles of faith, take my comfort and resolution from hearing God's word and receiving the sacraments. Let people pin what party label on me they will, I recognize no name but Christian.[57]

What is striking is that these statements are so simple that they are interchangeable. Except for the biographical details, Rihel could have used Schütterlin's words, or Schütterlin Braun's. In the last third of the sixteenth century a Catholic, a probable Lutheran, and a possible Calvinist all chose to express their faith in the broadest possible terms. They might just as well have stood up and recited the Apostles' Creed. They had faithfully reproduced the content of the Senate and XXI's 1529 statement on the essentials of Christianity, and their fellow magistrates found their explanations quite adequate. There was no close questioning, no attempt to pin a colleague down and force precision on him. They all agreed on the essentials, and it was better to stop there than to push on to the areas where they disagreed.

Jacob Sturm was perhaps the only magistrate of the first generation to appreciate the subtleties of the doctrines in dispute, and he was

[55]AST 100, unnumbered piece (1570).
[56]RP 1577, f. 357r-v.
[57]AST 326/22 (1595).

well aware that his colleagues did not share his interest. As he said in 1534, they could not be expected to sit through a reading of the Tetrapolitan Confession, nor to remember what was at the beginning if they did reach the end. Sturm wanted his colleagues to vote on the Confession and wanted them to vote intelligently, so he proposed that each man take home a copy and study it for a week. The result demonstrated that his colleagues were not prepared to turn themselves into theologians. The XIIIer Jacob Meyer, the XVer Hans von Blumenau, and Stettmeister Philips von Kageneck said that they would accept any decision reached by the majority. Carl Mieg hoped things would be kept simple, while Peter Sturm, Jacob's brother, dodged the question and said only that the preachers' sermons were too violent.[58] This same sort of attitude would crop up again in the next generation, for example in Johann Carl Lorcher's refusal to read the whole Formula of Concord because it was too long and too complicated.[59]

This distaste for theology should not be construed as an indifference to religion or willful ignorance of the ideas in the Bible, since the magistrates could quote Scripture to their purposes. Senator Nicolas Götz retold the parable of the good Samaritan to justify the admission of a French refugee.[60] In 1574 the Senate and XXI defended the lay supremacy with an ingenious gloss on the story of Moses, Aaron, and the golden calf.[61] In 1580 it sent a delegation to the Alsatian town of Obernai to protest the suppression of Protestant services there. In a single day these four magistrates worked up a sophisticated appeal, citing both the Old and New Testaments, as well as the writings of Augustine.[62] Nor were the magistrates' lay subjects indifferent to religion. Postmortem inventories of their possessions made in the early seventeenth century show that half the pictures they chose to decorate their homes portrayed religious scenes.[63]

What the magistrates wanted from Lutheranism was not confessional precision but peace and salvation. They avoided doctrinal de-

---

[58]*TAE*, vol. 2, no. 523 (1534). See Brady, *Ruling Class,* pp. 192–93.

[59]RP 1577, ff. 727v–728v.

[60]RP 1572, ff. 910r–911r.

[61]RP 1573, ff. 878r–881v.

[62]RP 1580, ff. 240r–241r, 259v–260r.

[63]Jean-Pierre Kintz, "La société strasbourgeoise du milieu du XVIe siècle à la fin de la guerre de Trente Ans, 1560–1650: Essai d'histoire démographique, économique, et sociale" (doctorat d'état, Strasbourg, 1980), p. 874.

bate in their own chambers because it fostered division, and they sought to prevent such debate among their subjects for the same reason. The Creeds provided an adequate statement of the Christian faith. A church that taught the fundamentals and no more could be a true church and yet a broad church that all Strasburghers could accept. It would not deny any belief necessary to salvation in the next life, but it would not destroy harmony in the present world. This was the church the magistrates wanted for Strasbourg.

The Senate and XXI urged its clergy to preach the barest minimum of doctrine. At a synod held in 1539 it cautioned the preachers to choose their texts from the Gospels and not to take up "the Prophets or other difficult books." The clergy's explanations of the Bible should not be about "subtle or high-flown materials, but about those which come within the understanding of the common people and are likely to contribute to their improvement." What they wanted the clergy to do was to enjoin their parishioners "to behave like pious Christians . . . to go to the sermons, to send their children to catechism classes, and not to neglect anything befitting pious Christians."[64] The lay rulers stressed ethics, not dogma. Policing behavior was a difficult task, and clergymen who preached on good morals could be of great help to the secular power. The practical result of sermons on doctrine might be doubt and division; the practical result of sermons on morality might be a more Godly city. Naturally the magistrates preferred the latter. As far as they were concerned, on matters of subtle doctrine it was better by far that the burghers remain in tranquil ignorance than that they take up a pugnacious certainty. This current in the magistrates' thinking fitted in well with the clergy's growing conviction that doctrine should be left to the experts.

Creeds, not confessions; ethics, not dogma: the magistrates' religion has a certain Erasmian cast. What Luther criticized in Erasmus was also characteristic of the rulers of Strasbourg, as both preferred to pursue peace rather than to defend an immodest dogmatism about God's mysteries.[65] The attitudes Erasmus set down in works like the *Handbook of a Christian Knight* and the *Education of a Christian Prince* were part of the intellectual climate of the sixteenth century; it is even likely that some of the magistrates knew his ideas at first hand. Yet Erasmus was no magistrate, and the magistrates' religion was not his.

---

[64]AST 75/52, f. 761r; RP 1574, f. 316r-v.
[65]Ernest F. Winter, trans. and ed., *Erasmus-Luther: Discourse on Free Will* (New York, 1961), p. 102.

In their church reform they outlawed a whole series of practices, including the mass, which the humanist would have defended and once the new order had been founded they went to war to protect it. Their solution to the religious crisis was dictated by pragmatism, not humanism.

A simple Bible-based religion that everyone could understand, good morals that everyone could appreciate and practice, a church in which the clergy served the laity and not the contrary—to secular Lutherans in Strasbourg this was the essence of the reformation. The clergy rejected none of this, but they demonstrated an irresistible need to make matters more precise, to insist on the absolute primacy of the spiritual over the secular, and to demand a degree of piety the people would not grant them. In their hands the reformation turned into a revalorization of the clerical office, which Bucer had already defined as the highest human calling in 1523, and an elaboration of simple Scripture into complex dogma.[66]

A real divergence between clerical and lay thinking can be found in the arguments about the use of compulsion to enforce orthodoxy. The clergy tended to intolerance and the laity toward greater charity. This was a divergence of tendencies rather than an absolute distinction. As we have seen, a streak of bigotry against other confessions ran through the Lutheranism of Strasburghers in both estates, and the city's legendary toleration has to be balanced against this current in both lay and clerical thinking. Just as we can collect evidence of lay bigotry, like Michael Lichtensteiger's attempt to leave Lambert Daneau and his family to freeze on a wintry night, we can produce evidence of clerical charity, like Martin Bucer's protection of the anti-trinitarian Michael Servetus, or Johann Marbach's initial acceptance of the Calvinist pastor Guillaume Holbrac.[67] These cases, however, were dramatic reversals of the norms.

Early in the reformation, Martin Bucer and Wolfgang Capito had both argued that the Christian magistrates must use their sword against heretics. As Bucer put it, it was a new and dangerous error to hold that the lay rulers ought not to concern themselves with their subjects' beliefs so long as the public peace was not endangered.[68] The clergy continued to feel that this error was all too widespread in

[66]*Das ym selbs, BDS*, 1:51.
[67]Eells, *Martin Bucer*, pp. 132–33; and Chapter 5, note 90, above.
[68]Philippe Dollinger, "La tolérance à Strasbourg au XVIe siècle," *Hommage à Lucien Febvre*, 2 vols. (Paris, 1953), 2:242–43.

Strasbourg.[69] Marbach complained in 1572, "These days we have unfortunately fallen into the habit of leaving everyone free to take up not just the old religion, but also those which are expressly forbidden by the Religious Peace, so that people join all the other sects, like the Anabaptists, the Schwenckfelders, and the Calvinists, and all this publicly and without any prejudice to them."[70] We know that things were scarcely that easy-going. In the twenties and early thirties the Senate and XXI had accepted the evangelical clergy's argument that it must take charge of religious life and reform the local church. Bit by bit the magistrates did just that, and they defended their new church at home as well as abroad. They sought to keep the Sabbath holy. They confronted dissidents with a choice: be still or be punished. With blasphemers they were uncompromising. They executed Thomas Saltzmann in 1527 for questioning the Trinity. Georg Silberrad they clapped in jail, pilloried, and ran out of town with a whipping. They expelled Andreas Irmbsteiner and his wife and threatened to drown them if they returned. They put Matthis Weigand on display in a cage and then banished him.[71]

Heresy, as we have seen, was more of a problem to the magistrates than was blasphemy. Catholics, sectarians, and Calvinists nevertheless all had reason to argue that they suffered for their faiths, and certainly official policy restricted or denied their right to public worship. Even so, there is something to Marbach's complaint, and Strasbourg did earn a reputation for toleration, or in modern terms, moderation.[72] Sebastian Franck's judgment has been repeated by nearly every commentator: "What is elsewhere punished by execution, in Strasbourg brings no more than a whipping." Refugees entering the city regularly told the magistrates that they had been attracted by the city's renowned mercy and charity toward the persecuted.

Not only did the Senate and XXI take in the oppressed from other lands, it defended the principle of freedom of conscience. As one of its members remarked in 1580, quoting the late emperor, Maximilian, "There is no greater tyranny than to dictate to conscien-

[69]RP 1545, ff. 35v–37v; RP 1548, f. 294r.
[70]AST 87/60, f. 13r.
[71]Saltzmann, *TAE,* vol. 1, nos. 110–14; Silberrad, RP 1540, f. 50r–v; the Irmbsteiners, RP 1544, ff. 98v–99r; Weigand, RP 1546, f. 337r–v.
[72]The distinction is Dollinger's ("La tolérance," p. 249). He attributes this moderation to the magistrates, not the pastors (pp. 243, 245).

ces."[73] The magistrates would forbid certain forms of behavior—blasphemy, disruption of the Sabbath, participation in the services of rival faiths—but they would not try to force Lutheran observances on any adults, other than the nuns. They usually granted their subjects the same privilege they granted each other, freedom from being forced to account for one's faith. Throughout the century the lay authorities remained true, truer than did their clergy, to the early Protestant notion that no mortal could or should usurp God's privilege to see into the human heart. Freedom of conscience in Strasbourg was just that, and it did not extend to the freedom to act. Yet what liberty there was here was the work of the laity, not the clergy.

For most men and women in Strasbourg in the sixteenth century, religion was fundamental to the understanding of the meaning of human life. To them the true religion was simple and hearteningly certain: "For God so loved the world that he gave his only begotten son, that whosoever believeth in him should not perish, but have everlasting life" (John 3:16). Intellectuals in and out of the clergy might inquire into the why and the how of this, but the ordinary people shared the magistrates' conviction that these elaborations were vain things, more likely to produce confusion than comfort. *Sola fide*, *sola scriptura*, and *sola gratia* were enough for them. Religious services should not drag on to the point of making people late for dinner.[74]

The attitudes of the laity toward religion conditioned the evolution of the reformation at every stage. Lay militants gave the early preachers the power they needed to demolish the old church, and lay anti-clericalism, apathy, and independence had unexpected effects on the formation of the new church. The laity in Strasbourg had frequent occasion to observe that the new preachers, like the old priests, demanded too much. They had had reason to dislike the old papacy and were not disposed to see a new one replace it. Their opposition to the clergy's dreams was precisely what pushed the preachers to put more and more stress on their obligation to discipline and direct the laity. Likewise, the laity's unwillingness to model their religious ideas entirely on their pastors', and their penchant for making up their own minds, contributed to the clergy's drive to work out exactly what was and was not orthodox Lutheranism. Their independence un-

[73]RP 1580, ff. 259v–260r.
[74]RP 1546, f. 252v.

doubtedly encouraged the Lutheran clergy to try to resurrect the old priestly monopoly on doctrine. When Lutheran orthodoxy finally carried the day in Strasbourg, it affirmed a resurgence of clerical power and imposed a complicated theology. Even then the great Church Ordinance of 1598 did not go forth as the law of the land according to Johann Pappus and the Church Assembly, but as the decree of "the Stettmeister, the Senate, and our friends the XXI." The clergy wrote it, but they wrote it as they did both for and because of the laity. It stands as a monument to the lay as well as the clerical values that shaped Strasbourg's long reformation.

CHAPTER EIGHT

The Christian Community

While clerical definitions of Christian doctrine increasingly shaped the Strasburghers' religious opinions, the city's laity continued to resist parts of their preachers' message about how good Christians must behave. Moral reform, like doctrinal accuracy, had been one of the cherished goals of the early reformers. The original reformation settlement transferred to the lay magistrates all power to enforce norms of behavior, just as it gave them control of doctrinal norms. For the next four to six decades the policing of doctrine and behavior followed similar paths, as two generations of magistrates defended the lay supremacy while the clergy struggled to undermine it. At the close of the century the third generation restored some of the clergy's lost authority, much less in matters of discipline than of doctrine. Throughout the century, lay and clerical notions of morality never coincided perfectly, and the lay ethos remained the dominant force in the Strasburghers' lives.

Each of the competing currents in the early reformation promised to put an end to the manifold sins and crimes that were said to disfigure late medieval society. Martin Bucer's first reforming tract, *No One Should Live for Himself, but for Others* (1523), offered a set of images of community life before and after an evangelical reformation. The old priests were perverse, the old rulers negligent, and the old commons slothful and mean. The reformed pastors were godly, the reformed rulers true fathers to their people, and the reformed people abounded in piety and charity. Let the Gospel be preached, concluded Bucer, and temporal as well as spiritual problems could be solved.[1] Bucer's colleagues in the ministry shared his conviction that their reformation would bring quick conversions, deep conversions, and a whole new society.

In this message the laity could hear a promise of freedom. The preachers offered relief from the confessional, from the myriad clerical fees, and from the thousand proscriptions on daily life.[2] Yet those who heard in the evangelicals' sermons only the gospel of freedom heard only what they wanted to hear. The preachers did indeed propose to remove the human inventions weighing upon Christians, but only to replace them with the yoke of Christ. From the beginning they expected a reformed society to be a disciplined society; Bucer was not yet in Strasbourg when he first called for the enforcement of the Mosaic laws.[3] As time wore on, the clergy showed more and more willingness to invent their own rules and institutions to discipline the laity, although the city of saints always eluded them. "We have been preaching the Gospel here for a long time," they wrote in 1547, "and still there is no proper disciplinary ordinance, nor punishment of depravity."[4]

The clergy knew whom to blame for the persistence of immorality in Strasbourg. It was not their fault, for they had preached the Gospel and carried out their pastoral responsibilities with devotion. What had stalled the moral regeneration of the city was the stubbornness of the lay Strasburghers. The commons had supported the evangelicals as long as it had been a question of destroying old obligations and imposing strict standards on the clergy's behavior. There they stopped. Their own behavior was another matter, and the new preachers found themselves endlessly repeating Geiler von Kaysersberg's old charges about adultery, fornication, prostitution, immodesty, theft, gluttony, drunkenness, vanity, blasphemy, carousing, and sharp business practices like usury and speculation. From the pulpits the good burghers often looked like a bad lot. The magistrates were most of all to blame for neglecting their God-given responsibilities to police the city. When the clergy tried to take action against the evils they saw around them they thus ran up against two walls: the magistrates' conviction that discipline was indeed their

---

[1]*Das ym selbs niemand sonder andern leben soll* (1523), BDS, vol. 1.
[2]Ozment, *Reformation in the Cities*, pp. 47–67, 117–18.
[3]*Das ym selbs*, pp. 56–57, and *Summary seiner Predig* (1523), BDS, 1:142.
[4]RP 1547, ff. 178v–183v.

own responsibility and the general lay conviction that the preachers' standards of behavior were impossibly rigorous.

The late medieval Senate and XXI had long labored to undermine the old church courts.[5] Through the bishop's and the archdeacon's officials the prereformation church had claimed jurisdiction over matters of faith, the clergy's behavior, marriage and sexuality, church property, charity, perjury, probate of wills, and usury. Although the officials retained a theoretical competence over these areas in the early 1500s, the Senate and XXI had already managed to nibble away bits and pieces from almost every section.[6] By 1530 the whole system had been destroyed and, with it, any hope the evangelical clergy might have entertained of inheriting some of the old priests' coercive powers.

The lay magistrates replaced the officials. The Senate and XXI itself took charge of church doctrine and property as well as of clerical morality, transferring perjury, probate, and usury to the existing secular courts. A lay board, the *Almosenherren,* now took full control of charity.[7] The Senate and XXI created two new courts, the Marriage Court and the Morals Board, to administer the remainder of its expanded jurisdiction.

The Marriage Court, set up in 1529, took control of who could marry and who could divorce, of marital disagreements, and of many sexual offenses.[8] Three Senators and two members of the XXI ruled on cases. Like the city lawyers, the clergy had only an advisory role; the judges could consult them but were under no obligation to accept their advice. The Court's records have been lost but evidence of its work surfaces in other sources. The lay judges prevented marriages; Ursula Lachenmeyer was forbidden to marry her widowed brother-in-law. They also forced marriages on people. When Wolff Gauske and Anna Ott were caught having an affair, the judges first clapped them in prison and then marched them off to the altar.[9] The Marriage

---

[5]Levresse, "L'officialité épiscopale," pp. 309–14.

[6]Levresse, "L'officialité," pp. 184–224.

[7]On the welfare arrangements, see Chapter 2, note 46, above, and for the courts, Chapter 2, note 41.

[8]François Wendel, *Le mariage à Strasbourg à l'époque de la réforme, 1520–1692* (Strasbourg, 1928). Köhler, *Züricher Ehegericht,* includes material on Strasbourg. Thomas Max Safley, *Let No Man Put Asunder: The Control of Marriage in the German Southwest: A Comparative Study, 1550–1600* (Kirksville, Mo., 1984) permits useful comparisons with the Catholic jurisdictions in the diocese of Constance, and with Basel.

[9]AMS N26, p. 414, and M67, p. 280; Kintz, "La société," pp. 223–24.

Court had to suspend its operations in the aftermath of the Schmalkadic War, but the Senate and XXI revived it six years later.[10]

The Morals Board, or *Zuchtherren,* was created in 1548.[11] The Senate and XXI delegated a Stettmeister, two members of the XXI, and two senators to oversee the execution of Strasbourg's morals laws. The clergy had no voice in this body, although it had been created in response to their complaints about the persistence of immorality in Strasbourg.[12] Its records are not extant, and its exact jurisdiction is difficult to reconstruct.

The reformation also attacked chunks of the canon law enforced by the old church courts. The evangelical reformers urged its replacement by the laws of Moses, which they thought should also take precedence over customary and imperial law. The Senate and XXI chose to ignore this advice and continued to use and modify definitions of crimes and proper punishments developed in Germany in the medieval period.[13] The principal collection of morals legislation in the sixteenth century was the "Constitution" of 1529, which codified the laws on blasphemy, cursing, gambling, drunkenness, and sexual offenses. The Senate and XXI reissued this long text in 1535 as the core of a disciplinary ordinance that added two statutes on the proper observance of the Sabbath and seven other laws. In the general preamble to this collection the magistrates explained that it had been promulgated to ensure that people lived up to their faith as it had been outlined in the Tetrapolitan Confession. Moreover, the magistrates ordered copies of the disciplinary ordinance printed for distribution to each guild hall and summoned the corporations to turn out for the hours-long reading of the full text.[14] Thirteen years later they again called all their subjects together to hear its provisions repeated.[15]

Strasbourg had laws and had the means to enforce its laws, so that everything seemed to be in place to make the city as godly a city as Geneva became, at least in reputation. Yet no Lutheran Knox ever came to exclaim over the holiness of the Strasburghers' lives, and

---

[10]RP 1550, ff. 30v–31r; RP 1556, f. 253r.

[11]RP 1547, f. 67r; RP 1548, f. 36r.

[12]Bellardi, *Gemeinschaft,* pp. 42–63.

[13]Compare the statutes in Johann Karl Brucker, ed., *Strassburger Zunft-und Polizei-Verordnungen des 14. und 15. Jahrhunderts* (Strasbourg, 1889), the sixteenth-century texts in AMS série R, and *Der Statt Strassburg Policeij Ordnung.* Safley, *Let No Man,* argues that much of the old canon law on marriage survived in both Catholic and Protestant jurisdictions.

[14]Text: Roehrich, *Mittheilungen,* 1:244–84.

[15]AST 84/59, 1548.

their own clergy preferred to stress their lapses. Again and again the preachers pleaded with the Senate and XXI to make Strasbourg a shining example of saintliness by compelling the people to complete the reformation of the clergy by a reformation of the laity.[16] What was at issue between the preachers and their parishioners was not entirely the definition of what was decent and what was wicked. Both took their inspiration from the Bible and agreed that offenses like murder, theft, and adultery were sinful and criminal. This still left a large grey area: was it wrong, for example, to practice archery on Sunday afternoon? Could something be licit for one group and illicit for another? How much immorality could the city tolerate? Where did the enforcement of norms of behavior veer off into the coercion of consciences? An examination of only a few areas—sexual misconduct, gambling, usury, and respect for religion—will reveal the pattern of disagreement.

Sexual activity was licit only between spouses. The clergy denounced everything else as sin, and the magistrates promised to prosecute everything else as crime.[17] We have seen that premarital intercourse could lead to forced marriages. An unwed mother whose partner could not be found might face prison and then exile after the birth of her child; fornication was to bring imprisonment and fines, while adultery might lead to exile. The clergy held that these penalties were too light. In place of imprisonment, fines, and exile they advocated a return to capital punishment as prescribed by Deuteronomy. Judged against Old Testament dictates, the penalties in Strasbourg were moderate. No one was stoned here for adultery, although the magistrates did employ the death penalty in other cases they found particularly heinous. Claus Frey was drowned for bigamy, Daniel Finck beheaded for incest, and two men burned for sodomy.[18] On the other hand, sometimes the guilty managed to go unpunished. Jerg Butz's daughter married in white, danced at her wedding reception—and had a child three hours later. The Senate and XXI decided that it would be unfair to single her out for punishment when so many were guilty.[19]

[16]See Appendixes C and D.

[17]Discussion of a new law for unwed mothers: RP 1569, ff. 492v, 493r; RP 1570, ff. 249v, 251r-v, 262r, 553v. RP 1541, ff. 94v, 181r, on a case of fornication. On adultery, RP 1540, ff. 71v-72r; RP 1584, ff. 5v-7r, 19r-v. For the clerical call for stiffer penalties see RP 1541, ff. 195v-196r; AST 84/83, 1571. See also Kintz, *La société*, pp. 210-17.

[18]*TAE*, vol. 2, no. 564 on Frey; RP 1585, ff. 413r-414r and ff. through 1588, f. 317v, on Finck. Büheler, "La chronique," no. 275 (1539).

[19]RP 1570, ff. 249v, 251r-v.

Were so many guilty? It seems not, despite the horrified observations that adultery was out of control and prostitution increasing daily. Given the rudimentary means of contraception available to the Strasburghers, the rate of premarital conceptions and the illegitimacy rate should provide a rough but reasonable index to illicit heterosexual activity. Some couples did practice premarital intercourse; in the 1560s about 8 percent of births took place within eight months of the marriage ceremony. In the latter part of the century a tiny number of babies was born outside wedlock, .67 percent of all births. Both rates are extremely low for an early modern city.[20]

The clergy's cries of "Wolf!" failed to stampede the magistrates into action. In 1572 pastor Johann Thomas criticized the authorities for allowing the wicked to flourish, and the Senate and XXI heard him out. Then they began to press him: just who were these wicked people? Thomas could name only one or two suspected fornicators. The magistrates sent him away.[21] Later the same year Wolf Sigismund Wurmser, a man no one would call excessively soft-hearted, made a point of informing his colleagues in the council that the pastors' claim that most of the women who gave birth in the Great Hospital were whores (that is, unmarried) was without foundation. He had been keeping track of births there for the past five or six years and could prove that the great majority of these mothers were honorably married. Moreover, even if there were a few bad types, "We must show mercy to them as well." His fellow hospital superintendents, Johann Carl Lorcher and Andres Graff, backed him up. They added that in their opinion the pastors frequently lacked charity in their sermons.[22]

The magistrates did not all share Wurmser's tolerance. Michael Lichtensteiger, a firm ally of the clergy in this as in most things, rose a few years later to attack his colleagues' leniency.[23] Unmarried mothers were not punished in Strasbourg with the same flourish as in Worms, Colmar, or Geneva, he complained. If something were not done, "We'll soon have a little Venice on our hands!" The Senate and XXI made its usual decision; the old laws were excellent, and all that needed to be done was to enforce them. Junker Ludwig Wolff von Renchen, on the other hand, tried to sway his colleagues in the op-

[20]Kintz, *La société,* pp. 210–17 on premarital conceptions and illegitimacy. The illegitimacy rate is calculated for 1561–90, and certain lacunae in the data make it artificially low. For the next thirty years the rate was 1.24 percent.

[21]RP 1572, ff. 369r-v.

[22]RP 1572, ff. 560v–561v.

[23]RP 1580, ff. 33v–34r, 42v–43r. Venice was a symbol of debauchery to the Alsatians.

posite direction. This senator twice tried to increase the number of brothels in the city to protect the virtue of married women and virgins from predatory delinquents. Once again the Senate and XXI refused to budge.[24]

The clergy sought—at least in public—to impose perfection as a standard. A single prostitute, a pair of adulterers, a lone bastard, were each one too many. God's wrath would descend on the city that tolerated such libertinage. In private the pastors were undoubtedly more interested in winning back sinners than in seeing them stoned, as Ludwig Rabus's concern for Ursula Lachenmeyer and her brother-in-law showed.[25] Yet although they knew that the natural human must always sin and that believing Christians thus had their lapses, immorality still enraged them. Its presence was a constant pain to them, a reminder of the shortcomings of the city's reformation.

The magistrates, on the other hand, took a more relaxed view. All their experience taught that crime would always be with them, and their purpose was to keep it within limits, since they trusted in God not to blast the city for a few reprobates. What was essential to them was to prevent public scandals and to keep the peace, and they were certain that a thorough crackdown on all manifestations of immorality would likely cause more trouble than did the odd brothel. Their position remained, "Since our predecessors made good laws against these crimes, we have only to stand by them."[26] Their collective attitude near the end of the century was what it had been in the 1520s and 1530s: moral perfection was an ideal unlikely to be realized in this life. As they told the clergy in 1534, "We must let the world remain worldly a little longer yet."[27]

While sexual misconduct was kept to a minimum in Strasbourg, gambling was a plague. All over the city people wagered: at the bakery, in the back offices of the episcopal notaries, in church, in the inns, in the guildhalls, around the orphanage, just outside the walls. Everyone seemed to do it—merchants on their way to the Frankfurt fair, an old priest who ostentatiously diced on Sunday to annoy Lutherans on their way to church, members of the city nobility, young apprentices, the commander of the Teutonic Knights (a genuine high-roller willing to stake up to 1,600 florins, it was rumored),

---

[24]RP 1553, f. 252r; RP 1554, f. 274r, 274v.
[25]AMS, N26, p. 414.
[26]For two late examples, RP 1572, f. 879r-v, and RP 1587, f. 260r.
[27]Brant, "Annales," no. 5057.

and people on the dole who bet their last pfennig.[28] The ropemakers' building was a special center. The magistrates frequently ordered raids there, without ever managing to put the gamblers out of business.[29]

What is interesting here is the clash between the clergy's view that gambling was wrong, whoever did it, and the magistrates' view that it was worse when the working classes and the poor did it. The crackdowns were always directed at the latter two groups; it is extremely unlikely that the Senate and XXI ever tried to disturb the noble commander of the Teutonic Knights. The principle of class justice, namely that the powerful might do what the humble might not, was entrenched in local jurisprudence. To the rich who could afford them went the furs and the sumptuous wedding receptions, while the poor were forced into the economy of coarse cloth and modest celebrations. The law punished rich and poor differently for the same offenses. A 1568 blasphemy statute, for instance, specified that the degree of mutilation imposed on the worst offenders would depend on the lawbreaker's rank as well as on the gravity of the offense. Similarly, commoners could be pilloried but nobles could not.[30] As a chronicler complained, "They punish the poor for drinking, while the rich and the nobles get away with it."[31]

The magistrates did make some effort to enforce their laws on gambling. But when it came to usury they did little more than cluck their tongues for form's sake. The pastors might well complain about usury, but they knew there was no hope of amendment since the magistrates themselves were usurers, many of whom drew sizeable portions of their incomes from lending money at interest to their subjects both in and out of town. The best the preachers could get from them were grudging promises to punish usurers "in so far as possible," or to regulate speculation and usury, "not all the time, but when there are shortages and the prices rise."[32]

The sorest question about the regulation of behavior revolved

---

[28]RP 1542, ff. 80r, 330r; RP 1543, f. 490v; RP 1544, f. 63r; RP 1547, f. 35r-v; RP 1548, ff. 21v, 22r.

[29]Among the raids, some of which had a distinct Keystone Kops flavor: RP 1543, f. 177r; RP 1545, f. 242r; RP 1548, f. 35v; RP 1553, f. 361r-v; RP 1560, f. 7v; RP 1562, ff. 138v, 139v; RP 1568, ff. 328r, 335v; RP 1577, f. 103r.

[30]BNUS R22/12, ff. 3v–4v.

[31]Brant, "Annales," no. 4988.

[32]Magisterial usury, Brady, *Ruling Class,* pp. 147–52; promises of action, RP 1539, ff. 219r, 235r–237r, 264v–265r.

around religious observances. Religion, after all, was considered to be the cornerstone of morality. To what extent could the regime force the Strasburghers to practice the Lutheran faith?

The magistrates accepted the evangelical clergy's initial position that faith could not be compelled and part of their argument that the secular powers could legitimately regulate outward observances. They did make baptism compulsory.[33] They also regulated behavior on the Sabbath. No one was to work "without special, pressing, and honest cause." No one was to sell anything except bread, milk, and fish until the morning services were over, and innkeepers were to keep their premises closed during the church services. No one was to promenade through the churches, to loiter outside them to gossip, or to practice shooting anywhere in the city, since all these things disrupted the services.[34] Critics of the established church and its clergy could expect punishment. The Senate and XXI dealt harshly with blasphemers who mocked the Christian religion. Georg Koch, a mercenary passing through the city, was foolish enough to announce, well into his cups, that the Romans would never have killed Christ if he had not done something to deserve it. The magistrates ordered him put to death. The public executioner chopped off his head, cut out his tongue, and burned his corpse.[35]

The magistrates never chose to regard church attendance as an external work that they could oblige people to perform. They ordered heads of households to send their underage charges to church, or at least to keep them off the streets on Sunday mornings.[36] They appealed to adults to come.[37] They bound themselves to set a good example by attending at least one of the weekly services along with their own families. They chose to work by example rather than by compulsion on the rather latitudinarian and semi-Pelagian ground that "faith is a work of free will and a gift of God." They were reluctant to demand church attendance, because such a law would be unenforceable, and unenforceable laws brought justice into disrepute. Any such law, as they well knew, would also make the burghers grumble about a "new papacy."[38]

If the pastors' testimony is to be believed, the Strasburghers took

[33]*TAE,* vol. 2, nos. 638, 645 (1535).
[34]Text of the 1535 Disciplinary Ordinance: Roehrich, *Mittheilungen,* 1:252–54.
[35]RP 1569, ff. 286v–287v, 305v–308v, 319v–320v, 327v–328v.
[36]Disciplinary Ordinance, pp. 256–57.
[37]AST 84/59, sig. Aiv recto.
[38]AST 84/19 (1534); AST 84/31 (1536).

full advantage of the magistrates' unwillingness to force church observances upon them. "Young and old alike rarely come to services," reported Bucer, Capito, and Hedio. Young people preferred lolling in the streets to attending their catechism classes. The special days of prayer and penance drew few parishioners.[39] Many people neglected to take communion. In 1541 the pastors drew the magistrates' attention to people who had not done so in fifteen, sixteen, twenty years, or more.[40] The little information we have about the reception of the eucharist confirms this charge. A list of those who came to the pastor of St. Wilhelm to prepare themselves for the Lord's Supper gives only 307 names spread over ten months in 1544–45. Given the probable size of the parish population, the list suggests a participation rate under 10 percent, although allowance has to be made for children too young to take the sacrament. Another list from the same parish for 1546 records many services at which only a single family, a lone woman, or a solitary couple took communion. In 1547, defeat in the Schmalkaldic War and fears about the emperor's intentions stimulated devotion to the Protestant cause, and the pastors were attempting to create *ecclesiolae* of dedicated laymen to ensure the underground survival of the faith if Catholicism returned. At St. Wilhelm, over three separate services, only sixty-five men participated in the Lord's supper.[41] While this reluctance to receive the sacrament could spring from pious motives—a sense of sinfulness, for example—it more likely signaled the laity's refusal to accept the clergy's piety wholeheartedly.

The preachers could not rest content while the laity misbehaved and neglected their religious duties. Their theology recognized the inevitability of sin, yet it also taught that the Old Adam must be trampled. They knew that human behavior would never be perfect, but they continued to feel that it could be made a great deal better. Martin Bucer voiced their common and enduring conviction when he told the Strasburghers that since what the clergy demanded of the faithful had been commanded by God, it must be possible in practice. "We ask for no discipline and penances in the Church other than those the Lord ordained and commanded. What the Lord commands,

---

[39]RP 1540, ff. 302v–304v; RP 1555, f. 239r; RP 1571, ff. 834v–835r.
[40]RP 1541, f. 413v; AST 80/39.
[41]AMS N24, pp. 61–73 for 17 June 1544 through 25 April 1545; pp. 125–26 for 25 December 1545 through 24 August 1546; and pp. 84–88 for 1547. Almost half those named in the last list were members of the parish fellowship.

he sends his spirit to accomplish, so that all is possible and all may be improved with his help."[42] What rankled the clergy was their sense that the magistrates could do more than they did to make Strasbourg a godly city.

The clergy tried to make the magistrates enact tougher laws and practice stricter enforcement of existing legislation. They used their powers of persuasion directly on their parishioners, trying to change their ideas and thus the roots of their behavior. Since neither of these tactics worked, they also tried to insinuate themselves back into the judicial system. They wanted two things: the right to exercise the full ban, that is, the right to name notorious sinners to their fellow parishioners, who should then shun them; and the right to examine all their parishioners on their beliefs and practices.

The use of excommunication for temporal ends, for example to compel debtors to make repayment, had made it a lightning rod for discontent at the beginning of the reformation. The laity loathed it, and Catholic reformers denounced its misuse before the evangelical condemned it.[43] But the evangelicals could not abandon excommunication. Even before the mass had been abolished in Strasbourg, the preachers argued that a "Christian ban" (so-called to distinguish it from the perverted "papist ban" of the old church) was part of the Apostles' teaching and necessary in a large church. As they put it, "A church without the ban is like a household without order."[44] When Anabaptist criticism of the evangelical church as a church of sinners grew, the clergy became more and more convinced that only public excommunication of reprobates could silence these opponents.[45]

Protestant church ordinances allowed excommunication, and apparently as a more dreadful weapon than the old papist ban. It could be used against sinners, but only for spiritual offenses and only when all else had failed.[46] Limiting its use might have made excommunication more terrible, but in Strasbourg the preachers could not tell their parishioners who had been excommunicated, and so the measure was gutted of the force of social ostracism. The clergy could refuse the

---

[42] *Von der waren Seelsorge* (1538), BDS, 7:192. Luther's familiar teaching on the impossibility of keeping the law is echoed in Bucer's recognition (p. 105) that the church will always contain sinners.

[43] For example, Thomas Murner, *Die Schelmenzunft* (1512), in *Thomas Murners Deutsche Schriften*, 3:49.

[44] *TAE*, vol. 1, no. 171, p. 214 (1529); Bucer, *Seelsorge*, p. 81.

[45] *TAE*, vol. 1, no. 235 (1530 ff.).

[46] Ozment, *Reformation in the Cities*, p. 159.

sacraments and burial services to those they judged immoral or heretical, but that was all the law allowed. The Senate and XXI balked at the full ban for several reasons. It reminded people of the old "papist tyranny," it introduced divisions within the community, and most important, it gave the clergy a sphere of action outside lay control. Armed with the ban, a preacher could call anyone—even a magistrate—to account. An adulterer or a gambler did not challenge the political status quo, but a pastor with the power to excommunicate threatened the lay supremacy.

It was much the same story with the clergy's demand to interview parishioners before allowing them to participate in the sacramental life of the church. For most of the century the Senate and XXI turned a deaf ear to these proposals. The magistrates postponed discussions and left the clergy hanging.[47]

In the late 1540s the pastors, too long rebuffed, tried a new tactic.[48] They decided to go ahead on their own initiative to gather the most committed members of their congregations into parish fellowships where good doctrine and morality could better flourish. The movement appalled the magistrates, who disliked any collective activity outside their direct control, and the more so one that seemed riddled with Anabaptists and religious zealots. The movement threatened to split the church by creating an elite body of "better" Christians within it, and clearly restored to the clergy extensive power to examine people's beliefs. These developments put the magistrates in an awkward position. The fellowships could not be allowed to go unsupervised, since the Senate and XXI insisted on supervising everything. If an elite body were going to appear, the magistrates, as self-proclaimed heads of the church, would have to belong to it, yet few ideas could have been more foreign to their sense of their own dignity than this notion of sitting down as equals with gardeners and fishermen to suffer fraternal correction at their hands. To the Senate and XXI the fellowships were a dreadful mixture of democratic and theocratic deviations from the proper order. The fact that the movement appeared at a time when the Schmalkaldic League was going down to defeat before the emperor reinforced their concern because Charles V would certainly object to it, as the clergy intended it to be a bulwark against his attempts to restore Catholicism. Aided by a split in the

---

[47]Requests include *TAE*, vol. 1, nos. 235, 244. Reactions, RP 1540, ff. 182r-v, 302v–304v; RP 1542, f. 460r.

[48]Bellardi, *Gemeinschaft,* analyzes the attempt in detail.

Church Assembly, not all of whose members were prepared to push on in the face of magisterial opposition, the magistrates destroyed the fellowships. Their only concessions were to republish existing morals legislation and to set up a new lay disciplinary body, the Zuchtherren, to enforce it.

The clergy soon tried a different approach. In 1554 they proposed an inspection of the city parishes, carefully arguing that it would be conducted in cooperation with the lay authorities, that it would involve no coercion, and that it could only enhance the magistrates' surveillance over their church. In short, it would be every bit as useful as the regular inspections the Senate and XXI had carried out in the rural parishes since 1535. The proposal came from the new president of the Church Assembly, Johann Marbach. Like all his petitions, it was well organized and drafted with some regard for official preoccupations.[49] This particular petition was also persuasive, and the magistrates decided to try the experiment. Unfortunately for Marbach, the inspection was marred by a nasty personal quarrel that pitted him against Pastor Beatus Gerung, who objected to taking orders from a man he regarded as a young whippersnapper.[50] The experiment was never repeated. If continued, it would certainly have enlarged the clergy's power to pressure their parishioners, since it allowed them to check on things like church attendance and participation in communion. The magistrates were not blind to this potential and they reminded themselves to keep a close eye on the clergy lest, under the cover of this inspection, they tried to smuggle back "the old servitude."[51]

At about the same time, the Senate and XXI also prevented Marbach from officially introducing his draft Agenda, which was an attempt to revise the 1534 Church Ordinance.[52] Among other things, it provided for a quizzing of communicants before the Lord's Supper. On the Saturday before the communion service those who wished to participate were to present themselves at a special service to strengthen their faith and to obtain absolution for their sins. The pastor would question them either as a group or individually, taking care to screen out the unworthy. Marbach defined the unworthy as: those without

[49]AST 45, ff. 477r–487r.
[50]AST 45, ff. 491r–534r.
[51]RP 1554, f. 232v.
[52]AST 201, pp. 101–82; AST 200, a variant copy belonging to Marbach's colleague Panacratius Keffel.

faith and love; notorious sinners; Catholics; blasphemers; those who shunned the church services; those who disobeyed their parents, masters, or rulers; those who did not raise their children and charges to be Christians; murderers, whores, adulterers, and gluttons; thieves, usurers, robbers, and gamblers. Although the magistrates never gave the Agenda their imprimatur, Marbach used it in his own parish and so did at least one of his colleagues.

The Church Assembly's next effort to secure itself a greater role in the policing of morality came in the form of an appeal to the Senate and XXI to establish a consistory in Strasbourg. The clergy first proposed such a body of "magistrates and other learned persons" to deal with marriage and other church business in 1556. The magistrates simply postponed discussion.[53] A year later the Lutheran theologians who assembled at the Frankfurt Colloquy endorsed consistories, and the Strasburghers present passed along the advice to their rulers. This time the magistrates talked about the idea long enough to know why they disliked it. They refused to set up any sort of mixed judicial body because "we shouldn't hand over our sword" to the clergy.[54]

In 1572 the clergy began a new campaign.[55] One Sunday the preachers announced their intention to institute a private absolution of sins to complement the general absolution in the liturgy. They intended to go from house to house to talk with their parishioners and then to pronounce public excommunications. They had not forewarned the magistrates of this plan, and the oligarchs resented the attempt to bypass their authority. On Monday the Senate and XXI ordered the clergy to say and do nothing more. The Church Assembly replied with a lengthy explanation of its position, telling the Senate and XXI that the recent wave of bad harvests and high prices was nothing other than divine punishment for the swearing, sinning, and heresy pullulating in Strasbourg. They claimed that the only hope of divine reprieve was to restore St. Peter's keys to their rightful owners by letting the clergy discipline the people. They indeed proposed to go from house to house, but only by invitation and not at all to those who had chosen to divorce themselves from the church. They intended to remind couples, parents, children, masters, and

[53]RP 1556, f. 266r. For the background to the Lutheran clergy's interest in consistories see Estes, *Christian Magistrate and State Church*, pp. 59–61, 70–80.
[54]RP 1557, ff. 267v–268r; RP 1559, ff. 326v–327r.
[55]RP 1572, ff. 107v–108r, 141v–142r; AST 84/85.

servants of their reciprocal obligations and to question them about their religious observances. As a second measure, they proposed again that an interview prior to communion be made obligatory. They were careful to distinguish this practice from a "papist confession" or any other compulsion"liable to distress the Christian heart," although they admitted that the distinction was subtle and that not all the laity would be able to see it. Their purpose was to teach, for the aim of the interview was to instruct the faithful in one of the central Christian mysteries. This pre-communion interview, they added, was neither a foreign idea nor a real innovation, as it was customary in the churches of the Augsburg Confession and had been practiced for years in Strasbourg at the church of St. Nicolas. All the clergy asked was that the magistrates confirm this good old custom. As a final means of discipline they proposed to use the ban against notorious, unrepentant sinners—not of course the "papist ban" but the method of multiple exhortation outlined in Matthew 18 (15–18). These measures, they stressed, would be applied only to Lutherans; heretics would be left alone. The magistrates thought all this over and decided to think some more. They again reprimanded the clergy for putting such ideas before the commons without having consulted the Senate and XXI, and then made the preachers swear on their burgher's oath to do nothing until the regime authorized them to proceed. After that the magistrates never again discussed the project.

The Senate and XXI remained convinced that the punishment of delinquents was by divine command a lay responsibility. In 1574, responding to clerical charges that the magistrates catered to popular error out of fear of the common people, the Senate and XXI ruled that:

> In the first place each magistrate who wants the title of Christian is particularly charged with establishing correct, true church services and, in the interests of this, with the protection of the pious and the repression of the godless. This is clearly to be seen in the Holy Bible, where it is obvious that the two tables of the law were given to Moses and not to Aaron. It was Moses who was ordered to make them known to the people and to enforce them. Moreover, it was Aaron, out of fear of the people, who let them set up the golden calf and worship it. It was Moses who destroyed the calf and punished its worshipers.[56]

[56]Decision of January 6, 1574 (RP 1573, ff. 878r–881v), to restrict Marbach's, and thus the clergy's, power.

The magistrates presented themselves as the heirs to a divine commission that the clergy could not be expected to discharge reliably. They knew where their duty lay and considered themselves fit to do it.

The pastors found ways around the magistrates' refusal to cooperate with their efforts to win the right to examine parishioners and to publicly shame incorrigible delinquents. Couples who wished to marry and parents with newborn infants had to turn to the clergy, and could be questioned about their faith.[57] In the 1540s the pastor of St. Wilhelm interviewed parishioners before giving them communion, and so did the pastors of St. Nicolas and Old St. Peter in later decades.[58] Certainly the clergy could remonstrate with sinners, as Matthis Negelin did with Hans Bizer, a drunkard in his parish.[59] In addition, the pastors were turning the church wardens into their assistants.

The wardens had been given extensive powers to police the laity in the aftermath of a synod held in 1533.[60] In 1539, after complaints by the clergy that the wardens' negligence and ineffectiveness encouraged people to turn their backs on the undisciplined Strasbourg church, the Senate and XXI resolved to deal itself with stubborn miscreants whom the wardens could not handle.[61] Thus in 1550, when the wardens at St. Thomas failed to get anywhere with Anastasius Kandel, whose treatment of his wife and children offended his neighbors, the Senate and XXI hauled him in to answer for his behavior.[62] By the 1570s the Church Assembly had worked a new wrinkle into the procedure. By then, cases that could not be dealt with at the parish level were transferred before the Assembly, rather than the Senate and XXI. The wardens brought Hans Hummerdinger and his wife, guilty of premarital intercourse, to the Assembly, not the Senate and XXI.[63] The wardens had shifted from being officers of the lay magistrates to being agents of the pastors.

The Church Assembly attempted to revive something of the old

---

[57]The best source for these interviews is AMS N26, parish registers of St. Wilhelm, 1552–68.
[58]AMS N25, pp. 61–73; AST 200, ff. 25v–32r (1553).
[59]AMS N26, p. 519 (1566).
[60]*Kirchenpflegerordnung*, in Roehrich, *Mittheilungen*, 1:257–60.
[61]RP 1539, ff. 26v–27r; AMS R3, ff. 262r–364r; RP 1539, ff. 27r–v; AST 79/45. Bellardi, *Gemeinschaft*, pp. 17–20.
[62]AST 84/64.
[63]AST 79/3, ff. 22v–29r (1576); AMS N136, p. 55 (1592).

jurisdiction of the bishop's and archdeacon's officials. In his 1576 description of the Assembly, Johann Marbach claimed that it had jurisdiction over cases of grievous sin, among which he included dealing with heretics, witchcraft and sorcery, blasphemy, marital and sexual offenses, usury, and difficult matters of conscience.[64] All were clear invasions of the jurisdiction of the lay courts. The clergy, without having received explicit permission to do so, were creating a system of double jeopardy. A couple accused of fornication, for example, would now have to answer to the Church Assembly as well as to the Marriage Court.

Furthermore, although the clergy had no legal right to identify unrepentant sinners to the general public, they could make a great show of welcoming back the repentant who had strayed in secret. In 1577 Ulrich Dietrich, who had been punished by the magistrates for "disorder, adultery, and incest," wanted to reconcile himself to the church. Pastor Johann Thomas summoned Dietrich to the altar of St. Nicolas church and there, before the parishioners, Dietrich acknowledged his sins, recognized the disciplinary powers of the church, and vowed to sin no more. Thomas admonished the parishioners to accept the prodigal and then offered him communion.[65]

The friction between magistrates and preachers over the control of discipline should not obscure the fact that both groups wished to see the delinquent and the disorderly forced to behave better. The magistrates expected the church wardens to join the pastors in the work of fraternal discipline and they consistently urged the clergy to preach against sin and crime. However, as magistrates and as defenders of the lay supremacy, they expected the clergy to act as an auxiliary, not a rival, to the secular courts.

At all levels of society some Strasburghers responded to their preachers' call to purify the community. Magistrate Michael Lichtensteiger, a well-to-do spice merchant and staunch supporter of the Church Assembly, was one such man. He would willingly have driven the last miserable bastard-bearing woman out the city gates.[66] His colleague Wolfgang Schütterlin, while no advocate of clerical control, thought the Zuchtherren farcical in their leniency.[67] The clergy had popular support as well. At least twice, prominent magis-

[64]AST 79/3, f. 28r–v.
[65]AMS N105, ff. 74r–78v.
[66]RP 1577, ff. 725v–732r.
[67]RP 1586, ff. 7v–8r.

trates had the unnerving experience of receiving anonymous letters by night, warning them that if they did not punish the gamblers, the singers of obscene songs, and the disrupters of the Sabbath, then the burghers would depose them and bring in magistrates who would.[68] The abortive fellowship movement of the late forties attracted mostly artisans and laborers, demonstrating that its ideals were not anathema to working-class laymen.[69] On certain specific issues the clergy probably had a great deal of support. The preachers who condemned usury and speculation no doubt struck a responsive chord. The magistrates' class justice must have stuck in many throats, although it is at least arguable that when their subjects dreamed of equality before the law, they hoped this would be achieved by extending the rules for the rich, not the more exacting clerical norms, over the whole populace.

The Church Assembly had enough support to get some of its disciplinary practices enshrined in law in the 1598 Church Ordinance. Old statutes confirmed the power of the church wardens to summon parishioners who misbehaved or mocked the sacraments and a new section recognized the Church Assembly's right to shame such people publicly.[70] The Ordinance confirmed the practice of holding special services on Saturday evenings before the Lord's Supper was to be celebrated, and urged those wishing to participate in the sacrament to present themselves to their pastor in private.[71] But even the 1598 Church Ordinance did not introduce anything like a consistory and did not give the clergy seats on the Marriage Court or the Morals Board. The courts remained the preserve of the laity.

The Strasburghers had largely rejected the clergy's program to create a city of saints. They listened to Protestant sermons on morality as their ancestors had listened to Geiler von Kaysersberg's exhortations and denunciations. There was a good deal for a Christian to think about in these sermons, and certainly the preachers ought to teach people to live decently. Most Strasburghers did behave properly and they were conscious of doing so. They listened to the sermons, but they did not storm out of the churches to clamor for mandatory church attendance, for the stoning of adulterers, or for the clerical policing of behavior. The clergy could not muster more than a minority of lay supporters for their disciplinary projects for two

---

[68]RP 1544, f. 15r-v.
[69]Bellardi, *Gemeinschaft*, pp. 175–98.
[70]*Kirchenordnung* (Strasbourg, 1598), pp. 318–25, 194–95.
[71]Ibid., pp. 159–60.

reasons. The first is obvious and requires no comment here: the pastors demanded too much and in their demands came to sound too much like the old priests.[72] At least as important was the preachers' failure to convince the lay Strasburghers that they were telling the truth about conditions in the city. Their congregations refused to recognize the picture of their city which the preachers painted in their jeremiads. About this the Strasburghers thought their clergy were wrong, and they were not about to be mobilized in support of error.

The clergy set themselves up for this defeat when their sense of mission led them to harp on the wicked while ignoring the good. They drew attention to parishioners who neglected their duties, but left the diligent unsung. They told the magistrates about the ignorant, but not about people like Bastian Klughertz, a gardener who had gone through the parish school at St. Wilhelm and then come eagerly to his catechism classes.[73] They complained about empty churches when the people of St. Thomas and New St. Peter knew theirs were stuffed to overflowing.[74]

By following the debate on discipline through clerical petitions and magisterial reactions, this chapter has lost sight of the sober, the faithful, the honest, and the decent. The clerical lamentations leave too little place for the warm family sense and the trust in God evident in the autobiographical notes of the magistrates Christoff Kolöffel and Johann Schenckbecher.[75] The minutes of the Senate and XXI resound with complaints about impiety, ostentatious living, and "überfleissig essen und trinken," but they also reveal something else: the modesty and sense of measure that prompted the council of XV to ridicule Michael Lichtensteiger for taking a carriage to meetings while the rest of his colleagues walked, or the generosity with which the parishioners regularly filled the collection plates passed around for poor students or for the victims of fires.[76] While no Knox ever came to immortalize the conduct of the Strasburghers, scores of lay refugees spoke of finding not a sinkhole of debauchery and irreligion, but a city justly known throughout Europe for its people's charity and piety.[77]

---

[72]Gerald Strauss develops this point throughout *Luther's House of Learning*.

[73]AMS N26, p. 417 (1564).

[74] RP 1560, ff. 279r, 280v; RP 1578, ff. 64v–65r.

[75]BNUS ms. 847; AST 1655.

[76]XV 1588, f. 17r-v. Kintz, *La société*, pp. 107–8, analyzes charitable giving.

[77]AMS V/14/28, testimony of Pierre Klein of Antwerp, 1571. RP 1571, ff. 716v–717r, testimony of Peter Kesten of Munich. Just as the pastors erred on the side of condemnation, the refugees tended to be overly fulsome in their praise. Nevertheless, they are closer to the mark.

The Strasburghers did not lay the foundations of a new Eden in the sixteenth century; instead, they went on with the job of building a city of good citizens. The surviving evidence about their private lives is scattered and fragmentary. Autobiographical material, like Kolöffel's and Schenckbecher's notes, is scarce, and only traces of the most spectacular court cases can be found, since the records themselves have been lost. Despite this, enough remains from the Strasburghers' own hands, from the lay authors whose works they bought, and even from the clergy's complaints to put together an outline of what the Strasburghers thought made a good citizen.

In Strasbourg, as in every early modern city, being a good citizen meant doing one's job competently and honestly. Here the standards of the city's artisans, preachers, and magistrates overlapped. The butcher's meat should be fresh, the weaver's cloth flawless, and the master carpenter's cabinet not just functional, but beautiful. In this lay the honor of the men and women of the guilds, and evidence of their skills is still easily found in the streets and in the museums of modern Strasbourg.[78]

Four hundred years after the reformation the Strasburghers' pride in their work stands out as one of their cherished values. Other aspects of their definition of a good citizen are more shadowy now, in part because we must pursue them through sources less tangible than houses and their furnishings, sources often at several removes from the Strasburghers' immediate lives, such as literary works more ambiguous than things of wood, metal, or cloth. The novels of Georg Wickram, a minor civic employee in the nearby Alsatian city of Colmar, enjoyed a vogue in Strasbourg around the middle of the century. His "bourgeois romances" are moralistic tales in which wooden characters march through predictable plots. The failings of his writings, common enough in German vernacular fiction in the sixteenth century, do not undermine Wickram's value as a spokesman for *bürgerlich* ideals. To use them as a mirror of actual behavior would be as indefensible as to read Sebastian Brant's *Ship of Fools* as a realistic description of life in Basel around 1500; still, Wickram does portray the model "good citizen" we are seeking.[79]

[78]See Recht, Klein, and Foessel, *Connaître Strasbourg.*

[79]Wickram's mid-century fiction is certainly idealized, but unlike late sixteenth-century English "bourgeois hero-tales" it deals not with princes in disguise but with genuine commoners. His virtuous merchants do practice the mercantile virtues. Compare the works of Thomas Heywood, Richard Johnson, and Thomas Delaney analyzed by Laura Stevenson O'Connell, "The Elizabethan Bourgeois Hero-Tale: Aspects of an Adolescent Social Consciousness," in *After the Reformation: Essays in Honor of J. H. Hexter,* ed. Barbara

One of his novels, *The Good and Bad Neighbors,* describes the func-
tioning of an institution central to the lives of real Strasburghers, the
Freundschaft of relatives and friends which surrounded each individual.[80] Wickram first presents Robert, an honored merchant, and
his virtuous wife, Sophia. On one of his commercial voyages Robert
rescues a young merchant, Richard, who has fallen ill at sea, and
brings him home. Richard promptly falls in love with Robert and
Sophia's daughter Cassandra. Their marriage reception is a most
restrained affair—no dancing, Wickram notes with approval. The
young husband is ambushed one night by thugs hired by a disappointed suitor of Cassandra, but is rescued by a goldsmith named
Lazarus; Richard soon returns the favor by saving Lazarus from
Turkish pirates. Eventually the two friends both have children,
Lazarus a son and Richard a daughter. Wickram describes how these
two learn to read and write together, how Amelia learns to be a
master embroiderer, and (at much greater length) how young
Lazarus junior learns the merchant's trade. Naturally after a few
hitches the two marry.

Wickram writes about the virtues of the lay life. Friendship is a key
quality; the novel revolves around the pairs formed by Robert and
Richard, Richard and Lazarus, Cassandra and Lucia (Lazarus's wife),
Amelia and Lucia, and Lazarus junior and Richard. It stresses the joys
of marriage, for Robert and Sophia live happily together for more
than twenty-five years. The main characters are intelligent, generous
with each other, charitable toward the unfortunate, and courageous.
They carry their wealth without ostentation. They value education,
for its own sake and also for social advancement. They respect God,
their parents, their spouses, and each other; they tell each other Bible
stories. What they do not do is to go to church. There are no scenes in
which the friends attend sermons, and none—except for the two
marriages of Richard and Cassandra and of Lazarus junior and Amelia, and a passing reference to young Lazarus's baptism—in which
they take the sacraments. The friends manage to lead exemplary
Christian lives almost without contact with the clergy. It is also
noteworthy that while Wickram and his Strasbourg publisher present
these characters to a Lutheran audience as ideal figures, they are in

---

C. Malament (Philadelphia, 1980), pp. 267–90. I am grateful to Miriam Usher Chrisman
for introducing me to Wickram's work. For her analysis of his work see *Lay Culture,* pp.
209–13, 218–20.

[80]*Von Güten und Boessen Nachbaurn* (1556), in *Werke,* vol. 4.

fact Catholics who live in Brabant and Lisbon. The good neighbors are good burghers at odds with the Lutheran preachers' demand for orthodox and church-going parishioners.

For all that, the piety and restraint with which Wickram's fictional heroes and heroines conduct their lives are reminiscent of clerical ideals, and distance Wickram's characters a little from many real Strasburghers. In the face of the famines, wars, fires, floods, and bankruptcies that disfigured their lives, real Strasburghers made life tolerable through pleasures Wickram's characters did not permit themselves. Sunday afternoon was the time for a walk in the country, for target practice, or for a street dance.[81] Baptisms and marriages provided an excuse to dress in one's best, to eat, drink, and party with friends and neighbors.[82] Toward the end of the century Johann Fischart's German version of *Gargantua* sold well, catering to the citizens' taste for buffoonery and tall stories.[83] A good yarn always found an audience. Wickram himself turned his back on piety and restraint in his *Travelers' Tales,* a work he proclaimed suitable for ladies and for decent ears generally. Decency apparently stretched to cover a complicated tale about a magistrate who pretended to be pregnant in order to conceal his adultery, along with risqué fables about drunken, ignorant, and lecherous priests, usually Lorrainers.[84]

Once the whole city had a chance to take part in a massive display of good will in which real life rivaled the inventions and happy endings of the story-tellers.[85] In 1576 the regime was trying to put together an alliance with several Swiss towns. To prove how speedily their people could come to the aid of the Strasburghers if danger arose, a group of Zurich magistrates rowed down the Rhine in record time, bearing a cauldron of cereal loaded hot on their boat at dawn. Their little craft swept up the Ill that afternoon, its small cannon popping cheerfully and its crew arrayed in their ceremonial best. The Strasburghers lined the quay to cheer, the city pipers played, and the

---

[81]What the Strasburghers did on Sunday can be reconstructed from the clergy's complaints and from notes in the weekly agenda of the Senate and XXI which appear in the RP on Mondays.

[82]Here the sources indicated in the preceding note can be supplemented by the inspection records of the rural parishes, AST 45.

[83]*Geschichtklitterung* (Strasbourg, 1582, 1590).

[84]*Rollwagenbüchlein* (1555), in *Georg Wickrams sämtliche Werke,* ed. Hans-Gert Roloff, 12 vols. (Berlin, 1967–75), 7:7 and stories 4, 3, 20, 34, 46, 47, 79.

[85]Ville de Strasbourg, *Zurich-Strasbourg* (Strasbourg, 1976) reproduces many of the documents.

Senate and XXI waited at the dock. The Zurichers unloaded their prize, the lid came off the pot, and soon samples of the still-warm breakfast were circulating through the crowds. Then much finer dishes made their appearance from the city kitchens. A high point of the visit saw Zurichers and Strasburghers troop off to the firing range to compete with marksmen from all over the German-speaking lands. As part of the fun, the city council organized a lottery in which hundreds of gamblers tried their luck. The big draw arrived and out came the name of the lucky winner—a little orphan girl.

Undoubtedly the Strasburghers did not all or always live up to the lay ideals of honest work, friendship, and moderation punctuated only occasionally by revels, just as they failed to measure up to the clerical standards of piety and austerity. The majority of them even so, were not louts, idlers, and delinquents, but hard-working and God-fearing women and men. Among this majority were some who accepted the clergy's standard of perfection, but most agreed with their magistrates that God was prepared to leave the world worldly a little longer. Life in Strasbourg throughout the sixteenth century reflected their values better than it did those of the clergy.

CHAPTER NINE

The Impact of the Reformation

Not long ago Gerald Strauss directed historians to reopen the question of the success or failure of the German reformation. He took as his measuring stick the aim of the early reformers: to improve humanity and society by teaching the true faith, which would change the attitudes and behavior of the Germans, bringing them closer to God.[1] He concluded that even by the end of the century, "Lutheranism had not succeeded in making an impact on the population at large."[2] Strauss was writing particularly about the failure of the clergy's reformation to reach the mass of the people, that is, the peasantry.[3] He was careful to point out that his evidence (essentially the visitation records) is very sparse for the cities, and speculated that the grim collage of ignorance, apathy, and resistance he constructed for the countryside might not describe the urban reformation.[4] Certainly it does not describe Strasbourg.

In evaluating the fundamental changes brought about during the reformation we need to bear certain truths in mind. In the first place, the reformation in Strasbourg was not just a Lutheran reformation. The Lutherans were ultimately victorious, but other currents had their adherents and their roles in the city's evolution. Within the Lutheran stream the reformation was not just the clerical reforma-

[1] Gerald Strauss, "Success and Failure in the German Reformation," *Past & Present, 67* (1975), 42.

[2] Ibid., p. 59; Gerald Strauss, *Luther's House of Learning,* pp. 249, 307–8.

[3] His conclusions do not apply to the peasants of Strasbourg's rural territories. See Kittelson, "Successes and Failures," pp. 153–75.

[4] "Success and Failure," pp. 48, 59–60; *Luther's House,* p. 294.

tion, for many members of the laity nourished rival notions of what Lutheranism should be. While the reformation was a spiritual event, it was also a secular process, and its effects can be traced in customs as well as in beliefs. Finally, the reformation affected different groups within the city in different ways. It meant one thing to magistrates, another to clergymen, and something else again to Strasburghers outside those elites. What was a defeat for the clergy was at times a victory for the laity, while in other cases a failure for the ruled was a success for their rulers. Class and gender complicate matters further. The answers to questions like "What was the reformation's impact?" and "Was it a success or a failure?" depend on whom one asks. The answers also depend on when one asks, for the balance of power among magistrates, clergy, and people was not constant throughout the century.

The magistrates in office in 1520 were not dreaming of anything like an evangelical reformation. Indeed their previous failure to support Bishop Wilhelm von Honstein shows that even conservative Catholic reform was not entirely to their taste, for if successful, it would have strengthened the hand of the bishop, and the bishop was their traditional rival for control of the city. Their original response to evangelical preaching also fell far short of warm support. Yet the magistrates turned out to be the obvious early beneficiaries of the evangelical reformation. In the initial settlement of the mid-1530s they confirmed their escape from subordination to the Roman hierarchy and gained wide new powers over the city's Protestant clergy. They had seen the destruction of the currents of social radicalism, those attacks on lordship which had been building in Alsace since the days of Joss Fritz's peasant revolts. By taking over the property and revenues of Catholic corporations, they had fattened the municipal treasury and provided themselves with the funds to operate overhauled educational and charitable systems. On the other hand, with new power and wealth went increased responsibility and danger. The magistrates' plunge into the regulation of religious life condemned them, and their successors, to incalculable hours of draining debate. They were frequently uncomfortable with this work, for they were ill-prepared to arbitrate doctrinal disputes and uneasy about the requirements of enforcing orthodoxy. To make matters more difficult for them, their conversion to Protestantism threatened their city's independence. It brought them the enmity of the emperor and later contributed to their vulnerability in the imperial-French struggles.

The gains the magistrates had made at the expense of the clergy, embodied in the lay supremacy established in the original reformation settlement of the early thirties, did not all endure intact. The ineffectiveness of the church wardens and the purposeful solidarity of the Church Assembly slowly returned administrative control of the Strasbourg church to its clergy. Meanwhile the increasing complication of the doctrinal issues underlying religious politics, in particular the intra-Lutheran and Lutheran-Calvinist disputes, forced the magistrates to rely on the expertise of their theologians. What had been established as the magistrates' church was more the pastors' church at the end of the century. This development paralleled other changes in the governance of the city which made the Senate and XXI generally more dependent on the advice of its professional servants, for example, the city lawyers.[5] The revival of clerical authority was not unwelcome to the magistrates of the third generation, and it was possible only with their consent. By the late sixteenth century they were ready to concede that what their grandfathers had bitten off was now more than they could, or cared to, chew.

The long-term results of the German reformation were disastrous for the Senate and XXI. Within the Empire the reformation contributed to the decay of the cities and the strengthening of the princes, in particular in the latter half of the century. The divisions within the Empire weakened it vis-à-vis France; Alsace and Strasbourg would fall victim to this in the next century. Louis XIV's seizure of the city in 1681 realized one of the haunting terrors of the patriots who had ruled it in the sixteenth century. Not only was Strasbourg weaned away from the Empire and made bicultural, the Senate and XXI lost its near-sovereign status. The overlordship of the Bourbon kings was a very different thing from that of the Habsburg emperors.[6]

The evangelical clergy who had begun what became the Lutheran reformation in Strasbourg temporarily achieved the near total destruction of the old church in the 1520s. Their initial victory was incomplete, and from their point of view, characterized more by the purging of the bad than by the creation of the good, because changes in doctrine, ritual, and church structure were not accompanied by the personal reformation of every Strasburgher. Their victory was won at a heavy cost, paid in the form of submission to the Senate and

[5]Crämer, *Verfassung,* pp. 33–38.
[6]Franklin L. Ford, *Strasbourg in Transition, 1648–1789* (Cambridge, Mass., 1958).

XXI. Strasbourg's preachers in the thirties and forties voiced the same disappointment and malaise Gerald Strauss documented for the Lutheran clergy in general. Their frustrations were the predictable result of overly ambitious goals, for they had expected the preaching of the Gospel to produce a rapid alteration in the whole life of the city. Pessimistic as their anthropology was, it had not prepared them for the strength of the Old Adam's resistance.

The gloomy reassessment the clergy made of their progress in the thirties and forties did not break their spirit. The Church Assembly continued its work, lobbying the magistrates, preaching to the people, and catechizing the children. Two generations later the balance sheet on their efforts was much more positive. Dissent remained and sin remained, but the majority of the Strasburghers now regarded themselves as Lutherans, and much of the authority ceded to the lay rulers in the first generation had now been won back. Granted, the president and the Church Assembly did not have precisely the same powers as the bishop and priests of the early sixteenth century, but then they had not sought to be exactly what the old clergy had been. Their goal on this score had been a reform of the clerical estate and a better distinction between the proper spheres of lay and clerical jurisdictions. In these matters the state of affairs described in the 1598 Church Ordinance was much more gratifying to the clergy than the initial settlement had been.

The 1598 Church Ordinance did not signal the absolute triumph of the clerical reformation, however. When the laity accepted it and called themselves good Lutherans they affirmed that "good Lutheran" was a term that stretched to cover people who still balked at their preachers' views on the interplay of the secular and the spiritual. Much has been written about the reformation as a secularization of life, and the early Protestants in particular have at times been presented as the advocates of this secularization.[7] Certainly the mix of the spiritual and the worldly prevailing in the early sixteenth century outraged reformers of several schools, yet it is at least arguable that the Lutheran clergy's solution was not to secularize religious life but to sacralize lay life.[8] Telling the clergy to emulate the lay practices of marriage and work beneficial to their neighbors is obviously different from telling the laity to model their behavior on the monastic prac-

[7]For example, Ozment, *Reformation in the Cities,* pp. 89, 119.

[8]James M. Kittelson, "Humanism and the Reformation in Germany," *Central European History,* 9 (1976), 320, 321.

tices of celibacy and contemplation. Behind the obvious difference is a unity of purpose. All Christians must bow to God's will and every human act must be undertaken to please God. The point in both cases was to minimize the difference between secular and spiritual life by imposing a single stardard, the demands of God. The Strasburghers, as we have seen, resisted the clergy's invitation to an all-encompassing piety, preferring, as their rulers put it, to keep their world worldly, at least in part.

The gains and the losses the local reformation brought to men and women who were neither magistrates nor clergymen are harder to pinpoint than its results for the two elites. The magistrates' lay subjects were, at least in the surviving records, much less articulate about their desires and much more divided than either the magistrates or the preachers, but a few general conclusions can be drawn. The Lutheran faith was more comprehensible than prereformation Catholicism, for several reasons. The development of a German liturgy and the wider availability of the Bible in Luther's translation made obvious contributions, as did the massive educational effort directed at the city's people. Lutheran theology could reduce itself to a simpler core—only two sacraments to explain, not seven, for example. The early reformers had stripped their message to its essentials in their urgency to communicate their theology, and their successors continued to concentrate on that essence when addressing the laity. Among the intellectuals the early simplification gave way to the joys of elaboration, but this was of little consequence to most Strasburghers. The chief impact of the elaboration was a body blow to the "everyman his own theologian" current of the twenties, but the priesthood of all believers had been an ambiguous notion from the start and those who tried to act it out a minority.[9]

The Strasburghers found their new faith not only simpler to understand, but cheaper to practice. It produced nothing like the cathedral canons, whose aristocratic tastes had had to be financed by the laity. There were no more indulgences to buy, no more masses to purchase, no more candles to pay for, no more statues to donate. In other ways as well, religion became less demanding. The marriage laws were changed, and divorce with a right to remarry was allowed in certain cases. Against all this must be set an intractable question: was

[9]Heiko Oberman, *Masters of the Reformation: The Emergence of a New Intellectual Climate in Europe,* trans. Dennis Martin (London, 1981), pp. 277–80.

salvation by faith alone really more comforting and comprehensible than works-righteousness? The Lutherans' continuing difficulty with the role of good works suggests the answer may have been no.[10]

The laity's great gain was a more satisfactory clergy. The decline in anticlericalism—rabid in the early reformation, persistent for at least another generation in fears that the clergy would forge a "new papacy," and virtually absent by the end of the century—is among the most striking shifts in Strasbourg's intellectual climate. At mid-century the novelist Georg Wickram could trot out tales of lecherous priests (who had their real-life counterparts in the city), but he found nothing to satirize on the Protestant side.[11] The Lutheran clergy in Strasbourg did succeed in winning the respect, and even the affection, of their parishioners. Strasburghers chose clergymen as godparents for their children, turned out for their pastors' funerals, and remembered them in their wills.[12] Many of them kept portraits of their pastors in their homes.[13] The continuing currents of dissent and indifference indicate that not all Strasburghers accepted the clergy's ideals, but there were no more complaints about clerical laziness, ignorance, immorality, or greed.

Within the laity different groups experienced the reformation in different ways and took different messages about their secular lives from it. The very rich at the top of urban society in the 1520s could have found little comfort in the preachers' ideas about economic life. The evangelicals had nothing good to say, then or later, to the accumulators and producers of great wealth. The clergy abominated usury and speculation, two props of local wealth. This and their persistent rejection of all arguments that religious policy must be shaped with an eye to its repercussions on commerce show how little sympathy they had for capitalist business. As Martin Bucer saw it, merchants "become rich without working, against God's commandment (Genesis 3:19) [and] seek their own profit through the exploitation and destruction of others."[14] Despite the preachers' attitude toward commercial capitalism, enough of the rich became evangelical

---

[10]For example, the disputes between Georg Major and Nicolas Amsdorf, taken up in the Formula of Concord; see Tappert, ed., *The Book of Concord*, pp. 475–77.

[11]*Rollwagenbüchlein*, in *Werke*, vol. 7, nos. 3, 20, 34, 46, 47, 79; AMS AA 1576 and AA 1587, f. 45r.

[12]Baptisms, AMS N168, p. 116; N213, f. 149r; N214, p. 140; N215, f. 19v. BNUS ms. 1266, f. 94r, on Marbach's funeral. Bequests: KS 227, ff. 231r–236v; KS 210, ff. 268r–270r, 302r–v.

[13]Kintz, "La société," p. 873.

[14]*Das ym selbs, BDS,* 1:59.

to swing the balance in the ruling class and make Strasbourg Protestant.

Three times the clergy forged extraordinary alliances with groups in the commons—in the early and middle twenties, the late forties, and at the time of the Bishops' War—and these alliances, the products of crises, were strongly colored by criticism of the city's rich. In normal times the clergy's sympathies remained with the poor, but their sympathy produced more talk than action. The clergy distanced themselves in 1525 from the partisans of the one forceful attempt to remake the secular status quo and redistribute wealth. Thereafter they almost always defended the established social order, for they had made compromises with the ruling class in order to destroy the old church. The reworking of the city's welfare arrangements in the early sixteenth century can no longer be seen as peculiarly evangelical; it was the local face of a larger European evolution.[15] Undoubtedly the clergy encouraged charity for the deserving poor, and themselves did what they could for individuals, but they assumed both the inevitability of poverty and its relative inconsequence before the great issue of salvation.

It was the middling sort of Strasburghers—the petty bourgeois and upper working-class families in the guilds—whose secular lives were most often validated by the reformers. Within the urban structure it was tradesmen in particular whom the clergy praised as model burghers. To quote Bucer again, "The Christian estates or occupations which are the most useful to others, and do them the least harm, [are] farming, the raising of livestock, and the necessary artisanal trades."[16] Translated into urban terms, Bucer's list would consist of those who supplied food, clothing, and shelter: butchers, bakers, gardeners, and fishermen; weavers, tailors, and shoemakers; masons, carpenters, and cabinetmakers. It was from this stratum that the clergy drew their strongest support, as is shown by the chronicles of the early reformation, the nominal rolls of the fellowship movement at mid-century, and the composition of the groups backing the preachers at the end of the century. The middling sort were those whose self-esteem the clergy flattered most, and of whose material interests they were most solicitous. This was, not incidentally, the milieu into which most of the clergy had themselves been born.

[15]Winckelmann, *Das Fürsorgewesen der Stadt Strassburg* is factually accurate but dated in its interpretations.
[16]*Das ym selbs,* p. 58.

This is not to argue that Lutheranism was the religion of the rising middle classes. Strasbourg had no rising middle class. Moreover, at every level of society, the majority converted. The city's economy was so saturated by the ecclesiastical presence that few Strasburghers did not have a direct interest in the fate of the church's financial empire, and economic self-interest undoubtedly influenced some people's response to the early reformation. Religious conversion, however, was not the result of a calculation of material gains and losses; it came rather from the conviction that the new faith was more Christian than the old. Secular interests played a powerful role not so much in the decision to join the evangelicals as in the interpretation of what the evangelicals were saying. Some Strasburghers cheered the destruction of the lordship and wealth of the Catholic clergy while their oligarchs were endorsing a Protestantism that muted its attacks on wealth and stressed obedience to secular lords.

The preachers' messages about family life and the proper relationships between men and women bit more deeply into private lives than did their advice on economic matters. Information about domestic life is rare and, except for demographic data, prescriptive or anecdotal.[17] Any reading of these sources will of necessity involve a noticeable amount of speculation.[18]

At the center of the effort to renew domestic life was the Lutheran message that sexual activity did not always drive the soul away from God.[19] The willingness of evangelical priests to put their doctrine into practice by taking wives struck a deep chord among many Strasburghers, convincing them that the long-desired reformation of religion was at last underway.[20] The evangelical clergy married because they were convinced that marriage was an estate pleasing to

[17]For the demographic data see Kintz, *La société,* in particular chap. 5. Miriam Usher Chrisman examines women's response to the early reformation in "Women and the Reformation in Strasbourg, 1490–1530," *ARG,* 64 (1972), 143–68.

[18]Working from published descriptive and prescriptive sources, and from prescriptive sources and court records respectively, Steven Ozment and Thomas Max Safley arrive at very different evaluations of sixteenth-century family life. Compare Ozment's *When Fathers Ruled: Family Life in Reformation Europe* (Cambridge, Mass., 1983) and Safley's *Let No Man Put Asunder.* Where Ozment sees change and liberation Safley finds continuity and community regulation.

[19]This is particularly clear in Luther's preaching. *Ein Sermon von dem ehelichen Stand* (1519) and *Vom ehelichen Leben* (1522), in *D. Martin Luthers Werke: Kritische Gesamtausgabe* (Weimar, 1883 ff.), 2:162–71 and 10²:267–304.

[20]Late in the sixteenth century Strasburghers chronicling their reformation frequently began with some sentence like "Anno 1524 [sic] the priests began to take wives." Berhard Hertzog, *Chronicon Alsatiae* (Strasbourg, 1592), p. 116.

God which allowed men and women to satisfy overpowering natural urges while ensuring the survival of the community. True celibacy, in their view, was such a rare gift that the unmarried had little hope of avoiding fornication. Therefore they encouraged early marriage and praised those who bore and raised children.[21]

The ideal Lutheran household was founded upon the reciprocal duties of the spouses to each other and of the parents and children. Husbands and wives were urged to welcome each other's sexual advances.[22] The labor of both was needed for their household to flourish, and they were expected to work together to strengthen their faith and improve their conduct. Parenting added a new dimension to these obligations, since fathers and mothers were expected to contribute to the Christian education of their offspring.[23] Some allowance was made for human weakness; in cases of adultery or desertion the offended spouse could have the marriage ended by the city magistrates.[24] Wives and husbands confronted by other difficulties were more likely to be told they must pray for the strength to endure their lives together.

Despite the emphasis on reciprocal duties, the reformed household was not an egalitarian household. The pious home had to have a head and that head had to be the husband and father. This insistence on masculine control reflected both the normal sixteenth-century view that all social groups, including the family, had natural leaders established by God, and the enduring conviction that women were simultaneously weak and dangerous. The 1598 Church Ordinance, echoing older attitudes, tempered its observations on reciprocity in marriage. Husbands ought to love their wives and provide for them, while wives must not only love and care for their husbands, they must also be sweet and meek. The Ordinance paid more attention to women's possible failings in marriage than to those of men and emphasized the dangers of female stubbornness, disobedience, disloyalty, bad temper, and negligence.[25] Male authority was not supposed to mean tyranny, and may often have been much tempered in practice. The idealized marriages of Georg Wickram's mid-century

[21]Ozment, *When Fathers Ruled*, chap. 1.
[22]Wendel, *Le mariage*, pp. 46, 56–57.
[23]*Tischgebete für die Kinder* (Strasbourg, 1557), sig. Aiii recto.
[24]Wendel, *Le mariage*, chap. 6.
[25]*Kirchenordnung* (Strasbourg, 1598), pp. 198–200. See also the marriage service, pp. 214–30.

fiction portrayed spouses who shared decision making, as Katherine and Matthis Zell seem to have done in reality.[26]

Men and women trying to live out the ideal of the evangelical household found they had duties other than authority and obedience determined by their gender. For women this meant motherhood, because, as the Church Ordinance put it, a woman's "greatest honor on earth is her fertility."[27] Pregnancy was dangerous, and Strasbourg's congregations regularly prayed for expectant mothers.[28] The pastors visited them and devised special prayers to strengthen them. These "consolations" made no secret of the impending pain of labor—"the fitting punishment of sin laid on the female sex"—but urged women to bear it stalwartly. After all, said the preachers, the pain did not last long, it was part of a God-pleasing vocation, it would produce children, and children were both a blessing from God and the future of the community. Angels would hover about the good Christian mother during her labor to protect the baby, for otherwise the red Dragon, the living Devil, would "gobble up the poor children and damn them for all eternity." This terrifying vision of spiritual combat waged around the obstetrical chair ended the pastors' official encouragement to expectant mothers.[29] The preachers frequently reminded mothers who survived childbirth and raised healthy infants of the importance of their work to society, and told them how pleasing it was to God.[30]

The Strasbourg preachers had rather less to say to husbands and fathers. While they were expected, as heads of their families, to oversee the moral guidance of their wives and children, the physical care of children was, by implication, women's work. The clergy's insistence that women's vocations were domestic and reproductive carried an undeveloped corollary. The good Christian husband and father had to be able to earn enough to support himself and at least two other people. His authority and the respectability of his household both depended on his economic success.

Individual Strasburghers of both sexes experienced difficulties in living up to the clerical ideals, and some of them fell into the hands of

[26]For Wickram's attitudes to marriage see Chrisman, *Lay Culture*, pp. 211, 219–20. For the Zells see Chrisman, "Women," and Roland Bainton, "Katherine Zell," *Medievalia et Humanistica*, n.s. 1 (1970), 3–28.

[27]*Kirchenordnung*, pp. 266–67.

[28]Ibid., p. 116. See also Kintz, *La société*, pp. 161–68, about obstetrics.

[29]*Kirchenordnung*, pp. 264–69.

[30]Waldemar Kawerau, *Die Reformation und die Ehe* (Leipzig, 1892), p. 3; Kintz, *La société*, pp. 219–21.

the magistrates, who punished their violations of clerical and social proscriptions. The stake awaited male homosexuals and men guilty of incest.[31] Men who fathered bastards could be forced into marriage if single, or imprisoned and fined if already married. Single mothers were labeled "whores," and those who could not be married might be exiled.[32] This was mild punishment compared to the fates reserved for women who attempted to procure abortions: death by decapitation, drowning, or flogging.[33] Women who forgot their duty to be meek might find themselves accused of witchcraft and possibly burned for their ill temper, while a husband who failed to assert his authority became the neighborhood joke. Women who resisted marriage and tried to make their own way in the world had little to hope for. An unmarried working-class woman found herself at the very bottom of the city's social pyramid, while the hostility to convents and beguinages closed the door on respectable work for more affluent spinsters.[34] One woman, who disguised herself as a man to find work as a baker's apprentice in the hard times of the 1590s, spent ten weeks in prison, then suffered the humiliation of being pilloried in her masculine clothing, and was at last beaten out of town.[35]

The reformation's ideal of family life created broader difficulties as well. The reiterated exhortations to women to practice meekness point to a widespread assertiveness among wives and daughters; certainly Susanna Wormser felt free to order her patrician husband to run errands for her.[36] Implicit in the preachers' praise for the married and the fertile was a condemnation of the unmarried and the childless. This must have created particular anguish among the women who could not conceive, or whose babies died, as so many did. Katherine Zell, whose own children did not survive, could only interpret her plight as divine punishment for her sins.[37] The city's contracting economy made it more and more difficult for one man alone to find

[31]Büheler, "La chronique," no. 275; RP 1585, ff. 413r–414r, 462v–463r.

[32]RP 1572, ff. 560v–561v; RP 1570, f. 553v.

[33]Kintz, *La société*, p. 217.

[34]*Der Statt Strassburg Policeij Ordnung*, p. 41, for working class spinsters.

[35]Louis Schneegans, *Strassburgische Geschichten, Sagen, Denkmäler, Inschriften, Künstler, Kunstgegenstände, und Allerlei* (Strasbourg, 1855), pp. 178–79, citing the lost original of Sebald Büheler's chronicle.

[36]Otto Winckelmann, "Strassburger Frauenbriefe des 16ten Jahrhunderts," *Archiv für Kulturgeschichte*, n.F. 2 (1904), 177–81.

[37]Bainton, "Katherine Zell," p. 6. Men were not immune to these feelings; Johann Schenckbecher's autobiographical notes frequently refer to his regret that his marriage was childless (AST 1655).

enough work to support his dependents. Early modern Strasbourg's economy was simply not rich enough to allow the city's laboring majority to shape its families entirely in accord with the Lutheran ideals. Some never married, most married late, and few could afford to restrict wives and daughters entirely to domestic work. The clergy's ideals, however, slowly became the middle-class standard.

For all the Strasburghers, in and out of the clergy, and of whatever estate or gender, the world changed slowly. Certainly in the first decade of the reformation there were revolutionary alterations in the externals of religious life. The clergy married; the liturgy came to be in German; the images disappeared from the churches, and the monks and nuns from the streets. The mass was gone, along with the processions, the indulgences, and the vigils. For all that, symbols and habits endured. The Strasburghers continued to listen for the ringing of the "Ave Maria bell" long after praying to Mary went out of fashion.[38] If people no longer prayed to the saints, they probably still cursed by them. Strasburghers who acquired official documents authenticated by the city seal could still admire the image of the Virgin on their papers.[39] In 1539, a decade after the abolition of the mass, some of the city's innkeepers remained oblivious to Protestant teaching about human law and berated guests who ordered meat on Fridays.[40] A young magistrate beginning his career in the courts might arm himself with a vernacular manual, Ulrich Tengler's *The Layman's Mirror of the Proper Ordinances of Civil and Criminal Law*. Well after the reformation had begun, he would find in it a careful distinction between lay and church courts, forms of oaths requiring witnesses to invoke the saints, and gruesome woodcuts showing monks who comforted the victims of all the diverse modes of execution current in the century.[41] This was not how justice was administered in Strasbourg, but there was no Protestant manual.

In a great many areas, including some parts of religious life, the reformation did not mean a complete break with the past. Geiler von Kaysersberg had condemned the wealthy monopolists and usurers in Strasbourg in terms as vehement as Martin Bucer's. The latter's *No One Should Live for Himself, but for Others* echoed prereformation

[38]RP 1544, f. 334v.

[39]Seals of 1537 and 1632 are reproduced in Crämer, *Verfassung*, plate 2.

[40]RP 1539, ff. 129v, 160v–161r.

[41]The last Strasbourg edition of Tengler's *Laienspiegel* was published in 1560. Its rival on the local market was another prereformation work, Sebastian Brant's *Richterliche Clagspiegel* (Strasbourg, 1553 [last local edition]).

judgments about the value of agriculture and the crafts, and the inherent dishonesty of commerce.[42] Much of the legislation on morality in sixteenth-century Strasbourg was simply a repetition of prereformation statutes.[43] There were continuities to be found in religious instruction as well. Johann Ulrich Surgant had pronounced preaching "the most effective agent for the conversion of mankind" well before Luther, and masters and parents were already being told to send their children to the clergy for catechism lessons before the Senate and XXI made this obligatory.[44] Even that supposedly typical Lutheran creation, the burgher's home as temple, was not so new; Dietrich Coelde and Stephen Lanzkrama had emphasized parental responsibility and family religious exercises in devotional manuals printed in the 1470s.[45] The reformers could not have found the audience they did if their message had been totally novel. The clergy knew this, and a constant theme of their reformation was that nothing was new. The reformers' ideas were very old, they said, for they were those of Christ and the Apostles. The Augsburg Confession agreed with the Tetrapolitan Confession; the Wittenberg Concord changed nothing, it only clarified things; the content of the 1598 Church Ordinance was traditional in Strasbourg. The desire to resist innovation had some odd results. In 1563 the magistrates decided they wanted to hear no more about the *Tetrapolitana* and they repealed it in 1598, but the members of two guilds were still sitting through an annual reading of it in 1611.[46] The ruts of familiar thinking slowed the progress of the clerical reformation more than once and confounded the clergy's early attempts to inculcate true doctrine. As late as 1534 the members of the Senate and XXI still agreed among themselves that "faith is a work of free will."[47]

Even where the reformers did break with the past, the ruptures were not necessarily lasting. Iconoclasm had been very much part of the early reformation, both clerical and popular, but in the latter part of the century images returned to the churches in the form of Biblical scenes and also in portraits of those saintly men, the first reformers.[48]

---

[42]For prereformation judgments see Janssen, *History of the German People*, 2:8–9, 81, 90–92, 96–97.

[43]See Chapter 8, note 13.

[44]Janssen, *History of the German People*, 1:36–37, 19–20.

[45]Ibid., 1:25, 31, 33.

[46]*BDS*, 3:24.

[47]AST 84/19, f. 1r.

[48]Bornert, *La réforme*, pp. 337, 487.

At first, all the holy days except Sunday were scrapped; by 1536 Bucer was grudgingly acknowledging some of the festivals of the early church. Christmas returned in 1537. By 1598 the Strasburghers were celebrating Easter, Pentecost, Christmas, and New Year's as full holidays, and St. Stephen's day, Good Friday, Easter Monday, Pentecost Monday, and Ascension as half-holidays.[49] In the latter part of the century a larger place was made for music in the church services, and Marbach revived polyphonic chant, performed for the congregation by student choirs.[50] Although only baptism and the eucharist were regarded as sacraments, a sort of quasi-sacramental status was restored to ordination and absolution.[51] The magistrates maintained meatless days—Friday, Saturday, and Lent—on economic grounds.[52] The clergy managed to restore private confession, even if they did not succeed in making it obligatory.[53] Prohibitions of sexual activity at certain periods of the year reappeared.[54] The result of all this, combined with the Catholic reformation, was to bring the religious lives of the Strasburghers and the people of the Catholic towns closer together than they had been in the second decade of the reformation. It is not unreasonable to speak of a re-Catholicization of some aspects of religious practice within Lutheranism, a down-to-earth parallel to the development of Protestant scholasticism.

Was the reformation a failure, then? To some extent yes, particularly if by the reformation one means the clergy's reformation. Yet it certainly made deep changes in the way the Strasburghers understood the Christian faith, and, however slowly and incompletely, had an undeniable impact on the way they lived their lives. In the end of reformation escapes the categories of success and failure. While we can roughly identify winners and losers at various stages, we must remember that the losers helped channel the reformation and that the winners had to make concessions to the losers and to each other. The religious settlement was a compromise in which everyone had yielded something. That compromise endured through conquest in 1681 and revolution in 1789; to this day Lutheranism has not exhausted its force in Strasbourg. As Georges Dor observed, in a quite

---

[49]Ibid., pp. 337–38, 491–93. The magistrates had made Christmas a secular holiday in 1532 (pp. 159–60).
[50]Ibid., pp. 227, 469–84.
[51]Ibid., pp. 187–88, 360–70, 335, 393.
[52]Kintz, *La société*, pp. 341–42.
[53]Bornert, *La réforme*, pp. 398–418.
[54]Kintz, *La société*, pp. 196–97, 205–6.

different context, "Survivre, c'était déjà vaincre."[55] In the risky conditions of the sixteenth century, the survival of their church was indeed a victory for the Lutherans.

[55]Georges Dor, "Les ancêtres," in *Poèmes et chansons* (Ottawa, 1968), p. 55. Dor refers to pioneers in the province of Québec.

Conclusion

Strasbourg's long reformation, nearly a century in the making, evolved through the interplay of magisterial, clerical, and popular designs for a Christian church. In the early decades of the sixteenth century the desire for church reform which had built up in the late middle ages produced a series of competing programs for reform in Strasbourg. The evangelical current, which rapidly became dominant here, had been begun by preachers and owed its success to their ability to capture popular support. Clergy and commons for a time united to win concessions from the magistrates, but their alliance proved short-lived, for the clerical program, with its insistence on a reformation of the laity as well as of the clergy, diverged from the popular sense of what a reformation should entail. To the laity the essential things were to tame the pretensions of the clergy and to reduce the demands they could make on the secular estates. By the time Strasbourg had broken with Rome the evangelical preachers had become pastors, eager to see doctrinal change accompanied by the moral regeneration of their parishioners, but the laity had little interest in this. Instead they accepted the lead of their secular rulers, who in the late twenties and early thirties organized a new territorial church, very much under magisterial control.

To the frustration of the clergy, the lay supremacy remained the dominant feature of local religious politics from the 1530s into the 1570s. For decades the commons and magistrates still nursed their old anticlericalism, ever watchful lest their pastors try to resurrect the old clerical dominance in a dreaded "new papacy." Magistrates and commons showed scant enthusiasm for the sort of all-pervasive piety favored by the clergy and rejected the preachers' attempts to impose their own standards on secular conduct. Significant minorities among the population at large preferred Schwenckfeld or Anabaptist leaders to their appointed pastors, others remained loyal to the old church, and Calvinist refugees created a third heretical enclave in the city. The delicacy with which the magistrates handled these rivals infuriated the clergy, but the complications of domestic and foreign policy made it imperative for the magistrates to act discretely. Strasbourg could not afford to become a citadel of pure Lutheranism; the pastors' anti-Catholicism and anti-Calvinism in particular violated the magistrates' sense of diplomatic realities. In these decades, too, the Lutheran preachers' attempts to monopolize the religious life of their city were hampered by the weakness and internal divisions that plagued their denomination between Luther's death and the creation of the Formula of Concord.

Starting in the 1570s, however, the Strasbourg clergy began to gain ground in their efforts to escape from magisterial tutelage and to win the trust of the majority of the lay Strasburghers. The evident success of the Catholic reformation in both the surrounding diocese and the Empire at large alarmed Strasburghers in all walks of life, renewing a concern for the safety of their church which had faded after the failure of the Catholic restoration temporarily imposed in the aftermath of the Schmalkaldic War. Attempts to create a pan-Protestant opposition to the resurgent Roman church served only to draw Strasbourg, its dependent villages, and its neighbors into the horrors of religious war. The Strasburghers became more and more convinced that Catholicism and Calvinism both bred ruin, while Lutheranism meant peace. Catholicism and Calvinism also seemed foreign, whereas Lutheranism could be identified with local patriotism. At the same time, the Lutheran theologians outside Strasbourg were at last arriving at the doctrinal consensus that, in the Formula of Concord, would end their internicene quarrels. The Church Assembly endorsed this peacemaking, and even though the magistrates of the seventies and eighties held themselves aloof from the theologians' efforts, the preachers were winning considerable popular support for the new Lutheran orthodoxy. They were also managing, without magisterial permission, to strengthen the office of president of the Church Assembly and to reduce active lay participation in the administration of the church.

In the 1570s a third generation came of age, children who had been catechized by pastors loyal to Lutherarism. Tales of clerical tyranny in Strasbourg were, for this generation, so old as to be nearly fabulous; the flesh and blood clergymen they knew had established themselves as trustworthy. The doctrinal issues of their day were arcane matters, and few of the laity showed any desire to master these intricacies; instead they found their pastors' argument that the laity should defer to professional expertise in these matters both sensible and convenient. In the late 1590s this generation suddenly took control of the dominant executive councils in Strasbourg's government. Men sick of the consequences of confessional strife, with no reason to continue to quarrel with their pastors over the ratification of the Formula of Concord, were prepared to make changes in portions of the original reformation settlement.

The acceptance of the Formula of Concord and the passage of a new Church Ordinance in 1598 marked the end of Strasbourg's reformation. The third generation to grapple with the dilemmas of doctrinal definition and enforcement, of church administration, and of the policing of morality summed up the laity's accumulated wisdom about what the reformation should mean for Strasbourg. While they willingly deferred to their pastors' doctrinal expertise and abandoned their fathers' quixotic attempts to construct a Protestant league against the Catholics, they preserved more than just external vestiges of the laity's reformation.

Despite the clergy's objections, Lutheran Strasbourg continued to extend a de facto toleration to the minorities who preferred rival Christian faiths. The reluctance to bully people into lying about their honest convictions which had always characterized the magistrates' enforcement of uniformity survived the reformation to provide a welcome protection for those among their subjects who could not yield to the pastors' persuasions.

Most Strasburghers had long ago become convinced that the man in the pulpit of their parish church was their best guide to understanding the true faith of Christ. The church these pastors administered, in close cooperation with the city's secular rulers, had resolved to teach according to the dictates of orthodoxy laid down in the Formula of Concord. For the laity the pastors had devised a simplified theology to brace and reassure men and women confronting life's difficulties. Sinners within the church might be brought to amendment by measured doses of shame administered by their pastors; those who persisted in their violation of community standards, along with annoying heretics, could also count on the attentions of the magistrates. If one great legacy of the laity's reformation was a limited local acceptance of honest dissent, another was the insistence that the ultimate control of behavior must be the preserve of the lay courts. Secular courts took charge of the actions of both clergy and laity, and what they enforced was the city's customary law, not the dictates of Moses.

The clergymen of the Church Assembly drafted the great Church Ordinance of 1598, and it would be wrong to minimize the role of its members and their predecessors in the evolution of the city's reformation. Yet in essence what happened in Strasbourg was the laity's reformation, for the Capitos, Bucers, Hedios, Marbachs, and Pappuses could accomplish no more than what the commons and rulers could be persuaded to accept. Lay support, first popular and then magisterial, was essential to sustain the rebel preachers' revolt against the old church's doctrines and practices. Thereafter the lay magistrates controlled the new territorial church and ensured its survival in the middle decades of the sixteenth century. Lay values left a strong stamp on the final resolution of the reformation debates. Throughout the six difficult decades that separated the first and second church ordinances, Lutheranism endured in Strasbourg because the laity wanted it to survive. They gave their loyalty to a church that was to them both faithful to the Bible and an escape from what they continued to regard as papal tyranny. Above all else, Lutheranism became their means to fulfill what they understood as God's design for his Christian people.

APPENDIX A

Magistrates Most Involved in
Religious Policy, 1539–1598

Appendix A summarizes the activities and, where possible, indicates the confessional leanings of the 115 men most active in setting and administering religious policy in the years for which the minutes of the Senate and XXI are extant. All served on both ad hoc and standing committees, but only the latter are given here. For information on other magistrates see Lorna Jane Abray, "The Long Reformation: Magistrates, Clergy, and People in Strasbourg, 1520–1598" (Ph.D. diss., Yale University, 1978), Appendix B.

Years of service are taken from Jacques Hatt, *Liste des membres du grand Sénat de Strasbourg, des stettmeistres, des ammeistres, des conseils des XXI, XIII et des XV du XIIIe siècle à 1789* (Strasbourg, 1963) as corrected by Thomas A. Brady, Jr., *Ruling Class, Regime and Reformation at Strasbourg, 1520–1555* (Leiden, 1978) for those whose terms in office began before 1555, and by the RP for those who took office thereafter. The offices are explained above, Chap. 2.

I have borrowed Brady's term "evangelical" to indicate an early supporter of the reformation. "Orthodox" describes a supporter of the unaltered Augsburg Confession and/or the Formula of Concord. Men who left Strasbourg in 1547 or 1548 favored compromise with the Catholic emperor rather than the continued resistance to him advocated by militant Protestants; for this, and for the terms "war party" and "peace party" see above, Chapter 4.

Abbreviations

admin.	administrator (*Pfleger*) of a convent or a beguinage
Amr.	Ammeister
convent board	set policy for dealing with surviving convents and monasteries
FC	Formula of Concord
ledige XXI	supernumerary member of XXI
mass committee	standing committee to achieve the abolition of masses allowed by the Religious Peace of 1555
Molsheim	Jacob von Molsheim's private papers (AST 65/15/10, f. 297r)
PS	Patrician Senator
scholarch	regent of Latin school
S	Guild Senator
St.	Stettmeister

Armbruster, Felix (= Erstein, genannt Armbruster).
  Sectarian board; admin. of a beguinage.
  S: 1542/43; XV: 1548; XIII: 1548–52.
  Early evangelical; favored resistance to Charles V in 1547 (Brady, *Ruling Class,* pp. 267, 313).
Auenheim, Hans.
  Morals board; convent board; church warden.
  S: 1581/82; XV: 1584–94.
  Peace party (XV 1592, ff. 109v–110r).
Baldner, Anselm.
  Admin. of St. Nicolas-in-undis.
  S: 1537/38; XV: 1535–63.
  Favored resistance to Charles V in 1547 (Brady, *Ruling Class,* p. 262).
Beinheim, Hans.
  School inspector; sectarian board; mass committee.
  S: 1583/84; XV: 1581–96; XIII: 1596–1602.
  Peace party (XV 1592, ff. 109v–110r).
Berss, Hans von.
  Admin. of a beguinage; sectarian board; morals board; admin. of St. Nicolas-in-undis; mass committee.
  S: 1552/53; Amr.: 1554, 1560, 1566; XV: 1551–54; XIII: 1557–69.
  According to Molsheim, an orthodox Lutheran.
Betscholdt, Martin.
  Church warden; admin. of a beguinage.
  S: 1522, 1526/27, 1532/33, 1536/37; XV: 1523–32; XIII: 1532–46.
  Late convert to Protestantism; supported the clergy about discipline in 1546 (Brady, *Ruling Class,* p. 300, and RP 1545, ff. 529v–530r, minutes of January 1546).
Bietenheim, Claus von.
  Admin. of St. Margaret; convent board.
  PS: 1586/87, 1589/90, 1592/93, 1595, 1598–99, 1601; XV: 1586–1601.
  Peace party (XV 1592, ff. 109v–110r).

Bietenheim, Sifrid von.
Sectarian board; convent board; admin. of a beguinage.
S: 1523/24, 1527/28, 1531/32, 1535/36, 1542; XV: 1539–44.

Bock, Hans.
Sectarian board; admin. of a beguinage, and of Knights of St. John.
PS: 1512/13; St.: 1506/07, 1509/10, 1515/16, 1518, 1522/23, 1525/26, 1529/30, 1532/33, 1535/36, 1539, 1541/42; XV: 1510–15; XIII: 1518–42.
Early evangelical and interested in theology, but did not impose Protestantism on his village of Gerstheim (Brady, *Ruling Class,* p. 303).

Boecklin, Gladi II.
Morals board; church warden.
PS: 1562/63; St.: 1565/66; ledige XXI: 1563–64; XV: 1564–65; XIII: 1565–66.
Volunteered to go fight with Andelot for the Huguenots (RP 1562, ff. 322v–323r).

Boecklin, Hans Philips.
School inspector; admin. of St. Nicolas-in-undis.
PS: 1575, 1578, 1580/81; St.: 1594; XV: 1593–94; XIII: 1594–1614.
Likely a member of the peace party (XV 1593, f. 222r-v).

Boecklin, Ulman.
Admin. of Knights of St. John.
PS: 1529/30; St.: 1532, 1534/35, 1537/38, 1540/41, 1543/44, 1546/47; XV: 1532–39; XIII: 1539–48.
Conservative evangelical who left in 1548 (Brady, *Ruling Class,* pp. 242, 283).

Braun, Hans.
Church warden; sectarian board.
S: 1554/55, 1558/59, 1562/63, 1566/67.
Presumably Lutheran, although the rest of his family was Catholic.

Brompt, Wolf von.
Church warden; sectarian board; morals board.
S: 1533/34, 1542, 1545/46, 1549/50, 1555/56.
Favored resistance in 1547 (Brady, *Ruling Class,* p. 270).

Christman, Jörg.
Morals board.
S: 1531/32, 1535/36, 1539/40, 1543/44, 1547/48, 1551/52, 1555/56, 1559/60.
Named to morals board as strict disciplinarian (RP 1560, f. 29r).

Conrad von Pfaffenheim, Hans.
Church Warden.
S: 1530/31, 1540/41, 1546/47, 1550/51.

Drenss, Augustin I.
Church warden; sectarian board.
S: 1536/37; XV: 1542–52.
In 1524, objected vehemently to a sister's marriage to Caspar Hedio (Brady, *Ruling Class,* pp. 231–32).

Duntzenheim, Batt von.
Convent board; admin. of St. Nicolas-in-undis.
S: 1521/22, 1525/26, 1533/34; XV: 1533–38; XIII: 1538–43.
Early, but perhaps conservative, evangelical (Brady, *Ruling Class,* p. 242); strict disciplinarian (RP 1542, f. 80r).

Appendix A

Duntzenheim, Jacob von.
  Convent board; morals board.
  S: 1534/35, 1540/41; XV: 1539–46; XIII: 1546–48, 1549–54; Amr.: 1548, 1554.
  Early evangelical; favored resistance to Charles V in 1547 (Brady, *Ruling Class,* pp. 242, 267).
Durckheim, Nicolas von.
  Sectarian board; admin. of Charterhouse; church warden; mass committee.
  S: 1567/68, 1579/80, 1583/84; XIII: 1585–96.
Erb, Bastian.
  Marriage court; sectarian board (?); admin. of a beguinage; church warden.
  S: 1517/18, 1525/26, 1531/32, 1539/40; XXI: ?–1542; XV: 1542–48.
  Interpreted defeat in Schmalkaldic War as punishment for the city's sins, and favored resistance (Brady, *Ruling Class,* p. 270, 262).
Erhard, Jacob.
  Morals board.
  S: 1567/68, 1573/74, 1577/78, 1581/82, 1593/94.
  Strict disciplinarian, annoyed by Church Assembly's campaign to create public support for FC (RP 1578, ff. 46r–48v; RP 1581, ff. 183r–185r).
Fenchell, Hans.
  Sectarian board; morals board; church warden?
  S: 1573, 1575/76, 1577, 1580.
  Recommended expulsion of Flacius Illyricus, a controversial Lutheran theologian (RP 1573, ff. 187v–190v).
Franck, Simon.
  Admin. of St. Nicolas-in-undis; church warden.
  S: 1534/35, 1538/39, 1542; XXI: 1544–48; XV: 1533–42; XIII: 1542–57; Amr.: 1543.
Fuchs, Blasius.
  Morals board; sectarian board; church warden.
  S: 1561/62; XV: 1563–69; XIII: 1569–75.
Fuchs, Nicolas.
  Morals board; school inspector; sectarian board; censor.
  S: 1571/72; XXI: 1572; XV: 1572–89; XIII: 1589–98; Amr.: 1583, 1589, 1595.
  A mainstay of the war party.
Full von Geispolsheim, Heinrich.
  Morals board; scholarch.
  PS: 1565/66; St.: 1568/69, 1571/72; XV: 1564; XIII: 1564–72.
Furst, Hans Adolph.
  Admin. of a beguinage; convent board; church warden.
  S: 1579/80, 1583/84, 1587/88; XV: 1590–98; XIII: 1598–1608.
  Orthodox Lutheran; approved historical section of 1598 Church Ordinance.
Geiger, David.
  Morals board; sectarian board.
  S: 1569/70; XXI: 1572–76; XV: 1576–89.
  Said the FC was over his head (RP 1577, ff. 725v–732v), but probably was an orthodox Lutheran; considered Jean Sturm's supporters to be Calvinist and denounced French "conventicles" (XV 1581, ff. 71v–72r, and RP 1582, ff. 67v–68r).

Geiger, Matthis.
Convent board; church warden; censor.
S: 1529/30; XV: 1532–33; XIII: 1533–49; Amr.: 1535, 1541, 1547.
Sought peace in 1547 (Brady, *Ruling Class,* p. 267).
Gerfalck, Diebolt.
Marriage court; sectarian board; church warden.
S: 1538/39, 1546/47, 1552/53, 1556/57, 1560/61; XXI: 1557–58; XV: 1539–?; 1558–64.
Sought peace with honor in 1547 (Brady, *Ruling Class,* p. 262); opposed compulsion in matters of faith (RP 1558, ff. 563r–564r).
Gloner, Gall.
Sectarian board.
S: 1560/61, 1564/65, 1568/69, 1572/73, 1576/77, 1580/81, 1584/85.
Opposed a loan to the Huguenots (RP 1577, ff. 609v–610r).
Götz, Nicolas.
Sectarian board; morals board.
S: 1566/67, 1572/73, 1578/79.
Recounted parable of good Samaritan to promote admission of refugees (RP 1572, ff. 910r–911r); sold arms to Johann Casimir in 1570 (AMS V/12/52).
Gottesheim, Friederich von.
Scholarch; censor; school inspector; mass committee.
S: 1547/48; XXI: 1547–48; XV: 1548, 1551; XIII: 1551–81.
Favored continued resistance in 1547, left in 1548 (Brady, *Ruling Class,* pp. 267, 338); frequently supported loans to the Huguenots; refused to let Marbach call himself "superintendent" (RP 1576, ff. 668r–669r).
Gottesheim, Matthis von.
Morals board; church warden.
S: 1571/72; XXI: 1572–77; XV: 1577–81; XIII: 1581–1610.
Strict disciplinarian (RP 1578, ff. 46r–48v); war party (AMS V/74/7).
Graff, Andres.
Church warden; morals board; school inspector.
S: 1564/65; XV: 1557–75.
Named to morals board as strict disciplinarian (RP 1560, f. 29v); believed Marbach's *De coena Domini* diminished the reputations of Bucer, Hedio, and Capito (RP 1565, ff. 55v–56r); said pastors lacked charity (RP 1572, ff. 560v–561v).
Hammerer, Hans.
Morals board; sectarian board; church warden.
S: 1536/37, 1544/45, 1550/51; XV: 1548–52; XIII: 1552–53, 1556–72; Amr.: 1553, 1559, 1565, 1571.
Orthodox Lutheran according to Molsheim; approved Speccer's work on predestination (RP 1558, ff. 88v–89r); complained about swearing (RP 1559, ff. 183v–184r); considered a plague to be punishment for the city's sins (RP 1565, f. 6r); but recommended keeping Jean Sturm as rector of Latin school (RP 1570, ff. 195v–196r), and opposed admission of a controversial Lutheran theologian, Tileman Hesshus (AST 177, f. 70r, 1565).
Held, Abraham.
Convent board; sectarian board; morals board; admin. of St. Nicolas-in-undis and of the Charterhouse; scholarch; church warden.

S: 1559/60, 1563, 1565/66; XV: 1564–69; XIII: 1569–94; Amr.: 1568, 1574, 1580, 1586, 1592.
Orthodox Lutheran (RP 1577, ff. 725v–732v); opposed alliance with Swiss (RP 1587, ff. 654v–656r) and wanted Calvinist refugee church closed (RP 1577, ff. 96r–99r); but said Marbach was no superintendent (RP 1576, ff. 668r–669r) and employed Anabaptists (Chap. 5, n. 35, above).

Herlin, Martin.
Marriage court; censor.
S: 1519/20; XV: 1521; XIII: 1523–47; Amr.: 1522, 1528, 1534, 1540, 1546.
Zealous evangelical by 1523/24 and favored resistance to Charles V in 1547 (Brady, *Ruling Class*, pp. 318, 268); sponsored move to shorten services lest they make people late for meals (RP 1546, f. 252r).

Heuss, Michael.
Admin. of a beguinage; morals board.
S: 1544/45, 1548; XXI: 1548; XV: 1549–52; XIII: 1552–56; Amr.: 1550, 1556.
Recommended that clergy be allowed to inspect city parishes (RP 1554, f. 8r).

Hohenburg, Hans von.
Admin. of a beguinage; sectarian board; mass committee.
S: 1580/81; XV: 1578–88; XIII: 1588–1607; Amr.: 1591, 1597.
Protested Jean Sturm's dismissal (RP 1581, ff. 530v–531v).

Joham von Mundolsheim, Conrad.
Admin. of a beguinage.
S: 1521/22; XV: 1522–30; XIII: 1530–48.
Feared resistance would ruin his business, and left in 1548 (Brady, *Ruling Class*, pp. 280–81); between 1550 and 1564, appointed Catholic priests to a benefice he controlled outside the city (Brady, *Ruling Class*, p. 323).

Joham von Mundolsheim, David.
Morals board; admin. of Unser Frauen Haus and of St. Margaret.
PS: 1571/72; St.: 1574/75, 1577/78, 1580/81, 1583/84; XV: 1572–77; XIII: 1577–85.
Orthodox Lutheran (RP 1577, ff. 96r–99r; XV 1581, ff. 66v–68v).

Joham von Mundolsheim, Diebold.
Morals board; admin. of Unser Frauen Haus; mass committee.
PS: 1556/57, 1559/60, 1562/63, 1581/82; St.: 1565/66, 1568/69, 1571/72, 1574/75, 1577; XV: 1559–72; XIII: 1572–77.
Left in 1548 (Brady, *Ruling Class*, p. 289); orthodox Lutheran (RP 1577, ff. 96r–99r), but between 1550 and 1564 appointed Catholic priests to a benefice he controlled outside the city (Brady, *Ruling Class*, p. 323).

Joham von Mundolsheim, Heinrich I.
Admin. of St. Margaret; morals board; mass committee.
PS: 1556/57, 1560/61, 1563/64; XXI: 1562; XV: 1563–73.
Left in 1548 (Brady, *Ruling Class*, p. 378).

Joham von Mundolsheim, Heinrich II.
School inspector; morals board.
PS: 1581/82; St.: 1584/85; XV: 1580–85; XIII: 1585–86.
Protested Jean Sturm's dismissal (RP 1581, ff. 530v–531v); negotiated with Swiss (RP 1584, ff. 625r–v).

Jung, Diebolt.
Church warden; sectarian board.
XV: 1575–84.

Orthodox Lutheran: owned a copy of the FC and of Brentz's Catechism and made bequests to two pastors in his will (KS 210, ff. 271r–272r and 276r–278r, 1584).

Jung, Sebastian.
Sectarian board; admin. of St. Margaret; church warden.
S: 1526/27, 1536/37, 1542/43, 1546/47; XV: 1548–54.

Kageneck, Bernhard von.
School inspector; morals board.
PS: 1583/84; St.: 1586/87, 1589/90, 1592/93; XV: 1583–86; XIII: 1586–94.
Peace party; forced to resign (RP 1594, ff. 326r–v, 330r–v).

Kageneck, Philips von.
Convent board.
PS: 1534/35, 1538/39; St.: 1541/42, 1544/45; XV: 1539–42; XIII: 1542–45.
Catholic at least until 1528; no opinion on *Tetrapolitana* in 1534 (Brady, *Ruling Class,* pp. 325, 193).

Keller, Barthel.
Morals board; sectarian board; church warden.
S: 1547/48, 1551/52, 1577/78.
Said the FC was over his head and hoped his conscience would not be bound to it (RP 1577, ff. 725v–732v).

Kettenheim, Hans Philips.
School inspector; scholarch; morals board; admin. of St. Margaret.
PS: 1573/74, 1576/77; St.: 1579/80, 1582/83, 1585/86, 1588/89, 1591/92, 1594/95, 1597/98; XXI: 1574; XIII: 1574–1602.
War party; strong opponent of Lichtensteiger (XV 1586, f. 244v).

Kips, Jacob.
Admin. of St. Margaret; scholarch; morals board.
XV: 1591–93; XIII: 1593–94; Amr.: 1594.
War party (AST V/74/7).

Kips, Veltin.
Admin. of St. Margaret; admin. of a beguinage.
S: 1537/38, 1542/43; XV: 1541–51.
Favored resistance in 1547 (Brady, *Ruling Class,* p. 262).

Kniebis, Claus.
Church warden; scholarch; censor.
S: 1512/13, 1516/17; XV: 1514–18; XIII: 1520–52; Amr.: 1519, 1525, 1531, 1537.
Zealous evangelical by 1522; leader of that faction in the 1520s; ready to sue for peace in 1547 (Brady, *Ruling Class,* pp. 327, 269).

Kniebis, Jacob.
Admin. of a beguinage; morals board.
S: 1588/89; XV: 1588–1602; XIII: 1602–6.

Kniebis, Nicolas Hugo.
Sectarian board; scholarch; morals board; censor; school inspector; admin. of a beguinage.
S: 1556/57, 1560/61; XV: 1562–84; XIII: 1584–88.
Wanted Marbach's attacks on Calvinism moderated (RP 1565, ff. 432v–433v).

Kolöffel, Christoph I.
Church warden; morals board; sectarian board.
S: 1556/57, 1564/65, 1568/69, 1572.

Lampartheim, Hans von.
  S: 1550/51, 1554/55; XV: 1554–62.
Lehen, Thomas.
  Morals board; sectarian board.
  S: 1539/40, 1543/44, 1547/48, 1553/54, 1557/58, 1561/62.
  Favored resistance in 1547 (Brady, *Ruling Class,* p. 261, n. 9).
Leimer, Georg.
  Church warden; morals board; sectarian board; admin. of Charterhouse and of
  a beguinage.
  S: 1552/53; XXI: 1553; XV: 1551–56; XIII: 1558–72; Amr.: 1556, 1562.
  Orthodox Lutheran according to Molsheim; also approved Marbach's book
  against Calvinists (RP 1564, f. 238v) and praised work of David Chytraeus (RP
  1567, f. 385r); but opposed admission of Tileman Hesshus, a controversial
  Lutheran theologian (RP 1565, f. 43v), and said Marbach's *De coena Domini*
  diminished the reputations of Bucer, Capito, and Hedio (RP 1565, ff. 55v–
  56r).
Lichtensteiger, Michael.
  Sectarian board; morals board; mass committee; church warden; admin. of St.
  Margaret and of Unser Frauen Haus.
  S: 1564/65; XV: 1562–69; XXI: 1570–72; XIII: 1572–89; Amr.: 1569, 1575,
  1581, 1587.
  Orthodox Lutheran (RP 1577, ff. 725v–732v); strict disciplinarian (RP 1580,
  ff. 33v–34r); major opponent of Jean Sturm; but in 1570 opposed Strasbourg's
  involvement in FC project (RP ff. 785v–787v), and in 1574 said Marbach was
  no superintendent (RP [1573], ff. 878r–881v).
Lindenfels, Hans.
  Admin. of St. Margaret; church warden.
  S: 1518/19, 1523, 1526/27; XV: 1521–31; XIII: 1534–48; Amr.: 1532, 1538,
  1544.
  Evangelical by 1524; led an iconoclastic riot in 1529 (Brady, *Ruling Class,* p.
  328); helped draft the XVI Articles summarizing local doctrine (AST 75/47, p.
  595).
Lorcher, Johann Carl.
  Censor; morals board; school inspector; mass committee; scholarch; admin. of
  a beguinage.
  S: 1562/63; XV: 1563–65; XIII: 1565–88; Amr.: 1567, 1573, 1579, 1585.
  Approved Chytraeus's book (RP 1567, f. 385r); anti-Calvinist (RP 1577, ff.
  353r–356r), but firm opponent of FC (RP 1577, ff. 722v–723v), and protested
  Jean Sturm's dismissal (RP 1581, ff. 530v–531v).
Messinger, Georg.
  Morals board.
  S: 1546/47, 1552/53, 1560/61.
Messinger, Hans Heinrich.
  Church warden; admin. of a beguinage.
  S: 1588; XV: 1584–88.
Messinger, Lux.
  Sectarian board?
  S: 1527/28, 1535/36, 1541/42, 1546/47; XV: 1548–51; Amr.: 1552.
  Wanted Strasbourg to seek peace in 1547 (Brady, *Ruling Class,* p. 267).

Meyer, Frantz.
  Admin. of St. Margaret.
  S: 1555/56; XV: 1553–62; XIII: 1562–65.
Meyer, Jacob (Maurer guild).
  Scholarch; censor.
  S: 1519, 1522/23, 1526/27, XV: 1521–24; XIII: 1525–62.
  Evangelical by 1523; no opinion on *Tetrapolitana* in 1534; favored resistance in 1547 (Brady, *Ruling Class,* pp. 193, 262, 331).
Meyer, Jacob (zur Blume guild).
  Sectarian board; morals board; church warden.
  XV: 1548–49; XXI: 1549–54; XIII: 1554–67; Amr.: 1549, 1555, 1561, 1567.
  Named to morals board as strict disciplinarian (RP 1560, f. 29r), but opposed the ban (RP 1557, ff. 267r–268r); according to Molsheim, orthodox.
Meyer, Nicolas.
  Church warden; censor; admin. of a beguinage.
  S: 1561/62; XV: 1560–78.
  Approved Marbach's attack on Zwinglians (RP 1564, f. 238v), but opposed admission of Tileman Hesshus (RP 1565, f. 43v) and was a friend of Jean Sturm (XV 1578, ff. 106v–107r).
Mieg, Andres.
  Sectarian board; admin. of Charterhouse; convent board.
  S: 1525/26; XV: 1532–43; XIII: 1543–51.
  Late convert, but evangelical by 1532 (Brady, *Ruling Class,* p. 332); took hard line on sects (e.g., RP 1545, ff. 372v–373r).
Mieg, Carl II.
  Sectarian board; scholarch; mass committee; censor; morals board.
  S: 1553/54; XV: 1552–57; XIII: 1558–72; Amr.: 1558, 1564, 1570.
  Orthodox Lutheran according to Molsheim (also RP 1568, ff. 5v–6v and AST 64/6, ff. 29v–30r, 1572), but wanted Marbach kept out of "political matters" (RP 1562, ff. 116v–117r).
Mieg, Daniel.
  Convent board; admin. of Charterhouse and of Unser Frauen Haus.
  S: 1520/21, 1526/27; XV: 1519–22; XIII: 1522–41; Amr.: 1524, 1530, 1536.
  Leading early evangelical (Brady, *Ruling Class,* p. 335).
Mieg, Sebastian I.
  Admin. of St. Margaret and St. Nicolas-in-undis; morals board.
  St.: 1587/88, 1590/91, 1593/94, 1596/97, 1599/1600; XV: 1558–63, 1586–87; XIII: 1563–85, 1587–1609.
  Belonged to peace party but opposed FC (XV 1592, ff. 102v–104v and RP 1577, ff. 725v–732v).
Mittelhausen, Adolph von.
  PS: 1547/48, 1551/52, 1554/55; St.: 1557/58, 1560, 1563/64; XV: 1552–60; XIII: 1560–65.
  Left in 1548 (Brady, *Ruling Class,* p. 379); orthodox according to Molsheim.
Molsheim, Jacob von.
  Morals board; sectarian board.
  S: 1563/64, 1571/72; XXI: 1569–75; XV: 1575–82; Amr.: 1577.
  Left in 1548 (Brady, *Ruling Class,* p. 379); strong supporter of FC and oppo-

nent of Jean Sturm (AMS VI/701a/8, his correspondence with Marbach, and AST 65/15, fragments of his private papers).

Mülnheim, Heinrich von.

Scholarch; convent board; admin. of St. Nicholas-in-undis; morals board; mass committee.

PS: 1537/38, 1543/44, 1546; St.: 1554/55, 1558/59, 1561/62, 1564/65, 1567/68, 1570/71, 1573/74, 1576/77; XV: 1543–48, 1553–59; XIII: 1559–78. Left in 1548, but had called for resistance in 1547 (Brady, *Ruling Class,* pp. 265–66, 379); approved Chytraeus's book (RP 1567, f. 385r); opposed Sturm (RP 1570, f. 130v); orthodox according to Molsheim; specifically requested that his funeral sermon be an oration against heresy (AST 169, ff. 516v–517r); but opposed the idea of a consistory (RP 1557, ff. 267r–268r), and rejected the FC (RP 1577, ff. 725v–732v).

Münch, Georg.

Morals board; sectarian board; mass committee; admin. of a beguinage.

S: 1567/68; XV: 1565–83.

Ally of Jean Sturm (RP 1570, ff. 195v–196r).

Münch, Sebastian.

Sectarian board; morals board.

S: 1556/57; XV: 1546–48, 1555–58; XIII: 1558–78.

Left in 1548 (Brady, *Ruling Class,* p. 379); approved Marbach's attacks on Zwinglians (RP 1564, f. 238v), but opposed Strasbourg's involvement in FC project (RP 1570, ff. 985v–987v).

Obrecht, Heinrich.

Admin. of St. Margaret and of a beguinage; convent board; church warden.

S: 1587/88; XV: 1585–94; XIII: 1594–1606; Amr.: 1596, 1602.

Peace party; orthodox Lutheran; approved historical section of 1598 Church Ordinance (RP 1597, ff. 623v–625v).

Odenstein, Michael.

S: 1544/45, 1548/49.

Odratzheim, Hans.

S: 1542/43, 1548/49, 1554/55, 1558; XXI: 1542–48; XV: 1548–53; XIII: 1553–58.

Urged resistance in 1548 (Brady, *Ruling Class,* p. 262).

Oettel, Hans.

Morals board; mass committee; sectarian board.

S: 1561/62, 1565/66, 1569/70; XXI: 1567–68; XV: 1568–85.

Wanted to cover up a scandal in which a Catholic Senator, Adolff Braun, had been caught smuggling an anti-Lutheran satire into the city; also wanted to destroy the papers of the anti-Calvinist Jacob Molsheim (RP 1570, ff. 544v–545v and 1582, ff. 555v–556v); favored charity to refugees, but thought Calvinism was heretical (RP 1572, ff. 910r–911r and 1577, ff. 96r–99r).

Ottlingen, Jacob von.

Sectarian board; morals board; church warden; admin. of a beguinage.

S: 1543/44, 1549/50, 1555/56; XXI: 1556–57; XIII: 1557–69.

Pfarrer, Matthis.

Convent board; church warden; morals board; scholarch; mass committee.

S: 1519/20, 1524/25; XV: 1523–25; XIII: 1525–68; Amr.: 1527, 1533, 1539, 1545, 1551, 1557, 1563.

Zealous evangelical by 1523 (Brady, *Ruling Class,* p. 340); opposed Catholic restoration (RP 1550, f. 31r-v and 1557, f. 281r); frequently complained about immorality; favored helping Marian and Huguenot refugees (RP 1554, f. 341v and 1562, f. 264r-v); orthodox according to Molsheim.

Pfitzer, Gregorius.
Marriage court; sectarian board; convent board; morals board; church warden.
S: 1525/26, 1529/30, 1533/34, 1539/40, 1543/44; XXI: 1541–49.
Played host to an Anabaptist leader, Wilhelm Reublin, in 1526 (Brady, *Ruling Class,* p. 248, n. 48).

Prechter, Friedrich.
School inspector; admin. of St. Nicolas-in-undis.
S: 1579/80; XXI: 1582–83; XIII: 1583–84; XV: 1584–94.
Leader of the peace party; accused of Catholicism.

Rechberger, Arbogast.
Scholarch; admin. of Charterhouse; morals board.
PS: 1564/65, 1567/68, 1570/71, 1573/74; St.: 1576/77, 1579/80; XXI: 1565–69; XV: 1569–78; XIII: 1578–80.
Opposed refugee church because it attracted foreigners (RP 1577, ff. 12r–13r); staunchly orthodox according to Pappus.

Rihel, Josias.
Scholarch; school inspector; sectarian board; admin. of a beguinage; church warden.
S: 1563/64, 1567/68, 1571/72, 1575/76, 1579/80; XXI: 1578–87; XV: 1587–90; XIII: 1590–97.
War party; possibly Calvinist (AST 326/22) and certainly not orthodox Lutheran.

Röder von Dierspurg, Egenolph.
Convent board; admin. of St. Margaret.
PS: 1515/16, 1519; St.: 1518, 1523/24, 1526/27, 1529/30, 1532/33, 1535/36, 1538/39, 1549/50; XV: 1525–29; XIII: 1530–50.
Evangelical by 1523/24 (Brady, *Ruling Class,* p. 343).

Römer, Stoffel.
Morals board.
S: 1553/54, 1557/58; XXI: 1557–65; XV: 1565–67.
Orthodox according to Molsheim, but said Marbach should keep out of "political matters" (RP 1562, ff. 116v–117r).

Rumler, Caspar.
Convent board; admin. of St. Margaret; church warden; mass committee.
S: 1517/18, 1521/22, 1527/28, 1537/38; XV: 1525–48; XIII: 1548–63.
Orthodox according to Molsheim, but opposed the ban (RP 1557, ff. 267r–268r).

Schacht, Sebastian.
Mass committee; church warden.
S: 1568/69, 1572/73, 1576/77, 1580/81, 1584/85, 1588/89, 1592/93, 1596/97, 1600–1601, 1604.
Wanted Strasbourg to stay out of theological controversy (RP 1589, ff. 70v–71v).

Schenckbecher, Johann.
Sectarian board; censor; school inspector; admin. of St. Nicolas-in-undis.
S: 1564/65; XV: 1564–75; XIII: 1575–90.
Friend of Sturm's; supported the Huguenots, but Lutheran in his views on the eucharist (AST 1655, 1656).

Appendix A

Schilling, Jacob.
Morals board.
S: 1579/80, 1583/84, 1587/88; XXI: 1588–95; XV: 1595–97.
Schimpff, Sebastian.
Morals board; admin. of St. Nicolas-in-undis; church warden.
S: 1575/76, 1579/80, 1583/84, 1587/88; XXI: 1589–99.
Schütterlin, Wolfgang.
Sectarian board; mass committee; morals board; church warden.
S: 1560/61, 1566/67; XV: 1568–72; XIII: 1572–1612; Amr.: 1572, 1578, 1584, 1590.
War party; probably Lutheran (RP 1577, ff. 357r-v); supported Jean Sturm (XV 1581, ff. 58v–59v); strict disciplinarian (RP 1576, ff. 7v–8r).
Schwencker, Michael.
Admin. of a beguinage; morals board.
S: 1543/44, 1551/52; XXI: 1544–48; XV: 1548–56.
Friend of Capito's; related to Zell through their wives (Brady, *Ruling Class,* p. 347).
Seupell, Heinrich.
Morals board; sectarian board.
S: 1567/68, 1573/74, 1577/78, 1581/82, 1585/86, 1591/92, 1598.
Annoyed by Church Assembly's campaign to create public support for FC (RP 1581, ff. 183r–185r).
Stedel, Christoph III.
Morals board; sectarian board; convent board; church warden.
S: 1565/66, 1569/70, 1573/74, 1577/78; XXI: 1575–78; XV: 1578–85.
Stoer, Jonas.
Sectarian board.
S: 1562/63.
Stoesser, Hans.
S: 1549/50; XV: 1551–58.
Stoesser, Hans Jacob.
Convent board; school inspector.
S: 1590/91; XV: 1589–93.
Storck, Veltin.
Convent board; sectarian board; church warden.
S: 1533/34, 1539/40, 1545/46; XV: 1543–59.
Sturm, Jacob.
Convent board; scholarch; admin. of Knights of St. John.
PS: 1524/25; St.: 1527/28, 1530/31, 1533/34, 1536/37, 1549/50; XV: 1525–26; XIII: 1526–53.
Evangelical by 1523, perhaps with Schwenckfeldian leanings (Brady, *Ruling Class,* pp. 351, 241–42).; Zanchi regarded him as a protector (AST 52/3).
Sturm, Peter.
Scholarch; convent board; admin. of St. Nicolas.
PS: 1524/25, 1527/28, 1530/31, 1533/34, 1536; St.: 1539/40, 1542/43, 1545/46, 1548/49, 1551/52, 1553, 1556/57; XV: 1533–63.
No opinion on *Tetrapolitana* in 1534 (Brady, *Ruling Class,* p. 193); objected to Speccer's book on predestination (RP 1558, ff. 83v–84r); orthodox according to Molsheim, but defended Zanchi (Brady, *Ruling Class,* pp. 352–53).

Sturm, Stephan.
  Marriage court; morals board.
  PS: 1536/37, 1539/40, 1542/43, 1545/46, 1548, 1551; St.: 1554/55, 1557/58, 1560/61, 1563/64, 1566/67, 1569/70, 1572/73, 1575/76, 1578; XV: 1544?–1548; XXI: 1551–62; XIII: 1562–78.
  Left in 1548 (Brady, *Ruling Class,* p. 379); orthodox according to Molsheim, but supported intervention in France (e.g., RP 1575, ff. 699v–702v).
Theurer, Michael.
  Admin. of a beguinage; censor; morals board.
  S: 1582/83, 1586/87; XXI: 1588–94; XV: 1594–1603.
  Schwenckfelder (XV 1594, ff. 4v–5r; AST 77/1).
Treubel, Gabriel zum.
  Admin. of St. Margaret; mass committee; morals board.
  PS: 1579/80; St.: 1582/83, 1585/86, 1588/89, 1591; XV: 1580–91.
  Son of the spiritualist Eckhart zum Treubel.
Volmar, Hans Heinrich.
  Sectarian board; church warden.
  S: 1558/59, 1567/68; XV: 1559–72.
  Lent money to Andelot (RP 1567, f. 35v).
Weicker, Mathis.
  Morals board; sectarian board; admin. of St. Margaret.
  S: 1554/55, 1560/61, 1564/65, 1570/71; XV: 1572–88; XIII: 1588–91; Amr.: 1576, 1582, 1588.
  Lent money to both French crown and Huguenots (RP 1573, ff. 709r-v and 1576, ff. 762v–763r); said refugees should be treated with charity (RP 1573, f. 34r-v); opposed FC project (RP 1570, ff. 985v–987v).
Wetzel von Marsilien, Jacob.
  Sectarian board.
  PS: 1533/34, 1536/37, 1540/41; XV: 1536–43.
  Converted an Anabaptist woman in 1536 (AA 399/26, f. 58v); opponent of Bucer and of the Wittenberg Concord (AST 69/144); dismissed from the regime partially on religious grounds (RP 1541, ff. 243v–248r through 1543, f. 385r-v); several members of his family were Catholic and he may have been as well; his relatives finally concluded that he was insane (RP 1545, f. 489r).
Wörlin, Philips.
  Morals board; school inspector; church warden?
  S: 1587/88; XV: 1585–91; XIII: 1591–94.
  Possibly war party (XV 1592, f. 97r), but told the clergy he was orthodox (BNUS ms. 998, pp. 97–98) and favored good discipline.
Wurmser von Vendenheim, Wolf Sigismund.
  Marriage court; morals board; admin. of Charterhouse and of Knights of St John; censor; scholarch.
  PS: 1552/53; St.: 1555/56, 1558, 1561/62, 1564/65, 1567/68, 1570/71, 1573/74; XV: 1554–56; XIII: 1556–74.
  Crypto-Catholic; regarded by his colleagues as pious (RP 1568, ff. 124v–125r); orthodox according to Molsheim, he received extreme unction on his death-bed from a Catholic canon (Brady, *Ruling Class,* p. 358).

APPENDIX B

Composition and Character of
the Church Assembly, 1536–1598

Appendix B shows the Church Assembly as it was in 1536, when the Wittenberg Concord was signed; in 1552, when Johann Marbach became its president; in 1567, roughly halfway through Marbach's tenure; in 1581, when Johann Pappus replaced Marbach as president; and in 1598, when the second Strasbourg Church Ordinance was promulgated. For individual biographies see Marie-Joseph Bopp, *Die evangelischen Geistlichen und Theologen in Elsass und Lothringen von der Reformation bis zur Gegenwart* (Neustadt a.d. Aisch, 1959).

The members of the Church Assembly were:

1536: Bucer, Capito, Firn, Hedio, Hubert, Lenglin, Mornhinweg, Johann Schmidt I, Schneid, Schwartz, Steinbach, Steinlin, and Zell.

1552: Brunner, Damarisk, Englisch, Gerung, Jacob Glocker, Hubert, L. L. Kyber, David Kyber, Lenglin, Marbach, Mornhinweg, Offner, Rabus, Reuchlin, Schwartz, and Söll.

1567: Englisch, Erasmi, Johann Faber I, Flinner, Nicolas Florus I, Frey, Greiner, Gründlinger, Hubert, Keffel, Kessler, Kretzmar, E. Kyber, Johann Liptitz, Marbach, Negelin, Offner, Rottmann, Schaller, Melchior Speccer, Johann Thomas I, and Walther.

1581: Carolus, Eberlin, Johann Faber I, Nicolas Florus I, Nicolas Florus II, Samuel Florus, Johann Frey, Georg Glocker, Heckel, Keffel, Kretzmar, Johann Liptitz, Negelin, Pappus, Caspar Poppius, Portius, Rottmann, Schad, Schaller, Johann Thomas I, Walther, and Zickel.

1598: Carolus, Crusius, Johann Faber II, Johann Frey, Greiner,

[242]

Herrenberger, Keffel, Krauch, Kretzmar, Lipp, Johann Liptitz, Daniel Liptitz, Münch, Nasser, Pappus, Portius, Reuter, Rottmann, Schaller, Scheuring, Schilling, T. Speccer, and Johann Thomas II.

Jean-Pierre Kintz and Bernard Vogler have published analyses of the Strasbourg clergy for slightly different periods. Compare Kintz, "Eglise et société strasbourgeoise du milieu du XVI siècle au milieu du XVIIe siècle," *Annuaire de la société des amis du vieux-Strasbourg*, 11 (1983), 33–69 and Vogler, "Recrutement et carrière des pasteurs Strasbourgeois au XVIe siècle," *RHPR*, 48 (1968), 151–74.

	Church Assembly date				
	1536	1552	1567	1581	1598
Number of members	13	16	22	22	23
Composition:					
pastors	7	5[a]	7	7	7
preachers[b]	1	2	3	1	3
assistants	5	9	12	14	13
Native Strasburghers	1	1	2	6	11
Other Alsatians	5	3	2		
Other	7	12	17	15	12
Unknown			1	1	
Studied at					
Strasbourg		6	14	16	18
Wittenberg		5	5	3	3
Freiburg	4	1			
Basel	3	2	1	3	1
Tübingen	1	2		3	1
Heidelberg	1				
Mainz	2				
Vienna	1	1			
Ingolstadt	1				
Erfurt	1				
Unknown	5	5	5	5	5
Highest degree to date:					
D. Theol.	4	5	7	4	4
M.A.	4	3	4	7	11
Some advanced study; no known degree	2	4	8	6	6
No known advanced study	3	4	3	5	2
Years of service to date:					
mean	9.3	8.6	10.4	12.3	17.6
median	13	6	6	13	16
Died in office	9	10	16	12	13

Appendix B

	Church Assembly date				
	1536	1552	1567	1581	1598
Retired			5	7	10
Dismissed	1	2		2	
Left Strasbourg	1	3	1		
Unknown	2	1		1	
Still active in next group analyzed	4	4	11	9	
Senior man began in	1521	1523	1531	1553	1561

[a]Composition of the Church Assembly in 1552 was still affected by the Augsburg Interim, which closed Old and New St. Peter to the Protestants, and forced the transfer of the cathedral congregation into the old Dominican cloister.

[b]Preachers = Cathedral preachers and *Freiprediger*.

Church Assembly Petitions,

1539–1597

Appendix C is an analysis of one hundred petitions presented to the Senate and XXI. First an overall view of their contents is given; then the petitions are divided into periods roughly corresponding to those used in Appendix B. The series begins in 1539, the first year for which the RP are extant; no significant petitions came forward in 1598.

"Morality" (M) covers all complaints about lay behavior: sexual misconduct, economic abuses, carousing, nonobservance of the Sabbath, swearing, and blasphemy. "Discipline" (D) refers to attempts to increase the clergy's power to discipline offenders, including their efforts to obtain a public form of excommunication. "Sects" (S) includes both Anabaptists and Schwenckfelders; like "Catholics" (RC) and "Calvinists" (C) it refers to complaints about the activities of these groups. "Church Ordinance" (CO) refers to attempts to impose a standardized liturgy or to obtain ratification of the Formula of Concord. The categories "Morals" and "Discipline" are closely related, as are "Calvinists" and "Church Ordinance."

Many of the petitions refer to more than one problem. Contents are expressed in percentages: "Morals 23" means that 23 percent of petitions in that period include complaints about behavior.

Appendix C does not exhaust the petitions to the magistrates. For example, routine requests concerning the details of parish administration have not been included.

Appendix C

Category of concern	Period				
	1539–51 (19 petitions)	1552–67 (38 petitions)	1568–81 (29 petitions)	1582–97 (14 petitions)	1539–97 (100 petitions)
Morality	37	21	45	43	35
Discipline	42	16	14	7	19
Sects	32	26	28	7	25
Catholics	21	45	28	21	32
Calvinists	0	18	34	36	22
Church ordinance	11	29	24	14	22

Date	Location	M	D	S	RC	C	CO
1539: 29 Jan.	RP 26v–27r	x					
16 Apr.	RP 89v		x				
5 May	RP 110v		x				
18 Aug.	RP 235r–237r	x					
1540: 18 Feb.	RP 42v–43v	x		x			
13 Aug.	RP 302v–304v		x	x			x
1541: 13 Mar.	RP 101r–v, AST 80/38	x					
11 May	RP 195v–196r	x					
24 Sept.	RP 413r–414v, AST 80/39	x					
1542: 8 Nov.	RP 448v–449r, AST 84/39	x	x	x			
1545: 4 Feb.	RP 35v–37v	x	x				x
1545/1546	AST 84/41		x	x	x		
1547: 11 Apr.	RP 178v–183v, AST 84/37 (?)	x					
9 Nov.	RP 600r–605r	x					
19 Dec.	RP 667r, AST 84/53	x					
1548: 5 Sept.	RP 449v–452r				x		
3 Nov.	RP 545r				x		
1549: 2 Feb.	RP 34v–39r, AST 84/60				x		
1550: 27 Jan.	RP 42v	x					
1552: 27 Aug.	RP 311v–313v	x			x		
17 Oct.	RP 395r, AST 84/65	x					
1553: 13 Mar.	RP 94r, 95r			x			
14 June	RP 209v–211r (290r–291r)	x	x	x			x
30 Oct.	RP 381v			x			
1 Nov.	RP 382r–385r	x			x		
1554: 13 Jan.	RP 4r, AST 200, AST 201						x
17 Mar.	RP 89v–90v			x			
23 June	RP 231v, AST 45, 491r–505v	x	x				
18 Aug.	RP 281v–285r, AST 87/43				x		
8 Sept.	RP 296d–296o, AST 177				x		
22 Oct.	AST 87/46				x		

Date			Location	M	D	S	RC	C	CO
1555:	12	Jan.	RP unpaginated, AST 87/50				x		
	6	May	RP 172v, 173v	x					
	10	June	RP 229v–230v			x			x
	26	Aug.	RP 346r-v, 346a						x
1556:	11	Jan.	RP 5r–6v				x		
	14	Mar.	RP 105r			x	x		
	11	Apr.	RP 146r–152r			x	x		
	6	June	RP 245r-v	x	x				x
	20	June	RP 264r-v	x	x		x		x
1557:	9	Aug.	RP 305r-v						x
	15	Dec.	RP 19. 1. 1558, 18r–21v				x		
1558:	21	Jan.	RP 27v–28v				x		
	16	Feb.	RP 83v–84r					x	
	16	Nov.	RP 575r–577r				x		
1559:	4	Sept.	RP 389v–393r					x	
1560:	15	Jan.	RP 7v	x					
	27	July	RP 299v–302v, AST 87/56				x		
1562:	24	June	AST 54/8, AST 75/59					x	
	21	Oct.	RP 352r-v					x	x
	26	Oct.	AST 54/12					x	
	1562		AST 84/114					x	
1563:	15	May	RP 178r–179v						x
1564:	28	Apr.	AST 84/78	x		x	x		
	8	May	RP 178r-v			x	x		x
1566:	9	Jan.	AST 55/15			x	x		x
1567:	25	May	AST 177, 28r–56v					x	
1570:	26	Apr.	RP 280r–281r	x					
	10	May	RP 320r–321v, AST 100				x		
	29	July	RP 1571, 323v–324r	x		x			
	7	Oct.	RP 1571, 323v–324r	x		x			
	25	Nov.	RP 1571, 323v–324r	x		x			
1571:	19	Mar.	RP 233v, AST 84/84	x					
	4	Apr.	RP 323v–324r, AST 84/83	x	x	x	x		
1572:	4	Feb.	RP 107v–108r	x	x				
	13	Feb.	RP 141v–142r, AST 84/85	x	x				x
	3	Mar.	AST 84/86						x
	26	Apr.	AST 63/1				x	x	
	1	Sept.	RP 762v–763r, AST 84/87, 88	x			x	x	x
	6	Sept.	AST 64/6				x	x	
1573:		June?	AST 63/2					x	
1575:	28	May	RP 312r–313v, AST 87/60, 61				x		
1576:	30	Jan.	RP 59v	x					
	26	Mar.	RP 176v–177v	x		x	x	x	
	27	Oct.	RP 632r–637v, AST 79/3		x				x
	29	Oct.	RP 639v–640v, AST 76/102		x				
1577:	1	Apr.	RP 198v, 199v–200v	x					
1578:	3	Feb.	RP 59r–60r						x
	5	Feb.	RP 61v, AMS VI/701a/7						x
	5	Mar.	RP 127r, AST 180/4						x
1580:	5	Mar.	RP 98v–99r					x	
	post-17	Mar.	AST 100				x	x	
	9	Apr.	RP 162r-v					x	
	18	July	RP 358v, 359r	x					
	8	Aug.	RP 399r–400r			x		x	x

Date	Location	M	D	S	RC	C	CO
1581: 29 July	RP 353r–355v					x	
1583: 5 Aug.	RP 331v–332v	x					
1585: 26 July	RP 281v, AMS II/84b/82					x	
30 Oct.	RP 427r–428r, AST 84/97	x	x		x	x	
1586: 11 June	RP 306v	x					
1589: 1 Mar.	RP 99r, AST 69/193						x
1591: 3 Mar.	RP 83r-v, AST 87/68				x		
1592: 23 Oct.	RP 512v, AST 135/5				x		
4 Nov.	RP 532v					x	
1593: 3 Feb.	RP 87v, AST 169, 39v–401r					x	
1594: 5 Jan.	RP 1593, 820r			x			
8 June	RP 221v	x					
1596: 21 June	RP 195r	x					
1597: 16 Feb.	RP 49r-v	x					
12 Nov.	RP 545r–546v, AST 90/23					x	x
TOTAL	(100 petitions):	35	19	25	32	22	22

Sermons, 1539–1594

Appendix D is an analysis of fifty-nine sermons preached in Strasbourg from 1539 to 1594, using the same categories as in Appendix C. The material is too unevenly distributed to break down by periods.

Appendix D includes only those sermons known to have come to the attention of the magistrates. It therefore tells more about what interested the magistrates officially than about what interested the clergy, and this may explain the different distributions of emphasis in Appendixes C and D.

The high proportion of sermons dealing with morality reflects the magistrates' conviction that policing abuses was part of their job, whereas the low number of sermons about discipline indicates that the clergy rarely went over the magistrates' heads to try to rouse popular support for their projects. The apparent upsurge in interest in the sects may be tied to the city inspection in the middle fifties. Attention to sermons against the Catholics increased in the Schmal-kaldic War and remained at a high level thereafter; concern about preaching against the Calvinists peaked during periods of local crisis—the 1560s and the end of the century. If there were sermons on the need for a new church ordinance, the magistrates took no official notice of them.

Subjects of concern in fifty-nine sermons, 1539–1594	
Morality	44%
Discipline	8%
Sects	10%
Catholics	42%
Calvinists	8%
Church ordinance	0%

Date	Location	M	D	S	RC	C	CO
1539: 4 Aug.	RP 219r	x					
1543: 29 Oct.	RP 469v	x					
1544: 3 Mar.	RP 96r	x					
7 Apr.	RP 153v				x		
18 Aug.	RP 380v				x		
1545: 30 Mar.	RP 129v	x					
31 Aug.	RP 348r	x					
1546: 19 Apr.	RP 244v				x		
13 Sept.	RP 460r	x					
20 Sept.	RP 469r	x					
4 Oct.	RP 490v	x					
1 Nov.	RP 533v	x					
1547: 21 Feb.	RP 63v				x		
30 Mar.	RP 153r				x		
9 May	RP 233v	x					
12 Sept.	RP 501v	x					
28 Nov.	RP 626b, recto				x		
12 Dec.	RP 653r		x				
19 Dec.	RP 667r, AST 84/53	x	x				
28 Dec.	RP 685v–686r	x	x				
1548: 5 May	RP 236r–v				x		
30 July	RP 374v, 375r–v				x		
6 Aug.	RP 386v, 387v	x					
20 Aug.	RP 416r				x		
10 Sept.	RP 456v, 457r	x					
3 Dec.	RP 586r				x		
1549: 18 Feb.	RP 63r–v				x		
1550: 9 June	RP 261v				x		
21 July	RP 319r				x		
1551: 17 Aug.	RP 263v			x			
12 Oct.	RP 322v, 323v	x					
12 Oct.	RP 322v, 323v				x		
1552: 15 Feb.	RP 43v	x					
24 Apr.	RP 126r	x					
22 Aug.	RP 310r				x		
1554: 31 Dec.	RP 408r				x		
1556: 9 Mar.	RP 98v			x			
1556	AST 80/53			x			
1558: 22 Jan.	RP 27v–28v, AST 173/48				x		
1560: 15 Jan.	RP 7v	x					
1562: 11 July	RP 212v–213r					x	
15 Nov.	AST 72/4				x		x
1566: 9 Jan.	AST 55/15				x	x	
1568: 24 May	RP 200v	x					
1571: 11 June	RP 534v				x		
20 Aug.	RP 748r–749r				x		
1572: 4 Feb.	RP 107v–108r	x	x				
21 Apr.	RP 369r–v	x					
14 July	RP 624r–625v, AST 72/5		x				
29 Nov.	RP 969v–970v, AST 75/7				x		
1573: 20 July	RP 492v–493r				x		
1574: 16 Aug.	RP 555r				x		
1575: 21 Nov.	RP 688v				x		

Date	Location	M	D	S	RC	C	CO
1576: 6 Feb.	RP 75v				x		
1580: 8 Aug.	RP 398r-399r			x		x	
1581: 17 May	RP 240r-v	x					
1587: 13 Nov.	RP 589r	x				x	
1588: 12 Feb.	RP 67v	x					
1594: 2 May	AST 84/108, 685r-v	x				x	
TOTAL	(59 sermons)	26	5	6	25	5	0

Bibliography

Abray, Lorna Jane. "The Long Reformation: Magistrates, Clergy, and People in Strasbourg, 1520–1598." Ph.D. dissertation, Yale University, 1978.
———. "La vie d'un anabaptiste strasbourgeois au 16e siècle: Michael Meckel." *Revue d'histoire et de philosophie religieuses*, 57 (1977), 195–207.
Adam, Johann. *Evangelische Kirchengeschichte der Stadt Strassburg bis zur französische Revolution*. Strasbourg: Heitz, 1922.
Alle alten Propheceien von keyserlich Maiestat. Strasbourg: J. Cammerlander, n.d.
Andreae, Jacob. *Abfertigung des Vortrabs Johan Sturmii*. Tübingen: Georg Gruppenbach, 1581.
———. *Kurtz Antwort . . . auff Herrn Johan Sturmii Buch Antipappus Quartus genant*. Dresden: n.p., 1581.
Bainton, Roland. "Katherine Zell." *Medievalia et Humanistica*, n.s. 1 (1970), 3–28.
Baldus, Elias. *Straszburgischer Augustus*. Strasbourg: E. Baldus, 1592.
Bekandtnus der vier frey und Reichstatt. Strasbourg: T. Rihel, 1579.
Bellardi, Werner. "Anton Engelbrecht (1485–1558): Helfer, Mitarbeiter und Gegner Bucers." *Archiv für Reformationsgeschichte*, 64 (1973), 183–206.
———. "Bucer und das Interim." In Marijn de Kroon and Marc Lienhard, eds., *Horizons européens de la réforme en Alsace. Das Elsass und die Reformation im Europa des XVI Jahrhunderts. Mélanges offerts à Jean Rott pour son 65e anniversaire*, pp. 267–311. Société savante d'Alsace et des régions de l'est, Grandes publications, vol. 17. Strasbourg: Istra, 1980.
———. *Die Geschichte der "christlichen Gemeinschaft" in Strassburg (1546/1550): Der Versuch einer "zweiten Reformation."* Quellen und Forschungen zur Reformationsgeschichte, vol. 18. Leipzig: M. Heinsius Nachfolger, 1934.
———. *Wolfgang Schultheiss: Wege und Wandlungen eines strassburger Spiritualisten und Zeitgenossen Martin Bucers*. Schriften der Erwin von Steinbach-Stiftung, vol. 5. Frankfurt am Main: Erwin von Steinbach-Stiftung, 1976.
Bernays, Jacob. "Zur Biographie Johann Winters von Andernach." *Zeitschrift für die Geschichte des Oberrheins*, n.F. 16 (1901), 28–57.
Bernhard, Marianne. *Hans Baldung Grien: Handzeichnungen, Druckgraphik*. Munich: Südwest, 1978.

Bibliography

Bizer, Ernst. *Studien zur Geschichte des Abendmahlstreits im 16ten Jahrhundert.* Gütersloh: C. Bertelsmann, 1940.

Bopp, Marie-Joseph. *Die evangelischen Geistlichen und Theologen in Elsass und Lothringen von der Reformation bis zur Gegenwart.* Neustadt a.d. Aisch: Degener, 1959.

Bornert, René. *La réforme protestante du culte à Strasbourg au XVIe siècle (1523–1598): Approche sociologique et interprétation théologique.* Studies in Medieval and Reformation Thought, vol. 28. Leiden: E. J. Brill, 1981.

Brady, Thomas A., Jr. "Jacob Sturm of Strasbourg and the Lutherans at the Diet of Augsburg (1530)." *Church History,* 42 (1973), 183–202.

_____. "Jacob Sturm of Strasbourg (1489–1553) and the Political Security of German Protestantism, 1526–1532." Ph.D. dissertation, University of Chicago, 1968.

_____. *Ruling Class, Regime and Reformation at Strasbourg, 1520–1555.* Studies in Medieval and Reformation Thought, vol. 22. Leiden: E. J. Brill, 1978.

_____. " 'Sind also zu beiden theilen Christen, des Gott erbarm': La mémoire de Jacques Sturm sur le culte public à Strasbourg (août 1525)." In Marijn de Kroon and Marc Lienhard, eds., *Horizons européens de la Réforme en Alsace./Das Elsass und die Reformation im Europa des XVI Jahrhunderts: Mélanges offerts à Jean Rott pour son 65e anniversaire,* pp. 69–79. Société savante d'Alsace et des régions de l'est, Grandes publications, vol. 17. Strasbourg: Istra, 1980.

_____. "The Social Place of a German Renaissance Artist: Hans Baldung Grien (1484/85-1545) at Strasbourg." *Central European History,* 8 (1975), 299–315.

Brandi, Karl, ed. *Der Augsburger Religionsfriede vom 25 September 1555: Kritische Ausgabe des Textes.* Munich: M. Rieger'sche Universitätsbuchhandlung, 1896.

_____. *Deutsche Reformation und Gegenreformation.* 2 vols. Leipzig: Quelle & Meyer, 1930.

Brant, Sebastian. *Richterliche Clagspiegel.* Strasbourg: W. Rihel & G. Messerschmidt, 1553.

_____ (attributed). "Annales de Sébastien Brant." Edited by Léon Dacheux. *Bulletin de la société pour la conservation des monuments historiques d'Alsace,* n.s. 15 (1892), 211–279, and n.s. 19 (1899), 33–260.

Brucker, Johann Karl, ed. *Strassburger Zunft- und Polizei-Verordnungen des 14. und 15. Jahrhunderts.* Strasbourg: J. Trübner, 1889.

Brunfels, Otto. *Almanach . . . von dem xxvj Jar an, bitz zuo Endt der Welt.* Strasbourg: n.p., 1526.

Bucer, Martin. *La correspondance de Martin Bucer.* Edited by Jean Rott. Leiden: E. J. Brill, 1979.

_____. *De Regno Christi.* In Wilhelm Pauck, ed. and trans., *Melanchthon and Bucer.* Library of Christian Classics, vol. 19. Philadelphia: Westminster, 1969.

_____. *Martin Bucers deutsche Schriften.* Edited by Robert Stupperich et al. Gütersloh: Gerd Mohn, 1960–.

Büheler, Sebald, Jr. "La chronique strasbourgeoise de Sébald Büheler." Edited by Léon Dacheux. *Bulletin de la société pour la conservation des monuments historiques d'Alsace,* n.s. 13 (1888), 23–149.

Bussière, Marie-Théodore de. *Histoire des religieuses dominicaines du couvent de Sainte Marguerite et Sainte Agnès à Strasbourg.* Strasbourg: Le Roux, 1860.

Calvin, Jean. *Calvini opera quae supersunt omnia.* Edited by Wilhelm Baum et al. 59 vols. Braunschweig: C. A. Schwetschke, 1863–1900.

Carion, Johann. *Practica und Prognostication.* Strasbourg: J. Cammerlander, 1545.

Bibliography

Chrisman, Miriam Usher. *Bibliography of Strasbourg Imprints, 1480–1599*. New Haven: Yale University Press, 1982.

———. *Lay Culture, Learned Culture: Books and Social Change in Strasbourg, 1480–1599*. New Haven: Yale University Press, 1982.

———. "Lay Response to the Protestant Reformation in Germany, 1520–1528." In Peter Newman Brooks, ed., *Reformation Principle and Practice: Festschrift for Geoffrey Dickens*, pp. 35–52. London: Scolars Press, 1980.

———. *Strasbourg and the Reform*. New Haven: Yale University Press, 1967.

———. "Women and the Reformation in Strasbourg, 1490–1530." *Archiv für Reformationsgeschichte*, 64 (1972), 143–68.

Christensen, Carl C. "Patterns of Iconoclasm in the Early Reformation: Strasbourg and Basel." In Joseph Gutmann, ed., *The Image and the Word: Confrontations in Judaism, Christianity and Islam*, pp. 107–48. Missoula, Mont.: Scholars Press, 1977.

Clasen, Claus-Peter. *Anabaptism: A Social History*. Ithaca: Cornell University Press, 1972.

———. "Anabaptist Sects in the Sixteenth Century." *Mennonite Quarterly Review*, 46 (1972), 256–79.

Confessio oder Bekantnuss. Neustadt: Mattheus Harnisch, 1580.

Courvoisier, Jacques. *La notion d'eglise chez Bucer dans son développement historique*. Etudes d'histoire et de philosophie religieuses publiées par la Faculté de théologie protestante de l'université de Strasbourg, vol. 28. Paris: Félix Alcan, 1933.

Crämer, Ulrich. *Die Verfassung und Verwaltung Strassburgs von der Reformationszeit bis zum Fall der Reichstadt, 1521–1681*. Schriften des Wissenschaftlichen Instituts der Elsass-Lothringer im Reich an der Universität Frankfurt, n.s. vol. 3. Frankfurt: Selbstverlag des Elsass-Lothringen-Institut, 1931.

Dacheux, Léon, ed. "Fragments de diverses vieilles chroniques." *Bulletin de la société pour la conservation des monuments historiques d'Alsace*, n.s. 18 (1898), 1–181.

Denis, Philippe. "La correspondance d'Hubert de Bapasme, réfugié lillois à Strasbourg (1545–1547)." *Bulletin de la société de l'histoire du protestantisme français*, 124 (1978), 84–112.

Dolan, John P., ed. and trans. *The Essential Erasmus*. New York: New American Library, 1964.

Dollinger, Philippe, ed. *Histoire de l'Alsace*. Toulouse: Privat, 1970.

———. "La population de Strasbourg et sa répartition aux XVe et XVIe siècles." In Werner Busch, Klaus Fehn, et al., eds., *Die Stadt in der europäischen Geschichte: Festschrift Edith Ennen*, pp. 521–38. Bonn: Ludwig Rohrscheid, 1972.

———. "La tolérance à Strasbourg au XVIe siècle." In *Hommage à Lucien Febvre*, vol. 2, pp. 241–49. 2 vols. Paris: Armand Colin, 1953.

Dor, Georges. *Poèmes et chansons*. Ottawa: Editions de l'Hexagone, 1968.

Duquesne, Joseph. *Les débuts de l'enseignement du droit à Strasbourg au XVIe siècle*. Strasbourg: Société des amis de l'université, 1923.

Edwards, Mark U. *Luther and the False Brethren*. Stanford: Stanford University Press, 1975.

Eells, Hastings. "Bucer's Plan for the Jews." *Church History*, 6 (1937), 127–36.

———. *Martin Bucer*. New Haven: Yale University Press, 1931.

Engel, Charles. *Les commencements de l'instruction primaire à Strasbourg au moyen âge et dans la première moitié du seizième siècle*. Strasbourg: Noiriel, 1889.

———. *L'école latine et l'ancienne académie de Strasbourg, 1538–1621.* Strasbourg: Schlesier & Schweikhardt, 1900.

Erasmus, Desiderius. *Collected Works of Erasmus.* Toronto: University of Toronto Press, 1974–.

———. *The Colloquies of Erasmus.* Ed. and trans. Craig R. Thompson. Chicago: University of Chicago Press, 1965.

Ernst, August, and Johann Adam. *Katechetische Geschichte des Elsasses bis zur Revolution.* Strasbourg: Friedrich Bull, 1887.

Estes, James Martin. *Christian Magistrate and State Church: The Reforming Career of Johannes Brenz.* Toronto: University of Toronto Press, 1982.

Febvre, Lucien. "La France et Strasbourg au XVIe siècle." *La vie en Alsace,* 4 (1925), 239–44, and 5 (1926), 32–39.

Fischart, Johann. *Geschichtklitterung.* Strasbourg: B. Jobin, 1582.

———. *Nacht Rab oder Nebelkraeh.* Strasbourg: B. Jobin, 1570.

———. *Ordenliche Beschreibung.* Strasbourg: B. Jobin, 1588.

———, trans. *Ausschreiben . . . der ubelfridigten Ständ inn Frankreich.* Strasbourg, B. Jobin, n.d.

———, trans. *Binenkorb desz heyl. roemischen Imenschwarms.* Strasbourg: B. Jobin, 1580.

Florus, Nicolas. *Der CXXXVII Psalm.* Strasbourg: K. Kieffer, 1587.

———. *Kurtze und einseltige Auslegung des 91 Psalmen.* Strasbourg: T. Berger, 1576.

Ford, Franklin L. *Strasbourg in Transition, 1648–1789.* Cambridge: Harvard University Press, 1958.

Fournier, Marcel, and Charles Engel, eds. *L'université de Strasbourg et les académies protestantes françaises.* Les statuts et privilèges des universités françaises, second part, 4, fasicule 1. Paris: Recueil générale des lois et des arrêts et du Journal du palais, 1894.

Franz, Gunther, ed. *Quellen zur Geschichte des Bauernkrieges.* Munich: R. Oldenbourg, 1963.

Fuchs, François Joseph. "Les catholiques strasbourgeois de 1529 à 1681." *Archives de l'eglise d'Alsace,* n.s. 22 (1975), 142–69.

———. "Droit de bourgeoisie à Strasbourg." *Revue d'Alsace,* 101 (1962), 19–50.

———. "L'immigration artisanale à Strasbourg de 1544 à 1565." In *Artisans et ouvriers d'Alsace,* pp. 155–97. Société savante d'Alsace et des régions de l'est, Publications, vol. 9. Strasbourg: Istra, 1965.

———. "Les relations commerciales entre Nuremberg et Strasbourg au XVe et XVIe siècles." In *Hommage à Durer: Strasbourg et Nuremberg dans la première moitié du XVI siècle,* pp. 77–90. Société savante d'Alsace et des régions de l'est, Collection recherches et documents, vol. 12. Strasbourg: Istra, 1972.

Geiler von Kaysersberg, Johann. *Die aeltesten Schriften Geilers von Kaysersberg.* Edited by Léon Dacheux. Freiburg im Breisgau, 1882; reprint edition, Amsterdam: Editions Rodopi, 1965.

———. *Die siben hauptsund.* Augsburg: H. Otmar, 1510.

Geisendorf, Paul-F. *Théodore de Bèze.* Geneva: J. Jullien, 1949.

Gensichen, Hans Werner. *Damnamus: Die Verwerfung von Irrlehre bei Luther und im Luthertum des 16ten Jahrhunderts.* Arbeiten zur Geschichte und Theologie des Luthertums, vol. 1. Berlin: Lutherisches Verlagshaus, 1955.

Gfrörer, Eduard. *Strassburger Kapitelstreit und bischöflicher Krieg im Spiegel der elsässischen Flugschriften-Literatur, 1569–1618.* Strassburger Beiträge zur neueren Geschichte, vol. 1². Strasbourg: Herdersche Buchhandlung, 1906.

Gottesheim, Jacob von. "Les éphémerides de Jacques de Gottesheim, docteur en droit, prébendier du grand-choeur de la cathédrale (1524–1543)." Edited by Rodolphe Reuss. *Bulletin de la société pour la conservation des monuments historiques d'Alsace*, n.s. 19 (1899), 267–81.

Hahn, Karl. "Das Aufkommen der Jesuiten in der Diözese Strassburg und die Gründung des jesuiten Kollegs in Molsheim." *Zeitschrift für die Geschichte des Oberrheins*, n.F. 25 (1910), 246–94.

_____. *Die kirchlichen Reformbestrebungen des strassburger Bischofs Johann von Manderscheid, 1569–1592: Ein Beitrag zur Geschichte der Gegenreformation.* Quellen und Forschungen zur Kirchen- und Kulturgeschichte von Elsass und Lothringen, vol. 3. Strasbourg: Karl J. Trübner, 1913.

_____. "Visitationen und Visitationsberichte aus dem Bistum Strassburg in der zweiten Hälfte des 16ten Jahrhunderts." *Zeitschrift für die Geschichte des Oberrheins*, n.F. 26 (1911), 204–49, 501–43, 573–98.

Hall, Basil. "Bucer et l'Angleterre." In Georges Livet, Francis Rapp, and Jean Rott, eds., *Strasbourg au coeur religieux du XVIe siècle: Hommage à Lucien Febvre*, pp. 401–30. Société savante d'Alsace et des régions de l'Est, Grandes publications, vol. 12. Strasbourg: Istra, 1977.

Hatt, Jacques. *Liste des membres du grand sénat de Strasbourg, des stettmeistres, des ammeistres, des conseils des XXI, XIII, et des XV du XIIIe siècle à 1789.* Strasbourg: Mairie, 1963.

Hedio, Caspar. *Radts Predig.* Strasbourg: J. Albrecht, 1534.

Hegel, Carl von, ed. *Die Chroniken der oberrheinischen Städte: Strassburg.* 2 vols. Leipzig: S. Hirzel, 1870–71.

Heitz, Robert. *La peinture en Alsace.* Strasbourg: Editions des Dernières nouvelles d'Alsace, 1975.

Hertzog, Bernhard. *Chronicon alsatiae.* Strasbourg: B. Jobin, 1592.

Himmelheber, Emil. *Caspar Hedio: Ein Lebensbild aus der Reformationsgeschichte.* Karlsruhe: G. Braun'schen Buchhandlung, 1881.

Hollaender, Alcuin. "Wilhelm von Oranien und Strassburg, 1568 und 1569." *Zeitschrift für die Geschichte des Oberrheins*, n.F. 21 (1906), 50–98.

Horning, Hans. *Daniel Sudermann als Handschriftensammler: Ein Beitrag zur strassburger Bibliothekgeschichte.* Tübingen Inaugural Dissertation, 1956.

Horning, Wilhelm. *Dr. Johann Marbach.* Strasbourg: Selbstverlag, 1887.

_____. *Dr. Johann Pappus von Lindau.* Strasbourg: Heitz, 1891.

_____. *Handbuch der Geschichte der evang.-luth. Kirche in Strassburg unter Marbach und Pappus.* Strasbourg: Selbstverlag, 1903.

_____, ed. "Auszug aus einer Copie des Protokoll-buches des strassburger Kirchen-convents, 1588–1618." *Beiträge zur Kirchengeschichte des Elsasses vom 16.–19. Jahrhunderts*, 5 (1885), Appendix, pp. i–72.

_____, ed. *Briefe von strassburger Reformatoren, ihren Mitarbeitern und Freunden über die Einführung des "Interims" in Strassburg (1548–1554).* Strasbourg: Selbstverlag, 1887.

Höss, Irmgard. "The Lutheran Church of the Reformation: Problems of Its Formation and Organization in the Middle and North German Territories." In Lawrence P. Buck and Jonathan W. Zophy, eds., *The Social History of the Reformation*, pp. 317–39. Columbus: Ohio State University Press, 1972.

Janssen, Johannes. *History of the German People at the Close of the Middle Ages.* Translated by M. A. Mitchell and A. M. Christie. 16 vols. London: Kegan Paul, Trench, Trübner, 1896–1925.

Jung, Otto. *Michael Philipp Beuther: Generalsuperintendent des Hertzogtums Zweibrücken (1564–1619)*. Veröffentlichungen des Vereins für pfälzische Kirchengeschichte, vol. 5. Landau: Im Verlag des Vereins, 1954.

Kawerau, Waldemar. *Die Reformation und die Ehe*. Schriften des Vereins für Reformationsgeschichte, vol. 39. Leipzig: M. Heinsius Nachfolger, 1892.

Kessler, Isaac. *Kurtz Examen und Underricht vom Sacrament des heyligen Abentmals . . . Für die Christliche Jugendt*. Strasbourg: S. Emmel, 1556.

Kintz, Jean-Pierre. "Eglise et société strasbourgeoise du milieu du XVIe siècle au milieu du XVIIe siècle." *Annuaire de la société des amis du vieux-Strasbourg*, 11 (1983), 33–69.

———. "La société strasbourgeoise du milieu du XVIe siècle à la fin de la guerre de Trente Ans, 1560–1650: essai d'histoire démographique, économique, et sociale." Doctorat d'état, Strasbourg, 1980.

———. *La société strasbourgeoise du milieu du XVIe siècle à la fin de la guerre de Trente Ans, 1560–1650: Essai d'histoire démographique, économique, et sociale*. Paris: Association des publications près les Universités de Strasbourg, 1984.

Kirchenordnung. Strasbourg: J. Martin, 1598.

Kittelson, James M. "Humanism and the Reformation in Germany." *Central European History*, 9 (1976), 303–22.

———. "Marbach vs. Zanchi: The Resolution of Controversy in Late Reformation Strasbourg." *Sixteenth Century Journal*, 8 (1977), 31–44.

———. "Successes and Failures in the German Reformation: The Report from Strasbourg." *Archiv für Reformationsgeschichte*, 73 (1982), 153–75.

———. *Wolfgang Capito: From Humanist to Reformer*. Studies in Medieval and Reformation Thought, vol. 17. Leiden: E. J. Brill, 1975.

Köhler, Walther. *Züricher Ehegericht und genfer Konsistorium*. 2 vols. Quellen und Abhandlungen zur schweizerischen Reformationsgeschichte, vols. 7 and 10. Leipzig: M. Heinsius Nachfolger, 1932.

Krebs, Manfred, and Hans Georg Rott, eds. *Elsass*. Part 1. *Stadt Strassburg, 1522–1532*. Quellen zur Geschichte der Täufer, vol. 7. Gütersloh: Gerd Mohn, 1959.

———. *Elsass*. Part 2. *Stadt Strassburg, 1533–1535*. Quellen zur Geschichte der Täufer, vol. 8. Gütersloh: Gerd Mohn, 1960.

Landmann, Florenz. "Die St. Sebastians-Brüderschaft an St. Martin in Strassburg: Ihr Verhältnis zu Sebastian Brant." *Archiv für elsässische Kirchengeschichte*, 16 (1943), 107–28.

LeRoy Ladurie, Emmanuel. *Montaillou, village d'Occitan*. Paris: Gallimard, 1975.

Levresse, René-Pierre. "L'officialité épiscopale de Strasbourg de ses origines à son transfert à Molsheim (1248–1597)." Doctorat d'Université, Strasbourg, 1972.

Lienhard, Marc. "Les autorités civiles et les anabaptistes: Attitudes du magistrat de Strasbourg (1526–1532)." In Marc Lienhard, ed., *The Origins and Characteristics of Anabaptism/Les débuts et les caractéristiques de l'anabaptisme*, pp. 196–215. Archives internationales de l'histoire des idées, vol. 87. The Hague: Martinus Nijhoff, 1977.

———, and Jean Rott. "Die Anfänge der evangelischen Predigten in Strassburg und ihr erstes Manifest: Der Aufruf der Karmeliter Tilmann von Lyn (Anfang 1522)." In Marijn de Kroon and Wilhelm Krüger, eds. *Bucer und seine Zeit: Forschungsbericht und Bibliographie*, pp. 54–73. Veröffentlichungen des Instituts für europäische Geschichte in Mainz, vol. 80. Wiesbaden: Fritz Steiner, 1976.

Linden, Friedrich Otto zur. *Melchior Hofmann, ein Prophet der Widertäufer*. Haarlem: De Erven F. Bohn, 1885.

Bibliography

Livet, Georges, Francis Rapp, and Jean Rott, eds. *Strasbourg au coeur religieux du XVIe siècle: Hommage à Lucien Febvre.* Société savante d'Alsace et des régions de l'est, Grandes publications, vol. 12. Strasbourg: Istra, 1977.

Luther, Martin. *D. Martin Luthers Werke: Kritische Gesamtausgabe.* Weimar: Herman Böhlaus Nachfolger, 1883 ff.

Lutz, Reinhard. *Verzaichnus . . . der kaetzerischen, und verdampten Leer Martin Steinbachs.* Strasbourg: Chr. Mylius, 1566.

Marbach, Johann. *Christlicher Underricht.* Strasbourg: Chr. Mylius, 1567.

———. *Christlicher und warhaffter Underricht.* Strasbourg: Chr. Mylius, 1565.

———. *Drey christlichen Predigen.* Strasbourg: Chr. Mylius, 1565.

———. *Von dem bischofflichen Ampt.* Strasbourg: J. Rihel, 1569.

———. *Von Mirackeln und Wunderzeichen.* Strasbourg: n.p., 1571.

Martin, Paul-E. *Trois cas de pluralisme confessionel aux XVIe et XVIIe siècles: Genève-Savoie-France.* Geneva: J. Jullien, 1961.

Meister, Aloys. "Akten zum Schisma im strassburger Domkapitel, 1583–1592." *Bulletin de la société pour la conservation des monuments historiques d'Alsace,* n.s. 19 (1899), 328–59.

———. *Der strassburger Kapitelstreit, 1583–1592: Ein Beitrag zur Geschichte der Gegenreformation.* Strasbourg: Heitz, 1899.

Mesnard, Pierre. "La pietas litterata de Jean Sturm et le développement à Strasbourg d'une pédagogie oecuménique (1538–1581)." *Bulletin de la société de l'histoire du protestantisme français,* 111 (1965), 281–302.

Meyer, Hans. *Die strassburger Goldschmiedezunft von ihrem Entstehen bis 1681: Urkunden und Darstellung.* Leipzig: Drucker & Humbolt, 1881.

Mieg, Philippe. *Histoire généalogique de la famille Mieg, 1395–1934.* Mulhouse: J. Brinckmann, 1934.

Mitchell, Charles B. "Martin Bucer and Sectarian Dissent." Ph.D. dissertation, Yale University, 1960.

Moeller, Bernd. "Die deutschen Humanisten und die Anfänge der Reformation." *Zeitschrift für Kirchengeschichte,* 70 (1959), 46–61.

———. "L'édit strasbourgeois sur la prédication du 1er décembre 1523 dans son contexte historique." In Georges Livet, Francis Rapp, and Jean Rott, eds., *Strasbourg au coeur religieux du XVIe siècle: Hommage à Lucien Febvre,* pp. 51–61. Société savante d'Alsace et des régions de l'est, Grandes publications, vol. 12. Strasbourg: Istra, 1977.

———. "Kleriker als Bürger." In *Festschrift für Hermann Heimpel,* vol. 2, pp. 195–224. Veröffentlichungen des Max-Planck-Instituts für Geschichte, vols. 36–37. Göttingen: Vandenhoeck & Ruprecht, 1971–72.

Moore, William Grayburn. *La réforme allemande et la littérature française: Recherches sur la notoriété de Luther en France.* Publications de la Faculté des lettres de l'université de Strasbourg, vol. 52. Strasbourg: Faculté des lettres, 1930.

Murner, Thomas. *Thomas Murners deutsche Schriften mit den Holzschnitten der Erstdrucke.* Edited by Edouard Fuchs et al. 9 vols. Berlin: Walter de Gruyter, 1918–31.

Nobbe, Heinrich. "Das Superintendentenamt, seine Stellung und Aufgabe nach den evangel. Kirchenordnungen des 16. Jahrhunderts." *Zeitschrift für Kirchengeschichte,* 14 (1894), 404–29, 526–77, and 15 (1895), 44–93.

Oberman, Heiko. *Masters of the Reformation: The Emergence of a New Intellectual Climate in Europe.* Translated by Dennis Martin. London: Cambridge University Press, 1981.

O'Connell, Laura Stevenson. "The Elizabethan Bourgeois Hero-Tale: Aspects of an Adolescent Social Consciousness." In Barbara C. Malament, ed., *After the Reformation: Essays in Honor of J. H. Hexter,* pp. 267–90. Philadelphia: University of Pennsylvania Press, 1980.

Olin, John C., ed. and trans. *Christian Humanism and the Reformation: Selected Writings of Erasmus with the Life of Erasmus by Beatus Rhenanus.* Revised edition. New York: Fordham University Press, 1975.

Oyer, John S. *Lutheran Reformers against the Anabaptists: Luther, Melanchthon, and Menius, and the Anabaptists of Central Germany.* The Hague: Martinus Nijhoff, 1964.

Ozment, Steven E. *The Reformation in the Cities.* New Haven: Yale University Press, 1975.

_____. *When Fathers Ruled: Family Life in Reformation Europe.* Cambridge: Harvard University Press, 1983.

Pannier, Jacques. *Calvin à Strasbourg.* Cahiers de la Revue d'histoire et de philosophie religieuses, vol. 12, 1925.

Pappus, Johann. *Bericht und Warnung . . . an eine christliche Burgerschafft.* Tübingen: Georg Gruppenbach, 1581.

_____. *Ein christliche Predigt.* Strasbourg: A. Bertram, 1592.

_____. *Christlicher und notwendiger Bericht von der zweybrueckischen zu Heidelberg newlich gedruckten Erklaerung des Catechismi.* Tübingen: Georg Gruppenbach, 1588.

_____. *Kurtzer und beständiger Bericht.* Strasbourg: Jost Martin, 1592.

Pariset, Jean-Daniel. *Les relations entre la France et l'Allemagne au milieu du XVIe siècle.* Société savante d'Alsace et des régions de l'est, Grandes publications, vol. 19. Strasbourg: Istra, 1981.

Pauck, Wilhelm. "The Ministry in the Time of the Continental Reformation." In H. Richard Niebuhr and Daniel D. Williams, eds., *The Ministry in Historical Perspective,* pp. 110–48. New York: Harper & Brothers, 1956.

Paulus, Nikolaus. "La liberté de conscience et les professeurs du séminaire protestant de Strasbourg au 16e siècle." *Revue catholique d'Alsace,* 9 (1890), 108–21, 158–61, 200–212.

_____. *Protestantismus und Toleranz im 16. Jahrhundert.* Freiburg im Breisgau: Herder, 1911.

_____. *Die Strassburger Reformatoren und die Gewissensfreiheit.* Strassburger Theologische Studien, vol. 2². Strasbourg: Herder, 1895.

Perdrizet, Paul. "La Vierge aux bras étendus." *Archives alsaciennes d'histoire de l'art,* 1 (1922), 1–29.

Peremans, Nicole. *Erasme et Bucer d'après leur correspondance.* Bibliothèque de la Faculté de philosophie et lettres de l'université de Liège, vol. 194. Paris: Société d'édition les belles lettres, 1970.

Peter, Rodolphe. "Les groupes informels au temps de la réforme, types rhénans." In René Metz and Jean Schickle, eds., *Les groupes informels dans l'eglise,* pp. 194–212. Strasbourg: CERDIC, 1971.

_____. "Le maraîcher Clément Ziegler, l'homme et son oeuvre." *Revue d'histoire et de philosophie religieuses,* 34 (1954), 255–82.

_____. "Les premiers ouvrages français imprimés à Strasbourg." *Bulletin de la société des amis du vieux-Strasbourg,* 2 (1974), 73–108.

Pfleger, Luzian. "Zur Geschichte der Strassburger Passionsspiele." *Archiv für elsässische Kirchengeschichte,* 13 (1938), 70.

Pollet, J.-V. *Martin Bucer: Etudes sur la correspondance avec de nombreux textes inédits.* 2 vols. Paris: Presses universitaires de France, 1959–1962.

Bibliography

Rapp, Francis. "Die elsässischen Humanisten und die geistliche Gesellschaft." In Otto Herding and Robert Stupperich, eds., *Die Humanisten in ihrer politischen und sozialen Umwelt*, pp. 87–108. Bonn: Deutsche Forschungsgemeinschaft, 1976.

———. *Réformes et réformation à Strasbourg: Eglise et société dans le diocèse de Strasbourg, 1450–1520*. Collection des hautes etudes alsaciennes, vol. 23. Strasbourg: Association des publications près les Universités de Strasbourg, 1975.

Recht, Roland, Jean-Pierre Klein, and Georges Foessel. *Connaître Strasbourg*. Strasbourg: Alsatia, 1976.

Reuss, Rodolphe, ed. *Die Beschreibung des bischöflichen Krieges, anno 1592*. Strasbourg: Treuttel & Würtz, 1878.

———. *Zwei Lieder über den Diebskrieg oder Durchzug des navarrischen Kriegsvolkes im Elsass (1587) mit historischer Einleitung und ungedruckten Beilagen*. Strasbourg: J. Noiriel, 1874.

Robinson, Hastings, ed. *Original Letters Relating to the English Reformation*. 2 vols. Cambridge: Cambridge University Press, 1846–47.

Roehrich, Timotheus Wilhelm. *Mittheilungen aus der Geschichte der evangelischen Kirche des Elsasses*. 3 vols. Paris: Treuttel & Würtz, 1855.

———. "Zur Geschichte der strassburgischen Widertäufer in den Jahren 1527 bis 1543." *Zeitschrift für die historische Theologie*, 30 (1860), 1–121.

Rott, Jean. "Artisanat et mouvements sociaux à Strasbourg autour de 1525." In *Artisans et ouvriers d'Alsace*, pp. 137–70. Société savante d'Alsace et des régions de l'est, Publications, vol. 9. Strasbourg: Istra, 1965.

———. "L'Eglise des réfugiés de langue française à Strasbourg au XVIe siècle: Aperçu de son histoire, en particulier de ses crises à partir de 1541." *Bulletin de la société de l'histoire du protestantisme français*, 122 (1976), 525–50.

———. "La guerre des paysans et la ville de Strasbourg." In Alphonse Wollbrett, ed., *La guerre des paysans, 1525: Etudes alsatiques*, pp. 137–70. Saverne: Société d'histoire et d'archéologie de Saverne et environs, 1975.

———. "Le recteur strasbourgeois Jean Sturm et les protestants français." In *Actes du colloque l'amiral de Coligny et son temps*, pp. 407–25. Paris: Société de l'histoire du protestantisme français, 1974.

Safley, Thomas Max. *Let No Man Put Asunder: The Control of Marriage in the German Southwest: A Comparative Study, 1550–1600*. Sixteenth Century Texts and Studies, vol. 2. Kirksville, Mo.: Sixteenth Century Journal Publishers, 1984.

Saladin, Johann Georg. "Die strassburger Chronik des Johann Georg Saladins." Edited by Aloys Meister and Aloys Ruppel. *Bulletin de la société pour la conservation des monuments historiques d'Alsace*, n.s. 22 (1908), 127–206, and n.s. 23 (1911), 182–281, 283–345.

Schadt, Wilhelm. "Wolfgang Schütterlin, Ammeister der Stadt Strassburg." *Die Ortenau*, 54 (1974), 257–59.

Schanz, Georg von. *Zur Geschichte der deutschen Gesellenvereine im Mittelalter*. Leipzig, 1876; reprint edition, Glashütten im Taunus: Detler Auvermann, 1973.

Schiess, Traugott, ed. *Briefwechsel der Brüder Ambrosius und Thomas Blaurer, 1509–1548*. 3 vols. Freiburg im Breisgau: Friedrich Ernst Fehsenfeld, 1908–12.

Schindling, Anton. *Humanistische Hochschule und freie Reichstadt: Gymnasium und Akademie in Strassburg, 1538–1621*. Veröffentlichungen des Instituts für europäische Geschichte in Mainz, vol. 77. Wiesbaden: Fritz Steiner, 1977.

Bibliography

Schmidt, Charles. *Histoire littéraire de l'Alsace à la fin du XVe et au commencement du XVIe siècle.* 2 vols. Paris: Sandoz & Fischbacher, 1879.

Schmidt, Charles G. A., ed. *Der Antheil der Strassburger an der Reformation in Churpfalz: Drei Schriften Johann Marbachs.* Strasbourg: Schmidt, 1856.

Schneegans, Louis. *Strassburgische Geschichten, Sagen, Denkmäler, Inschriften, Künstler, Kunstgegenstände, und Allerlei.* Strasbourg: Dannbach'schen Druckerei, 1855.

Schraepler, Horst. *Die rechtliche Behandlung der Täufer in der deutschen Schweiz, Südwestdeutschland, und Hessen, 1525–1618.* Schriften zur Kirchen- und Rechtsgeschichte, vol. 4. Tübingen: E. Fabian, 1957.

Schwenckfeld, Caspar. *Corpus Schwenckfeldianorum.* Edited by Chester David Hartranft et al. 19 vols. Leipzig: Schwenckfelder Church, 1907–61.

Scribner, R. W. "Civic Unity and the Reformation in Erfurt." *Past & Present,* 66 (1975), 28–60.

———. *For the Sake of Simple Folk: Popular Propaganda in the German Reformation.* Cambridge: Cambridge University Press, 1981.

Speccer, Melchior. *Auslegung des Evangelii Matthei am XIV Capitel.* Strasbourg: T. Rihel, 1568.

———. *Von der herrlichen Zukunfft Jesu Christi.* Strasbourg: S. Emmel, 1555.

Specklin, Daniel. "Les collectanées de Daniel Specklin." Edited by Rodolphe Reuss. *Bulletin de la société pour la conservation des monuments historiques d'Alsace,* n.s. 13 (1888), 157–360, and 14 (1889), 1–178, 201–404.

Spitz, Lewis W. *The Religious Renaissance of the German Humanists.* Cambridge: Harvard University Press, 1963.

Stafford, William. *Domesticating the Clergy: The Inception of the Reformation in Strasbourg, 1522–1524.* American Academy for Religion Dissertation Series, vol. 17. Missoula, Mont.: Scholars Press, 1976.

Der Statt Strassburg Policeij Ordnung. Strasbourg: Johann Carolus, 1628.

Strauss, Gerald. *Luther's House of Learning: Indoctrination of the Young in the German Reformation.* Baltimore: Johns Hopkins University Press, 1978.

———. "Success and Failure in the German Reformation." *Past & Present,* 67 (1975), 30–63.

Strohl, Henri. *Le protestantisme en Alsace.* Strasbourg: Editions Oberlin, 1950.

Sturm, Jean. *Communitio oder Erinnerungschrift.* Neustadt: Matheus Harnisch, 1581.

Tappert, Theodore G., trans. and ed. *The Book of Concord.* Philadelphia: Fortress, 1959.

Tengler, Ulrich. *Laienspiegel.* Strasbourg: J. Rihel & G. Messerschmidt, 1560.

Tischgebete für die Kinder. Strasbourg: S. Emmel, 1557.

Torrance, T. F. "Kingdom and Church in the Thought of Martin Bucer." *Journal of Ecclesiastical History,* 6 (1955), 48–59.

Trausch, Jacob, and Johann Wencker. "Les chroniques strasbourgeoises de Jacques Trausch et de Jean Wencker." Edited by Léon Dacheux. *Bulletin de la société pour la conservation des monuments historiques d'Alsace,* n.s. 15 (1892), 3–207.

Tüchle, Herman. "The Peace of Augsburg: New Order or Lull in the Fighting." In Henry J. Cohn, ed., *Government in Reformation Europe,* pp. 145–65. New York: Harper & Row, 1971.

Vierling, Joseph Fridolin. *Das Ringen um die letzten dem Katholizismus treuen Klöster Strassburgs.* Strassburger Beiträge zur neueren Geschichte, vol. 8. Strasbourg: Herdersche Buchhandlung, 1914.

Ville de Strasbourg. *Zurich-Strasbourg.* Strasbourg: Mairie, 1976.

Virck, Hans, et al., eds. *Politische Correspondenz der Stadt Strassburg im Zeitalter der Reformation.* 5 vols. in 6. Urkunden und Akten der Stadt Strassburg, Part 2. Strasbourg: Karl J. Trübner, 1882–89 and Heidelberg: Carl Winters Universitätsbuchhandlung, 1928–33.

Vogler, Bernard. "Recrutement et carrière des pasteurs strasbourgeois au XVI siècle." *Revue d'histoire et de philosophie religieuses,* 48 (1968), 151–74.

Warhafftige und Eygentliche Vertrags Articulen. Cologne: Johann Christofel, 1605.

Weigand, Wilhelm, ed. *Urkunden und Stadtrechte bis zum Jahre 1266. Urkundenbuch der Stadt Strassburg.* Strasbourg: Karl J. Trübner, 1879.

Wendel, François. *L'Eglise de Strasbourg, sa constitution et son organisation, 1532–1535.* Etudes d'histoire et de philosophie religieuses publiées par la Faculté de théologie protestante de l'université de Strasbourg, vol. 38. Paris: Presses universitaires de France, 1942.

———. *Le mariage à Strasbourg à l'époque de la réforme, 1520–1692.* Collection d'études sur l'histoire du droit et des institutions de l'Alsace, vol. 4. Strasbourg: Imprimerie alsacienne, 1928.

Weyrauch, Erdmann. *Konfessionelle Krise und soziale Stabilität: Das Interim in Strassburg, 1548–1562.* Spätmittelater und Frühe Neuzeit, vol. 7. Stuttgart: Klett-Cotta, 1978.

Wickram, Georg. *Georg Wickrams sämtliche Werke.* Edited by Hans-Gert Roloff. 12 vols. Berlin: Walter de Gruyter, 1967–75.

Widmaier, Alfred. *Friedrich Prechter und der strassburger Kapitelstreit.* Strassburger Beiträge zur neueren Geschichte, vol. 1⁴. Strasbourg: Herdersche Buchhandlung, 1910.

Williams, George H. *The Radical Reformation.* London: Weidenfeld & Nicolson, 1962.

Winckelmann, Otto. *Das Fürsorgewesen der Stadt Strassburg vor und nach der Reformation bis zum Ausgang des sechzehnten Jahrhunderts.* 2 vols. in 1. Quellen und Forschungen zur Reformationsgeschichte, vol. 5. Leipzig: M. Heinsius Nachfolger, 1922.

———. "Strassburger Frauenbriefe des 16ten Jahrhunderts." *Archiv für Kulturgeschichte,* n.F. 2 (1904), 172–95.

———. "Strassburgs Verfassung und Verwaltung im 16ten Jahrhundert." *Zeitschrift für die Geschichte des Oberrheins,* n.F. 18 (1903), 493–537, 600–642.

Winter, Ernest F., trans. and ed. *Erasmus-Luther: Discourse on Free Will.* New York: Frederick Unger, 1961.

Wolff, Christian. "Une liste nominative des habitants de Schiltigheim en 1575." *Bulletin du cercle généalogique d'Alsace,* 15 (1971), 43–47.

Zell, Katherine. *Ein Brieff an die gantze Burgerschafft.* Strasbourg: n.p., 1557.

Zeydel, Edwin. *Sebastian Brant.* Twayne's World Author Series, vol. 13. New York: Twayne, 1967

Ziegler, Oskar. *Die Politik der Stadt Strassburg im bischöflichen Kriege.* Strassburger Beiträge zur neueren Geschichte, vol. 1³. Strasbourg: Herdersche Buchhandlung, 1906.

Zimmermann, Jean-Robert. *Les compagnons de métiers à Strasbourg du début du XIVe siècle à la veille de la réforme.* Société savante d'Alsace et des régions de l'est, Collection recherches et documents, vol. 10. Strasbourg: Istra, 1971.

Zuber, Roger. "Les Champenois réfugiés à Strasbourg et l'église réformée de Châlons: Echanges intellectuels et vie religieuse, 1560–1590." *Mémoires de la société d'agriculture, commerce, sciences et arts du département de la Marne,* 79 (1964), 31–55.

Index